# Work and Worship

The Economic Order of the Shakers

Edward Deming Andrews
and Faith Andrews

New York Graphic Society
Greenwich, Connecticut

# Photographic Credits

...ook were taken by Armin Landeck, a personal ... Landeck's photographs have not only recorded ... movement, but also reveal the spirit that animat- ...andeck was kind enough to supply the publishers ...ing photographs: p. 2; p. 9; pp. 10-11; pp. 38-39; ...33; p. 136; pp. 160-161; p. 180; p. 182; pp. 188-189;

The Edward Deming Andrews Memorial Library is a seemingly endless source of rich material on the Shakers, representing fifty or more years of selective collecting and research by the Andrews. The library staff gave their assistance and time unstintingly in gathering and documenting the photographs. The following photographs were reproduced courtesy of The Henry Francis du Pont Winterthur Museum, The Edward Deming Andrews Memorial Shaker Collection: SA245 (73.932), p. 9; p. 15; p. 19; p. 26; p. 27; p. 34; SA311, p. 46; SA1420.2, left, p. 55; SA1420.4, p. 57; SA1420.1, left, p. 58; SA1420.3, right, p. 58; SA1043.3, right, p. 61; SA1042.5, left, p. 62; SA1417.11, left, p. 66; SA1048.4, right, p. 66; SA1048.2, left, p. 67; p. 74; p. 78; 62.128, left, p. 82; 62.127, right, p. 82; SA1412.90a, bottom, p. 86; SA588, p. 92; SA501, p. 93; SA201, p. 108; SA199, p. 109; SA56, p. 112; SA245 (73.930), p. 113; SA122, left, p. 115; SA485, p. 116; SA1426, top, p. 119; SA2, p. 120; SA4, p. 121; SA1328.5, p. 124; p. 126; SA212, p. 127; SA1004b, left, p. 129; SA1004k, right, p. 129; SA179, p. 130; AS, bottom, p. 133; AS165, p. 138; both, p. 140; p. 142; SA546c, top, p. 144; bottom, p. 144; p. 148; right, p. 149; T.C. Env. 2, p. 150; SA34.1, left, p. 151; AS290, p. 162; SA166, p. 167; SA245 (73.932), p. 169; SA245 (73.934), p. 175; SA1412.30a, p. 185; p. 187; SA245 (73.935), p. 193; SA172, p. 195; SA245 (73.931), p. 197; SA245 (73.929), p. 201; SA245 (73.933), p. 206; SA1435, p. 208.

Mrs. Andrews supplied the publishers with the following photographs: p. 61; p. 62; p. 68; both, p. 71; p. 76; p. 79; p. 80; p. 81; p. 83; p. 85; both, p. 88; p. 91; p. 94; p. 95; p. 96; p. 97; p. 98; both, p. 99; p. 100; p. 102; p. 104; p. 110; p. 111; right, p. 115; p. 117; both, p. 125; both, p. 147; left, p. 149; right, p. 151; both, p. 154; p. 199.

All photographs used in this book are on file at The Henry Francis du Pont Winterthur Museum.

Endpapers: Electrotypes and stereotypes from mid-nineteenth century were used on Shaker seed packages.

International Standard Book Number 0-8212-0593-5
Library of Congress Catalog Card Number 73-89949

Designed by Betsy Beach

Manufactured in the U.S.A.

# Contents

This book is dedicated to the "World's people" in the hope that they may better understand the Shaker heritage and find inspiration and courage to put their hands to work, their hearts to God.

# Introduction

The Shakers . . . developed a fully articulated and homogeneous culture, with a value-system and a way of life which was expressed not only in their religion, but was reflected in their unique social organization, their economic system, and their educational pattern. Their writings, their music, their pictorial art, their crafts, their household furnishings, and their architecture all display variant facets of a closely integrated culture. I am convinced that the Shakers offer unusual opportunities for study because of this fact that they do present in manageable compass—in microcosm—all the elements of a full-blown culture. This culture represented a deliberate alternative to the prevailing American culture, and therefore it offers a perspective upon American culture at large.

—David M. Potter

In temporal affairs as in spiritual, the Shakers were separatists. They went their own way, following principles which they believed were the true guides to Christian perfection. Although the United Society, in point of time, was co-eval with the American republic, and although the Shakers admired the ideals of the founding fathers, they nevertheless in their status as an order separate from the world, "a Kingdom of Christ," pursued a course at variance, and often in conflict, with the prevailing mores. The world's mores or morals, they held, were frequently based on selfish materialism, a desire, on the part of individuals or parties, to get ahead at any cost. Their own proclaimed purpose was to set an example of how men and women, in a voluntary association, should work and worship, in peace, humility, order, and brotherhood. The Shaker covenant states, "We believed we were debtors to God in relation to Each other, and all men, to improve our time and Tallents in this Life, in that manner in which we might be most useful."

Although our chief concern in the present study is with their economic system, its values and its influence, it should be emphasized that the industrial life of the Shaker order was distinctive in that it served not a secular but a religious purpose. In a true sense, work was a ritual, a calling, a form of worship. At first, in the face of distrust and persecution on every hand, it was a question of survival. But when the society became firmly established, the "temporalities" found their subsidiary place as the foundation of a social structure which in essence was dedicated to spiritual ends.

No motive of profit or material gain was involved; there were no wages, no reckoning of hours, no cost accounting. Surplus capital went into improvements, expansion (in buildings, equipment, and land), and notably into works of charity. As long as the society held to its basic doctrine of separation from the world, it remained, in the quality of its workmanship and the spirit that animated its labors, an exemplary institution attracting attention far and wide.

In the principles which the Shakers practiced with such devotion of mind and spirit lay the secret of their success. These were rooted in the practices of the primitive church in Jerusalem—where all those that believed held all things in common—and in the conviction that they were called from the world to build a millennial society superior to that world.

Central was the principle of union, or cooperation—within a given "family" and between families and communities. As in the monastic orders, it was not based on economic theory but rather on a singleness of purpose, the advancement of a cause. There were many contributing factors, among which may be mentioned:

1.  The recognition and use of native aptitudes and skills. Regulation of trades, reminiscent of the medieval guilds. A system of apprenticeship. The practice of division and rotation of labor. The ability—accruing from combined labor—to produce on a large scale.

2.  Respect for hand labor. Hand labor was a sacred privilege, a test of faith. Everyone worked, including the spiritual lead. The idea of rank was "repugnant to the spirit of Christianity."

3.  Recognition of the equality of the sexes, in rights and responsibilities. Of inestimable value to the economy was the elevation of the sisters to equality with the brethren.

4.  The doctrine of perfectionism. It was the Shakers' desire to excel the world in all good works, including standards of industrial workmanship. As one result, the products of their lands and shops commanded a premium in the market. It is significant that the deacons in charge of the trades, and the trustees in charge of finances, were appointed by and responsible to the ministry or bishops.

5.  Order, utility, and improvement as determinants of the economy. "Where there is no order, there is no God."

6.  The right use of property. The Shakers believed that "the true

followers of Christ are one with him, as he is one with the Father. This oneness includes all they possess; for he who has devoted himself to Christ, soul, body and spirit, can by no means, withhold his property." "The earth is the Lord's, and the fulness thereof." Property belonged to God, and should be used not to further man's personal ends, but His work in the world.

Such were the guideposts of Shaker industry. Being human, the reach of the Shakers may have been beyond their grasp. In striving for perfection there were failures, set-backs, and disillusionments. In the end, the line of separation between the Church and the world became obscured, the ramparts breached. Compromises were made or forced upon them. Prosperity contained the seeds of worldliness. Yet the fact that this holy experiment is destined to end should not overshadow the splendid example and accomplishments of the order nor the worth of principles which for so long a time sustained and illuminated a truly Christian community.

# I   Hearts to God

"Labor to make the way of God your own;
let it be your inheritance, your treasure,
your occupation, your daily calling."

—Ann Lee, c. 1783

The roots of Shaker culture—the principles by which the Believers lived and the practice of those principles—lay not only in the unusual personality and teaching of Ann Lee, the founder of the society, but also in the interpretation of her testimony by her immediate successors. Hers was the generating force, but it was left for others to give that force direction and a foundation. The human factors must also be viewed in the light of the religious and political conditions prevailing at the time of the origin of the society and its early development in America. It was the interaction between the world and the unworldly Shakers that determined the nature and significance of the movement.

Ann Lees (shortened to Lee after she settled in America) was born on February 29, 1736, the daughter of one John Lees, a poor blacksmith living on Toad Lane (now Todd Street) in Manchester, England. She had no schooling, and at an early age began work in a cotton factory preparing cotton for the looms and cutting velvet. Little is known about her childhood and youth. "She was the subject," it was said, "of religious impressions" and had "great light and conviction concerning the sinfulness and depravity of human nature, and especially concerning the lusts of the flesh." Such convictions involved her in altercations within her family, which consisted, besides her parents, of five brothers and two sisters. It was doubtless unhappiness and friction at home and disagreements over religion that led her to join, at the age of twenty-two, an obscure sect living in Bolton-on-the-Moors, near Manchester. The sect was led by two Quakers, James and Jane Wardley, who had come under the influence of the French Prophets, or Camisards, a radical sect of Calvinists. The Prophets, a number of whom had sought refuge in England after the revocation of the Edict of Nantes in 1685, were pre-millennialists fanatically confident that the second coming of Christ was imminent. Their worship was ecstatic, accompanied by singing, shouting, and dancing, visions and prophecies. They practiced confession of sin and preached the necessity of taking up "a full and final cross against all evil in their knowledge." Here, with the Wardleys, Ann Lees "found a good degree of that protection which she had so long desired."

Even though celibacy was one of their doctrines, it did not deter her, three years later, in 1761, from marrying Abraham Stanley, a blacksmith. The step may have been taken under pressure from her family, or because, as Shaker history has it, she had not then "attained to that knowledge of God which she so early desired." In any case, the outcome was tragic.

12

She had four children, all of whom died in infancy.

The next ten years of her life are somewhat obscure. According to her own account she underwent great suffering of mind and body, and in spite of a strong constitution was at times near death. Subject to visions and revelations, and doubtless conditioned by her own marital misfortunes, she became convinced, more than ever, that the "lustful gratifications of the flesh" were the foundation of human depravity. Militant, persuasive, magnetic—and, as she proclaimed, now divinely commissioned as Christ's successor—she came to assume a dominant role in the Wardley society. In meeting, she bore an "open testimony" against sin, and on the streets of the town incited the poor to rebel against their lot. As her influence increased within the society, so did abuse and outright persecution of the sect.

Direct conflict with the law was inevitable. Shaker meetings, held in the houses of members, were noisy affairs, resulting in "disturbances" and damage to property when the "wicked" tried to break them up. On July 14, 1772, called to quell "a breach of the Sabbath," the constable arrested five persons, among them Ann and her father, who were subsequently imprisoned. In October, on two occasions, the constable was again summoned to disperse "mobs" interfering with the Shaker meetings. Affairs reached a climax the following year. One Sunday, in late spring, when the congregation was assembled for morning prayer in Christ Church, Ann Lees, with three companions, "wilfully and contemptuously" interrupted the service. The record is silent on what they did or said. But the result was another prison term.

Persecution and imprisonment strengthened Ann's hold on the nascent Shaker movement. There is no evidence, however, that at this time she had formulated any positive or specific doctrine. She was *against* the order of prevailing conditions, it is true—the established church, poverty and economic injustice, the privileged classes, all forms of inequality—but essentially a dissenter without a program. She lived in a period of awakening and social ferment. William Pitt, coming into power in 1757, was beginning to make people conscious of their political rights. Ann had heard the revivalist George Whitefield preach in Manchester. Lancashire was being stirred by the Wesleys. But Ann's message, confined principally to diatribes against the sin of concupiscence, bore little relationship to current issues and therefore lacked popular appeal. Few were interested in her preachment that to be regenerated, to be born again into the kingdom of Christ, one must repent and forsake all that was carnal. Few believed her claim to be the leader of a new dispensation. Although the Shakers were not molested after Ann's last imprisonment, membership in the society remained limited. Failure to expand on its native soil was doubtless what led to the decision to carry the gospel to America. Only eight members accompanied "Ann the Word" when she sailed from Liverpool in May of 1774.

13

After a stormy passage, the little band of "Shaking Quakers" disembarked in New York on August 6, 1774. With the prophetess were her husband, her brother William, and her chief disciples—the youthful James Whittaker, the elderly John Hocknell (the only propertied member of the sect), his son Richard, James Shepherd, Mary Partington, and Nancy Lee, a cousin. On arrival, the company, in order to earn a livelihood, scattered into different parts of the country. Soon afterward, Abraham Stanley renounced his faith, abandoned his wife, and "joined himself to the world." Hocknell, with William Lee and Whittaker, went up the Hudson, where they purchased a piece of low swampy land in the "wilderness" of Niskeyuna, or Watervliet, near Albany. Lee found employment as a blacksmith in Albany, and Whittaker as a weaver. Hocknell returned to England to bring out his family and the family of John Partington. In the meantime Mother Ann remained in New York, taken in by a family by the name of Smith living on Queen-street (now Pearl Street), where she earned a scanty living washing and ironing.

There is some evidence that during the period before the Shakers were reunited at Niskeyuna in the spring of 1776, they explored other places to settle. In a history of Bucks County, Pennsylvania, the author relates that about 1773:

> Anna Lee, with her embryo sect of Shakers, eight or ten in number, passed through Falls and stopped at the home of Jonathan Kirkbride, while himself and wife were at Yearly Meeting at Philadelphia. The children, seeing a number of friendly-looking people ride up, invited them to spend the night. Anna took possession of a chamber and the others of the kitchen, where they commenced to iron a quantity of clothing from their saddlebags. At a given signal all dropped their work, to the astonishment of their young hosts, and, falling into ranks, went round and round the room in measured tread, shouting
>
> > As David danced before the Lord,
> > So will we, so will we;
> > There was a woman sent from God,
> > Her name is Anna Lee.[1]

With their Quaker background in England, it is understandable that the Shakers should seek out Quaker country in the colonies. That they were investigating sites in or near Philadelphia is supported by another source. In his *Literary Diary*, under the date of February 14, 1781, Ezra Stiles, president of Yale College, wrote that the first Shakers arrived in 1774, and the rest [the Hocknell and Partington families?] who came in 1776 [1775?] went to Philadelphia and traveled through Pennsylvania to New York where twelve came together.[2]

At Niskeyuna, three-and-a-half years were to pass before the Shakers found the long-sought opening for their testimony. The time was spent building, first a log cabin and then a frame house, felling trees, draining swamps, and tilling the land. Though they were often discouraged by their failure to attract converts, preparations for the prophesied reception of "great numbers" never slackened. In the spring of 1779, they started to lay up surplus stores of provisions. "We shall have company enough before another year comes about," Mother Ann promised, "to consume it all."

Agencies were already at work through which the promise was to be fulfilled. One was the Revolution. In 1780, Americans were still at war with Great Britain, with loyalties divided and hopes of political independence not yet materialized. Soon after Mother Ann left New York in the spring of 1776, General William Howe with a fleet under his brother, Lord Howe, appeared off the city, and Washington was forced to withdraw his army. Four years later, the war was still on in the south. The doom of Cornwallis was not sealed until 1781, nor the treaty of peace until 1783. Though the Shakers were left undisturbed at first, before the conflict came to an end, as we shall see, it brought the obscure sect into public notice.

The Tree of Life, *a drawing by a Shaker sister, Hannah Cohoon.*

Paralleling the wide-spread concern with war and politics was another revolution of sorts, a shifting of allegiance in religious affairs. As Vernon Parrington noted, the Great Awakening of the 1740s, in which the revivalist George Whitefield and Jonathan Edwards were the chief figures, was "the single movement that stirred the colonial heart deeply during three generations. . . . Theology was still of greater popular interest than politics."[3] As an aftermath of the Awakening, separatist congregations sprang up, particularly in New England, which challenged the theocratic Calvinistic doctrine of predestination, election, and depravity, and asserted the freedom of the human will. People everywhere deserted the Congregational churches to join the Baptists and Methodists.

One such sect was the Free Will Baptists, founded in 1780 in New Hampshire by an itinerant preacher, Benjamin Randall, who had been converted by Whitefield. Randall founded a number of churches, and in the wake of the revivals he promoted, the "Merry Dancers" or "New Lights," as they were called, spread from central New Hampshire and Vermont into southern Maine, western Massachusetts and Connecticut, and eastern New York. To be regenerated or saved, they held, one must repent and completely abandon all sin. Through the medium of direct inspiration, regeneration brought one into personal union with God. Christian perfection, perfect sanctification, was possible, but only through one's own efforts—sustained by the hope of the Second Coming of Christ.

The covenant of the church at New Durham, New Hampshire (April 13, 1791), contained the following articles:

> *Non-conformity to the world.* Christians are commanded not to
> conform to the world in its customs, fashions, and idle
> conversation. . . .

> *Liberality.* They are to do good to all, communicate to the Church
> Stock, and admonish the covetous.

> *Pride.* They should not exalt themselves, debase others, or adorn
> their person with ornaments or superfluous apparel.

> *Bearing arms.* True Christians cannot "bear carnal weapons. . . ."

> *Business.* They should not follow the customs of the world in trade,
> but do as they *would be* done by, and not as they *are* done by.[4]

Except for the principle that sexual relationship was the cardinal sin, these doctrines were analogous to those evolving in Shaker thought and practice. They were a preparation—as those of the French Prophets and Quakers had earlier been—for the opening of the Shaker testimony in America.

This came about in the following way. In New Lebanon, New York, and in surrounding towns, New Light revivals were at their height in the late 1770s. Those who held the meetings included Joseph Meacham, a lay preacher from Enfield, Connecticut; Calvin Harlow, one of his associates; and the Reverend Samuel Johnson, pastor of the Presbyterian church in New Lebanon. The meetings were heavily attended by the farmers, artisans, and small tradesmen in the neighborhood. Excitement was high. "What shall I do to be saved?" was the anxious recurrent question. Since Christ was about to appear a second time, the soul should be purified in preparation for His coming. But when He failed to appear, the afflatus generated in these meetings died away, and instead of being "awakened," disillusioned subjects of the revival apostatized or reverted to their former faiths.

Two of these "seekers," Talmadge Bishop and Reuben Wight, were on their way westward in March 1780, when they chanced upon the Shaker settlement at Niskeyuna. Here, for the first time, members of a New Light congregation received the astonishing intelligence that the millennium they longed for had already begun, that Christ, the Christ spirit, had made its second appearance in the person of the Shaker prophetess. Bishop and Wight were told that they, the Shakers, had "actually risen with Christ, and travel with Him in the Resurrection." Laboring in the work of regeneration, they had confessed their sins and left off committing them. But the cost was high. Flesh was at war with spirit; to be purified, to attain perfection, to be saved, one must forsake "the marriage of the flesh." The ecstatic "operations" of worship witnessed by the two travelers seemed to set the seal of conviction on this strange testimony.

Returning to New Lebanon, they reported their experience to Meacham, who delegated Harlow to inquire further into the Shakers' belief and practice. He in turn was almost persuaded that their leader, although a woman—and women, St. Paul had said, should keep silence in the churches—was indeed the herald of a new dispensation. Harlow's glowing account of his conversations was so convincing that Elder Meacham decided to see for himself this "woman of the new birth." On a May day in 1780, accompanied by Amos Hammond and Aaron Kibbee, he made the historic contact with the wilderness sect.

The ensuing dialogue was long and searching. The dancing and singing were never more joyful and exalted. And when the day was over, the leadership of one branch of the New Lights had been won over to the Shaker faith. Mother Ann at last had found her "opening," and soon, as she had foretold, people came "in droves" to Niskeyuna. On May 10, 1780, the first public meeting was held.

Events moved fast to publicize the Shaker cause. Less than two months after that meeting, three converts—David Darrow, Daniel Green, and Joseph Potter, New Lebanon farmers—were seized by patriotic neighbors as they were rounding up some sheep preparatory to driving them to the New York colony. Brought before the Commissioners for Detecting and Defeating Conspiracies in the State of New York, then meeting in Albany, they were charged with "disaffection to the American cause" on the grounds that the sheep were intended for the British. Suspicion spread to include other members of the sect, and in spite of the Shakers' protest that theirs was a gospel of peace, several of their leaders, including Mother Ann, her brother William, and Father James Whittaker, were committed to jail. After posting bonds for their good behavior, they were subsequently released, except for Ann, who, with a companion, was jailed at Poughkeepsie. It was not until December, through the intercession of Governor George Clinton, that she was freed.

Public attention, not always favorable, spread in the wake of "persecution by the wicked." As more and more inquirers flocked to the Niskeyuna colony, the Shaker leadership decided to undertake a mission into parts of eastern New York and New England. Starting out in May 1781, Mother Ann, with William Lee, Whittaker, and others, traveled by foot and horseback into a number of towns in Massachusetts and Connecticut, holding meetings wherever a few gathered to hear the gospel. Headquarters were established at Harvard, in eastern Massachusetts, to which place delegates from separatist churches all over New England came to hear the millennial tidings. The mission, lasting two years, met with constant harassment and often violent persecution, but served in the end to lay the foundations for communities in many places: New Lebanon in New York, Hancock and Tyringham in western Massachusetts, Enfield in Connecticut, Harvard and Shirley in eastern Massachusetts, Alfred and New Gloucester in Maine, and Enfield and Canterbury in New Hampshire, the seedbed of the New Light faith.

Besides physical afflictions, the early Shakers—even before the death of Ann Lee in 1784 and some time before they were able to formulate their own testimony in writing—were subjected to abuse of another kind. Apostates—Valentine Rathbun in 1781, 1782, and 1783, Amos Taylor in 1782, and Benjamin West in 1783—published in pamphlet form scurrilous diatribes against members of the sect, ridiculing their form of worship, accusing them of delusions, denunciation of non-believing relatives, ignorance, witchcraft, naked dancing, Catholicism (belief in celibacy, confession, perfection, miracles, obedience, etc.), the exploiting of common members, undermining the "civil power" of the American government, and so on. In a letter dated February 19, 1783, another critic, William Plumer, later governor of New Hampshire, wrote from Canterbury to a friend:

> Several persons who had valuable farms have sold them and given the money to support the common cause. The Elders dispose of

the people at the different houses, who are treated and reverenced as fathers. The common class receive only their food and clothing; the Elders do no labor, nor take any care to provide for their subsistence; they live freely, traveling from place to place....

[Members were so confident that in three years] their religion will universally prevail throughout North America and Great Britain... that they offered to give absolute deeds of their lands and houses for the same sums as for a three years lease.

The women and children are under the most abject submission to the master of the house where they live; the laborers and men to the tutors and Elders; and those to the church. A woman cannot give away a meal's victuals to a friend or relative without the express permission of the governor of the house,—even though he is her husband.[5]

Contemporary accounts, though often biased, give credence to the fact that the early Shakers were indeed extremists in doctrine and often fanatical in their forms of worship. But if one searches the records objectively, one sees emerging, during these years, principles that were to form the foundation of an ordered, industrious society. In the "sayings" of Mother Ann

*Each society selected a nearby hill or mountaintop for sacred rituals, which included singing and dancing around an enclosed hexagonal plot called the "fountain," marked by a large slab, the Lord's Stone.*

and her successor, James Whittaker (d. 1787), one glimpses, amid their constant diatribes against the "filthy works of the flesh," "lustful gratifications," "carnal nature," etc., their vision of a way of life consonant with the example of Christ and the apostolic church.

"There is no witchcraft but sin," the prophetess said on one occasion. And by sin she meant more than a "fleshly sense." Covetousness, uncleanliness, gluttony, pride, envy, waste, idleness, drunkenness, deceitfulness, abuse of wealth, politics, contention, war—all worldliness—such must be repudiated if one would walk as Christ walked.

From the beginning the Shakers eschewed both politics and war. "You never will kill the devil with the sword," Ann told General James Sullivan at Harvard in 1782. "The spirit of party is the spirit of the world," Whittaker declared at the time of Shay's Rebellion, "and whoever indulges it ... is off from Christian ground."

Charity was also a Christian duty. "If I owned the whole world," Ann told Nathan Goodrich at Hancock, "I would turn it all into joyousness; I would not say to the poor, 'Be ye warmed, and be ye clothed,' without giving them wherewithal to do it." "Once I served God through fear," she said, "but now I serve Him by love."

Industriousness, too. "It was always held up as a doctrine of truth ... that those who were unfaithful in temporal things could not find the blessing and protection of God in their spiritual travel."[6] "Cut your grain clean," Father James adjured a group of farmers; "God has caused it to grow, and you ought to be careful to save it. In this country you abound in good things, therefore you are lavish and wasteful."

Mother Ann also came to modify her opposition to marriage. "Do not go away and report that we forbid to marry," she said on one occasion, "for unless you are able to take up a full cross ... I would counsel you ... to take wives in a lawful manner, and cleave to them only ... for, of all lustful gratifications, that is the least sin."[7]

In occasional statements by these two early "witnesses" we find the first evidence that they looked forward to a time when property would be held in common and devoted to the "united interest." "After I have done my work in this world," Ann prophesied, "there will be a great increase in the gospel. It will be like a man's beginning the world and raising up a family of children, gathering an interest, then dying, and leaving his interest with his children, who will improve thereon and gather more." To some Believers from Enfield, New Hampshire, who thought they were to continue in this world only a few years and were therefore "squandering" their property, Mother Ann said: "Go home and set out apple trees, and raise calves, and make provisions as though you were to live a thousand years, and gather something to do good with." In conversation with Lucy

Wright, who was destined to be her successor in the female line, she said, speaking of the faithful:

> If you are faithful to take up your crosses against the world, the flesh, and all evil, and follow Christ in the regeneration, you shall receive an hundred fold, now, in this time, houses, and Brethren and Sisters, and mothers and children, and lands, and in the world to come, eternal life. You shall be blessed in your going out, and in your coming in; in your basket, and in your store.[8]

On the subject of common property, Father James was more specific. "The time is come," he announced at a meeting in Ashfield, Massachusetts, "for you to give up yourselves and your all, to God—your substance, your temporal property—to possess as though you possessed not." And in a letter from Ashfield, dated February 1782, he counseled Josiah Talcott, a Hancock farmer, to shake off "sloth and idleness" and put his farm in readiness, for he had land enough, when improved, "to maintain three families or more." During the Whittaker regime, the Believers were scattered. Some lived at home, conducting their own business and remaining in a "flesh relation." Homeless individuals were often taken into families which had united their domestic concerns. "The poor and destitute were taken in with those more able and shared equally." But during that regime, lands, goods, and money were already being consecrated to the cause, and converts "entertained at free cost" in the incipient communities. Darrow's sheep were an early pledge of support.

Although the communal idea had not originally entered into Ann Lee's social and religious doctrines, an oral agreement on basic principles of property rights was made soon after the organization of the New Lebanon society. It had been agreed that no one should buy or sell in the church, "nor trade with those not of the Church, except by the union of the Trustees." In business management it had been from the start assumed that the sisters should have equal privileges and equal responsibilities with the brethren, and union meetings for consultation were frequently held. The first covenant to commit to writing such agreements and the rules for membership was signed in 1795. This document illuminates the principles of communism and the religious basis of the "Joint Interest" idea as they first developed in the Shaker order.

The following is the Covenant of the Church of Christ, in New Lebanon, relating to the possession and use of a Joint Interest

In the year of our Lord 1788, the year in which most of the members of the Church were Gathered. The following order and Covenant was then, and from time to time after, made known and understood, received and entered into by us as members of the

Church, agreeable to an understanding of the order and Covenant of a Church in Gospel order.

For it was and is still our Faith, and confirmed by our experience, that there could be no Church in Complete order, according to the Law of Christ, without being Gathered into one Joint Interest and union, that all the members might have an equal right and privilege, according to their Calling and needs, in things both Spiritual & temporal. . . .

Firstly, The Conditions on which we were received, as members of the Church, were in Substance as follows. All or as many of us as were of age to act for ourselves, who offered ourselves as members of the Church, were to do it freely and Voluntarily as a Religious duty, and according to our own faith and desire.

Secondly, Youth and Children, being under age, were not to be received as members, or as being under the immediate care and government of the Church, But by the request or free consent of both their parents, if living, except they were left by one of their parents to the care of the other, then by the request or free Consent of that parent, and if the Child have no parents, Then by the request or free Consent of such person, or persons, as may have Just and Lawful right, in Care of the Child; Together with the Child's own desire.

Thirdly, All that should be received as members, being of age, that had any substance or property that was free from debt, or any Just demand of any that were without, either as Credittors or Heirs, were allowed to bring in their Substance, being their natural and Lawful right, and give it as a part of the Joint Interest of the Church, agreeable to their own faith and desire, to be under the order and Government of the Deacons, And overseers of the Temporal Interest of the Church, and any other use that the Gospel requires, according to the understanding and discression of those members with whom it was Intrusted, and that were appointed to that office and care.

Fourthly, All the members that should be received into the Church, should possess one Joint Interest, as a Religious right, that is, that all should have Just and Equal rights and Priviledges, according to their needs, in the use of all things in the Church, without Any difference being made on account of what any of us brought in, so long as we remained in Obedience to the order and Government of the Church, and are holden in relation as members. All the members are likewise Equally holden, according to their abilities, to maintain and support one Joint Interest in union, in Conformity to the order & Government of the Church.

Fifthly, As it was not the duty or purpose of the Church, in uniting into Church order, to gather and lay up an Interest of this Worlds goods; But what we become possessed of by Honest Industry, more

Than for our own support, to bestow to Charitable uses, for the relief of the poor, and otherwise as the Gospel might Require. Therefore it is our Faith never to bring Debt or blame against the Church, or each other, for any Interest or Services we should bestow to the Joint Interest of the Church, but Covenanted to freely give and Contribute our time and Tallents, as Brethren and Sisters, for the mutual good one of another, and other Charitable uses, according to the order of the Church.

The foregoing is the true Sense of the Covenant of the Church, in relation to the order and manner of the Possession and use of a Joint Interest, understood and supported by us the members. . . . We believed we were debtors to God in relation to Each other, and all men, to improve our time and Tallents in this Life, in that manner in which we might be most useful. Experience of Seven years Travel and Labour, and Received a greater Confirmation and Establishment in our faith, that the order and Covenant in which we have gathered, and Solemnly entered into, is a greater privilege, and Enables us to be more useful to ourselves, and others, than any other State in our Knowledge, and is that, that was Required, and is accepted of God. . . . In Testamony whereof, we have, both Bretheren and Sisters, hereunto subscribed our names in the year of our Lord 1795.

It was the conviction of the early Believers that the true Christian principle called for equal rights and privileges "in things both Spiritual and temporal" and that no difference should be made on account of the original contribution of the members. The phrase—"We believed we were debtors to God in relation to Each other, and all men, to improve our time and Tallents in this Life, in that manner in which we might be most useful"— summarizes what is meant by the term "consecrated industry" so often used in Shaker literature. Twenty-one brethren, headed by David Darrow, and twenty-two sisters, led by Ruth Farrington, signed their names to the document. The name of Joseph Meacham, the probable author, appears on an identical instrument signed at Enfield, Connecticut, the following year.

What was needed, after the deaths of Ann Lee and James Whittaker, was organization and definition of purpose. This was supplied largely by the gifted Joseph Meacham and his associates, under whom, beginning in 1787-88, the movement entered a new phase.

Through the executive genius of Joseph Meacham, the scattered, disorganized members of the Shaker faith were finally bound together in a carefully ordered union. Through his instrumentation, the Believers were gathered "into a body religious, not a body politic, or a body corporate. . . . Their real and personal estate could not be treated as a joint tenancy, nor a tenancy in common, therefore it was made a consecration—a consecrated whole." Because the institution of Shakerism was thus believed to be a derivative from divine rather than civil or political authority, the society could not "connect itself with the world; from this it must ever remain in isolation."

Separation from the world was the result of two forces: persecution and religious conviction. As converts to the new faith encountered opposition from the civil and military authorities as well as their own relatives, they found protection and temporal support in quasi-unions separated from their former associations. Such moves were inevitable, for they were also justified by the New Light–Shaker doctrine of nonconformity with the world. The world was full of sin. Only by withdrawal from the world could one realize the hope of salvation and perfection, complete freedom to obey the laws of God. The theme of the day, wrote Isaac Youngs, was mortification and separation from the world; many were overzealous, engaging in "excessive bodily hardship . . . in hand labor, exercising long and violently in the worship, going without needful sleep, eating but little. . . ."[9]

Joseph Meacham's idea, inspired it was said by the Jewish temple in Jerusalem, was to set up an inner court for those with "the greatest faith and abilities in things spiritual." The second court was for those "second in faith and abilities," chiefly young men and women skilled in or accustomed to manual labor. In the third or outward court were the elderly people, together with those appointed to carry on business relations with the world. Serving as the nucleus of the community was the meetinghouse built in 1786 and dedicated by James Whittaker the following year. In 1788, an oral covenant was adopted and a large dwelling raised for the accommodation of the members. In order to provide an interlude of peace for the establishment of the church in "gospel order," for a decade or more, active proselytizing ceased and the testimony was "withdrawn" from the world.

Supreme authority was vested in a four-member central ministry. By mutual agreement, Lucy Wright, a native of Pittsfield, Massachusetts, whose exceptional talents Mother Ann had earlier acclaimed, was elevated to co-leadership with Meacham. Serving with them, in 1787, were Henry Clough and Rebecca Kendal. In the ministry, the doctrine of the duality of the Godhead was given, for the first time, institutional recognition.

This was a belief in a dual deity—God was both male and female—and in a dual messiahship—Christ, one of the superior spirits, appeared in both Jesus, representing the male principle as the son of a carpenter, and in Mother Ann, the female principle, the daughter of a blacksmith. Thus the quaternity of Father-Son-Holy Mother Wisdom-Daughter was formed.[10]

The central ministry was a self-perpetuating body with appointive and regulative powers over every branch of the United Society. Under it the New Lebanon community gradually developed, with many changes, a definite organization. From 1787 to 1791, the Church consisted of the First and Second Orders. The First was Meacham's "inner court." The Second was an outgrowth of the outer court, which was concerned with temporal affairs; David Meacham, Joseph's brother, was appointed first deacon, with Jonathan Walker as associate. Assisting them were Richard Spier and Joseph Bennett. Membership was 105 persons, 57 brethren and 48 sisters, increased by 89 members in 1788, and 46 in 1789. In 1791, an "Order of [six] Families," reflecting an earlier arrangement, was instituted, under the leadership of Rufus Clark, John Bishop, Jonathan Walker, David Shapley, Israel Talcott, Moses Bacon, and Sanford Barker.

The first family to be *fully* organized was the so-called "Order of the Church," in 1792, with David Darrow as first elder, Ruth Farrington as first eldress, and David Osborne as "office deacon," to act "in union" with David Meacham and Jonathan Walker. About the same time, Lucy Bennett and Jane Spier were appointed "first deaconesses of the Church to direct and superintend the domestic concerns on the part of the sisters." In the same year, the Order of Families was consolidated under Elder Rufus Clark and Eldress Zeruah Clark, and a third family, taking the name of Second Order, was established under Elders Samuel Fitch and Elizur Goodrich (formerly Lucy Wright's husband) and Eldresses Mary Harlow and Elizabeth Chase. In June 1791, a house was built for aged members (Meacham's "second court"), and in August 1792, one for the youth.

In consequence of the growth of these orders or families it was found necessary, in 1814, to change their titles. The order formerly called the First Family received the title of First Order, being the first in gospel order (1792). The order formerly called the Second Family was now called the Second Order, "being the second part of the Church, which is considered as but one family, and the first in gospel establishment." The Order of Families (1792) received in 1814 the title of the Second Family, and the Young Believers' Order, first instituted in 1799-1800, became fully organized as the North Family. Eventually there were six families at New Lebanon, each with its own covenant: the Church (consisting of the First Order—including the Office—and the Second Order), the Second, South, West, East (or Hill), and the North, whose names were based on their location in relation to the central Church family, the site of the common meetinghouse; two branches of the North were organized in the neighboring town of Canaan, New York, and called the Lower and Upper Canaan Families. By the end of the first quarter of the nineteenth century, total membership of the community was between five and six hundred.

The society at New Lebanon (called Mount Lebanon after the post office was installed in 1861) was, for many decades, the largest society; it served as a pattern when other societies were established; it was the home of the central ministry or religious government; in fact, it was the "fountainhead" of Shakerism. A study of the organization of this commune is therefore in effect a study of each of the other 18 societies and 51 families. Each of the Shaker villages was like the others, not only in the organization of its religious and temporal affairs, but in its architecture, in its customs and folk ways, in its dress and the speech of its inhabitants, and in the general nature of its agricultural, horticultural, and industrial art activities. Such similarities were brought about and augmented by the rigid regulations of the central ministry, the periodical visitation of this ministry to the several societies, the cooperation of different communities in constructional enterprises, the frequent movement of members from one village to another and the interchange of goods. Although each family (and each community) was economically an independent unit with its own business managers or trustees, and although circumstances of location and native talent led to some differentiation in occupations and economic well-being, such variations were accidental rather than fundamental.

The term "family," in Shaker usage, referred to a group of brethren and sisters living in the same dwelling, autonomous as regards their industrial pursuits, and organized under the dual leadership of elders and eldresses (usually two of each sex), deacons (or trustees) and deaconesses, who had charge of the "temporalities," and "caretakers" of children, also of each sex. The family was the socioeconomic unit in the society, with membership ranging from as few as 25 to as many as 150. Experience taught the order, however, that the optimal number was about 50. If more, there was danger of its becoming "a petty municipality." If less, the advantages of combined labor would be curtailed.

In the period 1790-1793, the central ministry appointed leaders of all the societies in New England. These were eventually organized into "bishoprics" under subordinate ministries: Hancock, Tyringham, and Enfield, Connecticut, in one; Harvard and Shirley in another; Canterbury and Enfield, New Hampshire, in a third; and Alfred and New Gloucester (Sabbathday Lake) in a fourth. Niskeyuna, or Watervliet, was closely associated with the parent colony at New Lebanon.

Meacham's genius lay in his ability to transform ideals and principles into actual practice. "To each act and step," it was said, "he joined a thought of its use." His was the concept of an organization of the Church into a society of families, with a hierarchy of dedicated leaders. His *Concise Statement of the Principles of the Only True Church* (Bennington, Vermont, 1790) was the first published exposition of the faith, and was also the first explanation of the Shaker doctrine of progressive revelation. And, as a final legacy he left, before his death in 1796, a number of guide lines, or "way-marks," for those "who were or should be called in spiritual or temporal care, In the church."[11]

These writings on church order and government dealt with many sub-

Songs were a crucial part of Shaker worship. From early in the nineteenth century, certain Believers were appointed by the Ministry to be "instruments," to interpret and record divinely inspired songs (many in unknown tongues), messages, and visions.

The leaf sketches were tokens of affection and esteem, presented by one sister or brother to another. This particular leaf, written in 1839, "a golden leaf . . . from the Tree of songs," is a message of love from Mother Lucy to Sister Molly B., written by Mary Hazard.

jects: the order of appointment in the ministry; the importance of union; perfect equality of rights between male and female; instructions to the elders and deacons of the church; instructions to the elderly people; instructions concerning the education of youth and children; instructions relative to military requisitions; the duties of Believers in relation to the world of mankind, and so on.[12]

In Meacham's mind—and afterwards in Shaker practice—*order* and *use* were fundamental values. Thus, "the first lot in the Ministry is to give order and counsel to the second lot in the same Ministry, and to the Elders of the first family, in their own order." "All things ought to be made according to their order and use; and all things kept decent and in good order, according to their order and use. All things made for sale ought to be well done, and suitable for their use." "All ought to dress in plain and modest apparel, but clean and decent according to their order and calling." "All the members of the Church have a just and equal right to the use of things, according to their order and needs." "We are not called to labor to excell, or be like the world; but to excell them in order, union and peace, and in good works—works that are truly virtuous and useful to man, in this life." "All yards and fences . . . ought to be according to the order of buildings." "He [Elder David] is also to establish trades, or the order of trades in the Church." "Deacon Jonathan is called to the chief care and oversight relating to the order of buildings, yards and fences . . . to see that the materials for buildings are suitable for their use, according to the order and use of the buildings, and that the work is done in due order." "All work in the Church ought to be done plain and decent, according to the order and use of things, neither too high nor too low, according to their order and use."

According "to the order of God in the creation," Meacham wrote, every member of the Church, both male and female, should have "an equality in every lot in church relation. . . . For altho our Blessed Lord and Redeemer, Jesus Christ, was complete in his own glorious person, and laid the foundation for the salvation of all souls, yet as God 'hath created man of two parts, the male and female, it was necessary that he should make his second appearance in the second part of man, that the order might be complete, in the new creation."

In a millennial society, the new creation, there should be perfect harmony, perfect justice. Perfection was a way of life, not a state of mind. Everyone should know what was expected of him or her, and the reason why. Everyone should know under what authority, human and divine, he served, and why. Although the law of God exacted duty, submission, and discipline, it gave peace and freedom. The Shakers' vision was one of "gospel order," an ordered society.

The concept of use was similar. Correctly interpreted, it did not mean a narrow, selfish utilitarianism. Useful for what, was the criterion. In Shaker doctrine, all time and effort, all things done, should sustain the society, serve a purpose, and "otherwise as the gospel might require." Waste of time and money was sinful. What was superfluous, in things made or the way they were made, was a departure from essential good. Industrial skills, as we shall see, were expended only on products basically useful to the society and to the world.

Shaker order required exact inventories of property dedicated to the Church, "discharges" or releases when a member apostatized, and indentures in the case of minors brought into the society.

The relinquishment of all personal and private property and of the right to receive wages for his services was the accompaniment of the individual's reception into church or "covenant relationship." It was customary for the prospective member to remain for a time in what was known as the novitiate order, where one might still live with his or her family. While maintaining this partial relationship to the society, the individual retained full control of any property possessed and the freedom to withdraw at any time. Entrance into "church relation" involved not only freedom from all involvements, but a full dedication of all personal property.

Gideon Turner's Inventory:

Memm- of Movebel Estate of Gideon turner Brote in to the church
& given by him to the Care of the Deacons & overseers of the
Church 1788—(viz)

| | |
|---|---|
| 1 pide Horse valued at £12—& one mare & Colt £14— | £26-0-0 |
| 1 yoke 4 year old Cattel at £16—two Cows at £10 | 26-0-0 |
| 8 Sheep at £2-8—four Bads [beds?] & Bading at £26-10 | 28-18-0 |
| Brass Iron puter household furniture etc. | 18-6-2 |
| 1 Set Carpenters tools & 1 Set Joiners tools | |
| plow irons Chans [chains] etc the whole partly wore | 8-0-0 |
| 40 Bushel wheat at 5/4— £10-13-4 | 10-13-4 |
| 1789 | |
| to the use of my farm 1 year paid by Wm Elies | 28-0-0 |
| to the use of the farm 3 years Let to Wm Andros | |
| and paid in the one half of the produce Estimated | 60-0-0 |
| also Received of Elif Wood for a lot of Land Sold him | |
| in the year 1795 one yoke oxen & two Cows | |
| & ten Dollars worth of pork all valued old way at | 30-13-4 |
| | 236-10-10 |
| Inventory taken this 31 day of March 1796— | |
| Deduct out for A Hammond trobel & Expence | £4-0-0 |

29

A covenant member was still free to withdraw at any time from the society. Although in this case no claim could later be made on property once dedicated, the trustees of the temporal interests of the Shaker church invariably exercised justice by making "donations to the full amount of property that such persons have brought in, or become heir to, on their withdrawal."

Jonathan Pearce's Discharge:

Whereas I Jonathan Pearce have heretofore professed myself to be of the Religious Society of Christians Called Shakers and have frequently Visited the Eld.rs of the Church and have from time to time freely Contributed for the Support of the Ministry and Table Expenses, for myself and Others that have Visited the Elders, and for the Support of the Poor of said Church and Society Which I acknowledg I gave or Contributed freely and voluntarily according to my own Faith and that it hath been Consumed in the Manner and for the purpose for Which I gave it—Notwithstanding, since I have departed from them, I have Conceived I have Contributed more than my Just and Equal proportion, While I professed to be in Union with them, and upon that Consideration I have applyed to the present Elders of the Church to Consider me on that Account and have Recd. of Elder David Meacham in behalf of the Church and society the Sum or Value of Three Pounds New York Currency as a Matter of Gratis on their part Which together with what I have heretofore Recd I do acknowledge it to be a Just and Equal Ballence.—Therefore I do by these presents Acquit and discharge the said Church and Society Jointly and Severally from any further Request, Charge or Demand of any kind or Nature Whatever. In Testamony Whereof I have hereunto Sett my hand and Seal this 24th Day of September Adomini One Thousand, Seven Hundred & Eighty Nine—
In presents of
Jonathan Pearce
Abiathar Babbit
Joseph Bennet

When, as sometimes happened, apostates sued the society for property they had brought in or services rendered, these discharges held up in courts of law. The first test case, a suit brought into the New York Supreme Court by Benjamin Goodrich in 1799, resulted in a judgment favoring the society since Goodrich had earlier signed a discharge. Nevertheless, in the covenant as reframed in 1801, the wording was strengthened to give more specific powers to the deacons.

Experience also taught the Shakers legal caution in the matter of indenturing children, or minors, to the deacons or trustees. The covenant of 1795 prescribed the basic conditions, but it was some time before standard forms were used. Indentures varied slightly with family, society, or period. Often a particular occupation was specified. Thus, a nine-year-old girl was to be taught "the art and mystery of Dress-making"; a twelve-year-old boy, "the art and mystery of Farming," and so on.

In the revised printed indentures at New Lebanon, beginning in the 1830s, the rights of both parties to the agreement are more fully specified. The terminal age remained at twenty-one years. However, care was taken to point out that the instrument conformed "to the civil institutions" of the state, and that the minor was "bound" with the consent of the father and of his own free will. There were also certain provisos. If the "infant" should "obstinately refuse to perform and conform in and to" whatever the Shaker trustee shall require of him, the father agrees to take him back without making any charge for the services rendered or "claiming any damages." The father also agrees not to "unlawfully take away" his son during the continuance of the indenture. The trustee of the society, on his part, agrees to provide the boy "with comfortable food and clothing," and teach him, or have him taught "to read and write, and to understand the principles of common arithmetic together with such other branches of education as are usually taught in the schools of the aforesaid United Society. . . . Also such manual occupation or branch of business as shall be found best adapted to his genius and capacity. . . . " and also to provide him with "two suits of good and decent wearing apparel" at the termination of the indenture. "The present good" and "the future benefit and welfare" of the minor—"according to the customs, principles and practice" of the society—were the society's sacred obligation. Although New York and other states sometimes passed prejudicial legislation, the indenture agreements, like the discharges, retained legal validity in most cases of challenge.

In the early period, leading members made out wills in which, in case there were unbelieving relatives, the society was properly provided for.

David Darrow's Will:

Where as I David Darrow of Canaan in the County of Columbia
and State of New York being a member of the Church of Christ Called
Shakers in Said Canaan Did in the year of our Lord one Thousand
Seven Hundred and Eighty Eight in a Solemn maner enter into
Covenant Relation With my Bretheren and Sisters in the Church in the
presents of God and Each other to give my Self and Services to
Support one Joint Union and Interest in Church Relation According
to the order and Covenant of the Church—And as I have Recived the
grace of God in this Day of Christ's Second Appearing which called
me from my former Sins and Seprated me from the Cours of this
World and that Relation which was of the flesh to Labour to Support

the Relation which is of the Spirit—I therefore Did at the Same time
Divote and give as a free will offering According to my one faith and
Desire into the hands and care of the Deacons and overseers of the
Church of my Communion, all my temporal Property to be by them
Improved for pious and Charitable Uses according to thir Direction
agreeable to the order and Covenant of the Church—And I Do here by
for bid all persons Ever here after makeing any Claim or Demand [as
heirs] upon the Said Deacons and oversears for aney property I have
thus Devoted. . . . And being of Sound Disposeing mind and memory,
I Do make and ordain this to be my Last Will and Testament there
by Conferming and Establishing all my former gifts here to fore given
to the Said Deacons and oversears it is also my Desire and will that
all the Remaining part of my Estate whether Real or personal that may
be found belonging to me at the time of my Decease be taken into
the hands and be under the government and Direction of David
Meacham Jonathan Walker and David Osborn Deacons and oversears
of the Church to be by them Improved to those Sacred and Charitable
Uses before mentioned after paying (if any) all my Just Debts—that is,
for the Support of the Gospel the Education and instruction of the
youth of Said Community and for the Relief of Such of the poor the
Widow and fatherless as they Shall Judg to be Real Objects of Charity,
all to be Done According to the faith and Understanding of my Said
Executors as they shall Direct and appoint—and in order that the above
purposes may be carried into full Effect I Devise my whole Estate Real
and Personal to the Said David Meacham Jonathan Walker and David
Osborn Deacons and oversears as affore Said their Successors and
Assigns Upon the Special trust and Confidance that the Same be
applied according to the trew Intent and Meaning above Expressed in
this my Last Will and Testament—
In testimony whereof I have here unto Set my hand and Seal this
twenty seventh Day of December In the Year of our Lord one
Thousand Seven Hundred and Ninety eight

                                        David Darrow


Signed Sealed pronounced and Declared by him the Said Testator—to
be his Last Will and testament in presents of Us the Subscribing Witnesses & the presents of the S$^d$ testator And Each other

                                Samuel Gilbert
                                Epaphras Mac Swerth
                                Eli Hand


The "order and arrangement" of the United Society underwent change
in the course of time. By 1830, however, with the publication of *A Brief
Exposition,* a definite pattern had emerged. In each community, according
to this statement, there were three "progressive degrees of order":

1.  In first, or novitiate, class were those who received the faith but chose to live in their own family order and manage their own temporal affairs. They were admitted to all the privileges of the society, temporal and spiritual, but the society had no control over their property or children. Donations were voluntary, but could not be reclaimed. However, the society expected that as long as they remained in the gathering order they should bear in mind "the necessity and importance of a spiritual increase."

2.  The second, or junior, class was composed of persons "not having the charge of families" who wished to enjoy the benefits of membership. On joining they signed a contract or covenant in which they agreed to devote their *services* to the order and not to claim pecuniary compensation for such services. They had the privilege, by contract, to give the *improvement* of any part or all of their property, but the property could be resumed (without interest paid) at any time; or, if they wished, they could consecrate a part or the whole of their property to the institution. It was a matter of free choice.

3.  Those in the third, or senior, class—Meacham's "inner court"—covenanted to devote themselves and services, with all that they possessed (after settlement of any legal claims by creditors or heirs) to the service of God and the support of the gospel, promising at the same time never to claim or demand against the society for any services or property thus consecrated.

By these means and statements of principles the society sought to establish itself on a sound legal or constitutional foundation. However, since the Shakers had devoted their property to sacred purposes and separated themselves from the world, their estate, they held, was "a consecrated whole," not a joint tenancy or a tenancy in common to be incorporated under civil or political authority. For this reason, as we shall see, they were to come into frequent conflict with that authority. The purpose of *A Brief Exposition* was to obviate a "defamatory" bill presented to the New York legislature which would subject Shaker property to judgments and executions against individual members, prohibit fathers turning over all their property to the society, and prevent evasion of the military law by the Shakers. The foundation of the "peculiar" institution remained insecure for a long time.

> Between 1800 and 1860 [revivalism] was the one great religious movement in America, overshadowing the progress of liberal theology. It entered so fully into the lives of ordinary men and women that it became almost equal in importance to the conquest

of the West, the struggle over slavery, the progress of mechanics, and other decisive movements of the time. Like them, revivalism had a share in creating the national character. It became part of the national background and left a mark on the mind and soul of America.[13]

About twenty-five years after the forces of revivalism in New England had laid the foundation of the first group of Shaker communities, another great awakening was the means by which the United Society extended its scope and enlarged its structure. In the early years of the nineteenth century, when the Great Southern and Western Revival (the Kentucky Revival) was at its height, the central ministry at New Lebanon followed its course with interest. They remembered Mother Ann's prophecy that the next opportunity to open the testimony would be in "a great region in the Southwest." In 1805, when schisms were dividing the revivalists and a period of reaction and disillusionment setting in, the ministry took advantage of the unrest to send three advocates of the Shaker faith—Benjamin S. Youngs, Issacher Bates, and John Meacham—to this fertile ground. There they made contact with Richard McNemar, John Dunlavy, Matthew Houston, and others who had broken with the Presbyterian Synod to form a new sect called Schismatic Christians, or New Lights. In the course of time these dissenters, with their followers, influenced by the Shaker teaching and worship and demonstrated success in communitarian practice, proclaimed their allegiance to the eastern faith. The upshot of the mission was the establishment

*Shaker communities were characterized by their trim, orderly appearance and functional simplicity.*

of seven colonies in the West: four in Ohio at Turtle Creek (Union Village), Whitewater, Watervliet, and North Union (now Shaker Heights); two in Kentucky at Pleasant Hill (Shakertown) and South Union; and one, short-lived, at West Union (Busro) in Indiana. After the pattern set by New Lebanon, these societies were organized into bishoprics, with leadership and substantial monetary assistance provided by the eastern churches.

With the establishment of the western communities, the structure of the United Society was virtually complete. One important colony was to be added later, at Sodus Bay, New York, which moved to Groveland in the same state in 1836. Although the covenants adopted by these communities varied somewhat from the earlier ones in the East, they were in substance the same, and resisted similar legal assaults on their constitutionality. That the movement expanded with such success in new territory, drawing people from varying conditions of life on the western frontier, was proof of its vitality. It had taken on the characteristics of a national crusade, appealing to thousands of men and women as the solution to economic problems as well as the promise of a more abundant life.

Out of the West came a much needed formulation of the purpose to which these thousands had dedicated their property and labor. Before Richard McNemar published *The Kentucky Revival* at Cincinnati in 1807, the only exposition of the Shaker faith was the small pamphlet written by Joseph Meacham in 1790. For twenty-five years, in treatises by Valentine, Daniel, and Reuben Rathbun, Amos Taylor, and Benjamin West, the "wicked" had circulated falsehoods and distortions about the sect. Prejudice was widespread, often erupting into violence. With the appearance of McNemar's work, and more importantly, the definitive statement of Shaker faith and practice, *The Testimony of Christ's Second Appearing* by Benjamin S. Youngs, published at Lebanon, Ohio, in 1808, the case for the Believers could be judged on its merits. Though opposition to the Shakers continued—in books, pamphlets, and in the courts—it was rooted in prejudice and self-interest, not ignorance of the principles on which the sect had based itself.

McNemar was a thoughtful scholar who was earnestly seeking for the true path to Christian perfection. He was impressed with the arguments of the three missionaries, but examined them scrupulously before he adopted the faith. Two passages among others in *The Kentucky Revival* are statements in Shaker doctrine which he found irrefutable. The way to obtain salvation, the missionaries had taught, was by self-denial,

> taking up a full cross against the world, the flesh and all evil in
> our knowledge, and following Christ; walking as he walked and
> being in all things conformed to him, as our pattern and head.
> Particularly according to St. Paul, become dead with Christ to the

rudiments of the world—dying unto sin once—Rising with him to
a more spiritual and holy life, and ascending step by step in a
spiritual travel, and separating farther and farther from the course
of a corrupt and fallen nature, until we arrive at the perfect stature
and measure of the sons of God.[14]

God is present within the soul, the Shakers taught.

With inward sense of the power, protection, and presence of God,
the Believer travels out of the use of shadows and signs, ceremonies
and forms of worship. . . . There is no more occasion for calling
upon God afar off, when he has taken possession of his body, and
lives and walks in him, nor for calling to his memory, a departed
saviour, by signs and shadows of his dying love; when the only
saviour that ever redeemed a lost soul, is formed and living in him,
and executing every branch of his office.[15]

Youngs's book, sometimes called the "Shaker bible," was an exhaustive
treatise on Christianity, from the "fall of man" to the second appearing
of Christ. Revelation, according to the author, was a progressive work. God's
will was partially revealed in the ministry of Jesus, the primitive Christian
Church, and the pentecostal concept that Christ's kingdom was not of this
world. Then the reign of antichrist, in the form of the Catholic Church,
set in; the redeeming spirit left the earth with the domination of Leo the
Great (450 A.D.), the union of Church and State, and the enslavement of
conscience. In this dark period, unrelieved even by the Protestant Reforma-
tion, which was also a persecuting force, only the aspirations of the so-called
heretical sects—the Cathari, Albigenses, Quakers, and others—represented
the truth.

Youngs's view of a progressive revelation of truth was amplified in a
later Shaker exposition, *A Summary View of the Millennial Church*, by Calvin
Green and Seth Y. Wells, first published in 1823. In this work, the two
New Lebanon elders found that despite the persecutions rampant during
the reign of antichrist, the general principle of religious liberty was gaining
adherents during the seventeenth century. They mention the proclamation
by William of Orange, in 1689, concerning liberty of conscience in England,
and the edict of Peter the Great, in 1721, establishing "a plenary liberty of
conscience" throughout the Russian empire. From that period "the principles of civil and religious rights and liberty continued to gain ground,
especially in England and other parts of Europe."

Though there seems to have been no direct influence, the Shakers, in
Youngs's interpretation, approved of the Manichean doctrine which denied
the miraculous birth, the incarnation, the divinity of Jesus. In Shaker
thought, the mission of Jesus was to make manifest the divine attributes
36   of man, which He did more fully than anyone who had ever lived. The

dualistic doctrine of the Manicheans—that flesh was at war with spirit, that the material world was evil, and that escape or salvation lay in inspiration, a mystical understanding of the will of God, and a life of asceticism—also found a response in Shaker belief.

In conclusion, Youngs described in detail the attributes of the true church of Christ, in which He appeared for the second time in the testimony of Ann Lee. She it was who was destined by the prophecy of Daniel in Revelations to usher in the millennium, the thousand-year Kingdom of Christ on earth.

From the West, therefore, came the rationale of Shakerism. Because the communities there were removed from a certain Puritan conservatism dominant in the East, there was also a freer expression in worship; the lively songs and "exercises" which were to distinguish Shaker meetings originated in the West and eventually were taken up by the societies in New York and New England. Doubtless it was because the frontier colonies in Ohio and Kentucky were situated in the paths of the westward movement and were less isolated from the world that as a group they dissolved earlier than the older orders.

In addition to the works of McNemar and Youngs, one other early exposition of Shaker doctrine came out of the West, John Dunlavy's *The Manifesto*, published at Pleasant Hill, Kentucky, in 1818. In this treatise was the first reasoned defense of the principle of a "Joint Inheritance in things spiritual as well as temporal," a theme taken up again in *A Summary View of the Millennial Church*, in a section on the "Right Use of Property." "The true followers of Christ," the authors point out, "are one with him, as he is one with the Father. This oneness includes all they possess; for he who has devoted himself to Christ, soul, body, and spirit, can by no means withhold his property."

Green and Wells were deeply concerned with the problem of poverty, and its relation to property. "There are many, very many of our fellow beings," they wrote, "as good by nature as ourselves, and doubtless as precious in the sight of God, who through misfortune, are suffering from the want of the good things which we enjoy; and shall we be justified before God, if we do not extend the hand of charity according to our ability?" And again: "How many are the favorites of fortune, who share largely in the things of this world, and yet expend the property entrusted to their charge, in gratifying their own selfish propensities?" "Experience has proved, in the United Society that . . . the right use of property . . . is best promoted . . . by uniting it in a common stock, where all belonging to the Society, can unite to make it an increasing interest, for benevolent purposes, and at the same time, enjoy a competency out of it, upon terms of equality. . . . The same experience also proves, that a little, with union and harmony, and under judicious management, suffices to supply many wants."

# II  Hands to Work

Before the eighteenth century closed, the temporal foundations of Shaker-ism had been laid firmly. It had emerged as a *United* Society, with a clear-cut pattern of social organization. Through the testimony of Ann Lee and the first witnesses, the "way-marks" of Joseph Meacham, and the principles of a written covenant, the members of the order were conscious of their "privilege" and what it involved in work and sacrifice. With the establish-ment of the western communities early in the next century, the society had greatly expanded its range and influence, and in the works of McNemar, Youngs, Dunlavy, Green and Wells, had been given a rationale and theology.

The fate of the movement, from the beginning, depended, however, on whether it could survive as an order separate from the world, the American world of its time. In subjecting themselves to a rigid discipline and a system of common ownership, the Shakers had adopted a course at variance with the forces of freedom, individualism, and "progress" prevalent in society at large. In the young republic, their chiliastic doctrine, their reliance on special revelation, and their emphasis on the role of celibacy seemed reac-tionary, if not subversive, when compared with American institutions.

Opinion regarding the sect gradually changed, once the character of the institution became better known. Sporadic violence, however, by "mobs" continued, particularly in the West. Anti-Shaker literature found avid readers. Legislatures passed laws detrimental to the society. But a more tolerant attitude was all the while emerging. Local communities were grant-ing the Shaker societies their share of school funds and recognizing them in general on the same basis as other separatist denominations. In the world at large there were also signs of greater understanding. As severe a critic as Timothy Dwight, president of Yale, acknowledged that by 1799, "policy was taking the place of extravagance." Here, it came to be felt, was just another example of voluntary action, an experiment in association which was *not* at variance with American tradition. In the United States, de Toc-queville was to note, there were an "immense assemblage of associations ... not only commercial and political associations but associations of a thousand other kinds, religious, moral, serious, futile, general or restricted, enormous or diminutive." The Shaker covenant was no more radical than, say, the Mayflower Compact, *The Bloudy Tenent* of Roger Williams, or *The Fundamental Orders* of Thomas Hooker. Youngs's *Testimony* may be com-pared with John Eliot's *The Christian Commonwealth*. They were all the signs of seeking.

It was the economic policy of the society which, more than any other factor, formed a bridge of understanding between the society and the world. The Shakers were not *economic* separatists. They realized that subsistence, indeed survival, depended on industry and trade. They sought to erect
40  barriers against worldly contamination, but at the same time welcomed

the opportunity to produce goods which the world needed, and which would excel what the world could produce. Their communities were always open to the traveler, even the tramps and the so-called "winter Shakers" who professed interest in the doctrine in the late fall but left with the advent of spring. Services in the meetinghouses were open to the public. Serious inquirers were welcomed in the novitiate order. Students of communism found the Shaker leaders well informed on the social problems of the day. In short, the society, in principle and by necessity in practice, did not cut itself off from the life of the times. By carefully controlled contact with the world, it sought to strengthen its material foundation as the means of expanding its spiritual mission.

The key people in this relationship were the trustees and deacons, those in charge of the "temporalities." Their place was in "the outer court," but they were responsible to the elders and ultimately to the ministry. In theory, there was a distinction between the two offices: the trustees administered the "fixed property," with power to give and receive deeds of warranty, represent the society in lawsuits, buy or sell property, and so forth; the deacons (and deaconesses) directed given departments of industry and supervised the temporal needs of the family.

In practice, however, the functions of the two offices often merged. In the *Millennial Laws, or Gospel Statutes and Ordinances* of the society,[1] first recorded at New Lebanon in 1821 and revised in 1845, the "deacons or trustees" were treated as one order, a stewardship embracing all business transactions. Among their duties were the following:

2.  It is the duty of the Deacons and Deaconesses, or Trustees, to see to the domestic concerns of the family in which they reside, and to perform all business transactions, either with the world, or with believers in other families or societies. All trade and traffic, buying and selling, changing and swapping, must be done by them or by their immediate knowledge and consent.

4.  All monies, book accounts, deeds, bonds, notes, etc. which belong to the Church or family must be kept at the Office. . . . Exceptions with regard to spending money are sometimes necessary, which must always be directed by the Elders, in union with the Ministry.

5.  The Deacons or Trustees should keep all their accounts booked down regular and exact, and as far as possible avoid controversies with the world.

6.  Believers must not run in *debt* to the world.

10. Believers should have no connection in trade or barter with those who have turned their backs to the way of God. . . .

19. The order of God forbids that Believers should lend money upon usury (or interest) to their brethren of the household of faith. . . .

20. Those appointed to transact business are required to keep all their transactions plain and open to their visible Lead, and when they sustain lapses, whether in money or other things, to lay it open before the Lead in its true light. They are also required before making any heavy purchases, to ask counsel and obtain union of the leading influence of the Church or family in which they reside.

22. When brethren or sisters want anything bought, or brought in from among the world, or from other families of Believers, or wish for any article or articles which it is the duty of the Deacons and Deaconesses to provide, they must apply to them for whatever they desire, those of each sex in their own order. . . .

29. It is the duty of the Deacons and Deaconesses to see that suitable furniture for rooms, and suitable food for the family are provided . . . and to see that the food is cooked with good economy.

In the performance of such duties, the Laws enjoined the deacons and trustees to hold "the line of separation" from worldly influence. For instance:

11. When you resort to taverns, and public places, you shall not in any wise blend and gather with the wicked, by uniting in unnecessary conversation, jesting and joking, talking upon politics with them, or disputing or enquiring into things which will serve to draw your sense from the pure way of God.

12. All who go out among the world, should observe as far as possible, the order of kneeling, and should always kneel in prayer twice each day, if they have to do it by the road-side, or in the waggon, while driving along. . . .

16. When two or more are out together, they should as far as possibly consistent, all eat at one tavern, and lodge in one room, and when you walk in the streets, you should keep so close together that there would not be room for even so much as a dog to run between you and your companion.

The dispatch with which the converts to the Shaker faith put principles into practice was phenomenal. Even before they were fully organized in covenantal relations or the duties of deacons and trustees fully defined, they were putting their hands to work in various occupations of shop and field. Inspired by the impulses of the revival and the teachings of the "first witnesses," the Believers were eager to embark on the great enterprise of salvation, to realize in full measure the gospel promise, to start building a new earth. In 1795, only two years after the communities at Shirley and Harvard were organized, the Reverend William Bentley observed in his diary: "To see a Sect advanced from such unformed state, to the more civilized condition of little Towns ... was an object which provoked my greatest curiosity."[2]

The people drawn into the movement came from no fixed social class or economic stratum, no particular religious affiliation. There were none who could be called rich, but on the other hand there were many who were fairly prosperous tradesmen and farmers with considerable landholdings. There was a scattering of professional men, doctors, ministers, and teachers, and many artisans, mechanics, tanners, tailors, blacksmiths, coopers, weavers, millers, and practitioners of other trades. There were, of course, also many who were poor, families without means, many others victims of the economic depression following the Revolution. But though some may have joined as an escape from poverty or marital troubles, with most it was a matter of serious conviction. They were not in any sense a proletariat, but rather seekers after a better way of life, a true Christian fellowship. As Richard Ely was to observe at a later period, "These simple people fail to see how those who profess to be followers of Christ can tolerate luxury and poverty side by side among brothers and sisters, for this does not seem to them compatible with Christian love."[3]

Within the organizational framework instituted by Joseph Meacham and others, property and skills were put to immediate use. The farms consecrated by David and George Darrow, Amos Hammond, John Bishop, and others at New Lebanon became the nucleus of a landed estate which was gradually increased, by donation or purchase, until in 1839 it embraced 2,292¼ acres. By that date the property at Watervliet had also increased from the few virgin acres purchased by the first Shakers to an estate of 2,547 acres, much of it cleared and cultivated by assiduous toil. The same pattern obtained in all the societies: one of the foundations of the Canterbury community was Benjamin Whitcher's farm; at Enfield, New Hampshire, James Jewett's; at Hancock, Daniel Goodrich's. The community at Shirley owed its location and start to the benefactions of four well-to-do citizens, Elijah and Ivory Wilds, John Warren, and Nathan Willard; and at Harvard, to Zaccheus Stevens and Isaac and Jeremiah Willard. Sometimes the gift was money. One wonders if the early buildings at New Lebanon—including the great frame dwelling erected in 1788—could have been built without the liberal contributions of Joseph Bennett, Sr., one of Ann Lee's first converts, a prosperous landowner and one of the first proprietors of the town of New Providence (now Cheshire), Massachusetts.[4]

The site for a community, thus determined by a bequest of "good tillage," 43 farm buildings, and money, was then expanded through further donations and the purchase of contiguous properties. Once the title deeds were secured, all available land was put to use. At the New Lebanon Church, though the society was at first handicapped by a shortage of horses and oxen and the "coarseness" of agricultural implements, sizable crops of wheat, rye, oats, barley, corn, flax, and potatoes were being grown by the late 1780s. In 1789, for instance, some 3,000 bushels of potatoes were harvested for the use of the family. The raising of garden seeds for the market began about five or six years later.

The nature of industry was likewise determined by the skills available. By 1788-89, the following trades were being practiced at New Lebanon: tanning, blacksmithing, shoemaking, coopering, "clothiering," "tayloring," hatting, saddle-, buckle-, button-, dipper-, and whip-making, "joinering" and carpentry. As time went on, industry became increasingly diversified, specialized, and organized. But no time was wasted or purposes diverted by what Bentley called the pursuit of "speculative knowledge" and theory. Though the motivation was at heart religious, in practice there was no conflict between technical knowledge and religious faith. In the pursuit of their high purpose, science was integrated with, and served the cause of, humanitarianism.

Bentley's experience at Harvard and Shirley in 1795 will illustrate how rapidly two typical communities put into effect Mother Ann's injunction of "hands to work." All the rooms at Harvard, he observed, were "furnished" with stoves, which the Shakers had cast themselves. The blacksmiths there were also making andirons, boxes for wagon wheels, iron and brass candlesticks, etc. The whitesmiths were working in tin. There were several clocks "of their own making." Bentley admired their blue and white checked handkerchiefs, their fine linens, their excellent diaper, the "stuff" for women's cloaks, the shoes made of lasting. He was given clay pipes, with stems called "stails" (stales) of osier. He saw some "excellent" whips, shoe brushes, hammers of "neat & sufficient workmanship," and even a surgeon's instrument "made with great exactness." He noticed with pleasure the gardens, the beds of "Sage & Baum" (balm), and the stone walls "as straight as they can be made," the hollows filled up "to preserve a horizontal line in the fence." At Shirley, he paid tribute to the sturdy construction of the meetinghouse. The rooms in the Shirley dwelling were clean, orderly, and well furnished. The "neatness of their employments" everywhere impressed him.[5]

In these communities, as in the others established in the last two decades of the eighteenth century, the concept of manual labor as a duty, a therapy, a ritual was at the root of achievement. It was also the test of character; for no one in the society could be elevated to "lots" of leadership before they had "gained a gift in hand labor." And once appointed to the positions of eldership or ministry they continued to contribute, in special shops, to the economic welfare of the society. Many a visitor, such as Theodore Parker, remarked on this trait in the course of the last century. "You have no *menial service,*" he wrote to a Shaker friend in 1848, "none of your community thinks work is degrading, while in Society at large many are now ashamed of men (and women) who work and make them ashamed of themselves. Now *the Shakers have completely done away with that evil* as it seems to me. —that is one of their great merits, and it is a *very* great one, at the same time they secure *comfort* and win *health.*"[6]

One must admire, with Bentley, the effectiveness with which a sect, widely opposed at first and loosely organized in many parts of the East, was unified into a viable economic community. Within a brief period, and apparently with no knowledge of earlier experiments in religious association, the Shakers developed a system of combined labor and expenditure which not only provided subsistence but allowed for a surplus market. What made the system particularly effective, apart from the custom of wisely utilizing and allocating all available skills, was the spirit of cooperation or union which animated the whole enterprise. It was a form of people's capitalism, as Emerson later noted, in which the capitalist never dies and in which every adherent had a stake, economic as well as religious.

Over and over again that spirit was manifest in the life of the people. Although families were economically autonomous, buying from and selling to other families in the same community, they came together in the meeting-house on the Sabbath, met together at funerals and other occasions, and always cooperated, with money and labor, when there was sickness or loss by fire, when a large building project was under way, or when the sharing of knowledge would advance the common good. Shaker records abound with examples. For instance, when the North house was being built in New Lebanon, "Timber and Bords" were provided by the other families. On June 6, 1804, the office donated chairs, looking glasses, shovels, hinges, books, etc. From Niskeyuna came shingles, lime, clapboards, and stuff for window frames. On November 27, 1809, the ministry at New Lebanon proposed and agreed that "as an act of liberality worthy of the faith which we profess, to put in practice the principles of a united interest so far as to having the dressing of cloth in the Society done freely for the whole Society, without charge. This being acceded to, it was next proposed to have all the tanning and currying done upon the same liberal principles. . . ." At a later date (July 24, 1843)—to cite one more example—"Five of us [from the Church] went over to the Second order to help raise a barn. There has a Mason come on today to plaster between Joice and finish the oven and chimneys that Family left unfinished in consequence of being taken sick with a fever."[7] When large projects, such as the building of the second meetinghouse at New Lebanon (1822-24), were undertaken, labor, materials, 45 and money flowed in from other communities. Thousands of dollars from the eastern societies helped to support those in the West during the critical years of their organization.

*The first Shaker meetinghouses were large white, gambrel-roofed structures. The two doors facing the street were for visitors; the Shakers themselves entered the doors at the side—the brethren used the right door; the sisters, the left door; and the ministry, the center door.*

# The Culture
# of the Land

When James F. W. Johnston of the University of Durham in England began gathering notes for his two-volume work on North America (1851), the common opinion of the Shakers "at home" was that of a sect "distinguished only for odd customs and forms of worship." He was surprised, therefore, on his arrival here, to be informed "that the only localities in this State [New York] in which farming is carried on systematically, on a large scale, are the Settlements of the Shakers."[1]

Some fifteen years later, when another Englishman, Hepworth Dixon, editor of the *Athenaeum*, visited America, he had a similar experience. He had heard that the Shakers were known "to scoffers as a comic institution." The word "Shaker," he knew, was a term of "mockery and reproach." But when he inquired about the best place to collect American shrubs and flowers, he was told that no one in New York or Massachusetts could match the New Lebanon Shakers in the production of seeds and plants. Curious as to why, in a region where "the best talents" were "invested.... in the art of producing plenty from the soil," the Shakers should be the only seedsmen in the state, he was told it was because "they give their minds to it."[2]

Except in those areas in which the Believers specialized, notably the garden seed and medicinal herb business, the *produce* of Shaker farms did not differ markedly from that of farms "in the world." Potatoes were an important crop from the beginning. Flax was grown both for seed and for fiber. Barley, rye, wheat, and oats were cultivated for domestic needs, although the society often had to buy flour and grain (especially wheat) to fulfill its requirements. Much of the acreage not used for fuel and timber was devoted to hay. At New Lebanon, poultry and livestock, especially Saxon and Merino sheep, were also raised chiefly for home use, although in some communities, in the West particularly, considerable attention was given to the breeding of superior strains of sheep and cattle.[3] Before the Shakers renounced the use of pork in 1845, hogs were also an important part of the livestock. Well-tended vineyards, berry fields, and orchards (apple, pear, quince, cherry, peach, etc.) dotted the Shaker lands. Each family had its kitchen gardens, which were separate from those devoted to the seed and herb industries.

Surplus from the family farms was sold at the office or store, and in some cases a considerable business resulted. At New Lebanon, Hancock, Harvard, and other communities, dried apples and cider apple sauce had a ready market. Dried sweet corn, a Shaker specialty, was first retailed and wholesaled at New Lebanon, beginning in 1828, and later sold at the other New York colonies at Watervliet and Groveland. In the community kitchens, preserves, jellies, and wines were put up for sale as well as for domestic use, and the Believers at New Lebanon and Watervliet carried on—some say originated—the canning of vegetables for the market. Honey, maple sugar, and other confections were sold in many of the societies, as well as cheese, butter, and eggs.

What made the Shaker agriculture distinctive was its diversity, the neatness of the tillage, the experimental attitude toward farming methods, the democratic manner in which labor was allocated, and the spirit pervading all farm operations.

The careful study of agriculture was exalted by the Shakers into a kind of religious ritual. They looked upon the soil as something to be redeemed from "rugged barrenness into smiling fertility and beauty."[4] This thought is expressed in many ways. Shaker land "is easily known," wrote one visitor, "by its superior cultivation, and by its substantial stone-wall fences."[5] Hepworth Dixon found the Shakers believing that "if you would have a lovely garden, you should live a lovely life," and in the introduction to the *Gardener's Manual*, published in 1843, the writer insists that the garden is "an index of the owner's mind." Dixon's conversation with Elder Frederick Evans illuminates this attitude of spiritual devotion to husbandry.

> This morning [he writes] I have spent an hour with Frederick in the new orchard, listening to the story of how he planted it, as to a tale by some Arabian poet. "A tree has its wants and wishes,"

48

said the Elder; "and a man should study them as a teacher watches a child, to see what he can do. If you love the plant, and take heed of what it likes, you will be well repaid by it. I don't know if a tree ever comes to know you; and I think it may; but I am sure it feels when you care for it and tend it; as a child does, as a woman does. Now, when we planted this orchard, we first got the very best cuttings in our reach; we then built a house for every plant to live in, that is to say, we dug a deep hole for each; we drained it well; we laid down tiles and rubble, and then filled in a bed of suitable manure and mould; we put the plant into its nest gently, and pressed up the earth about it, and protected the infant tree by this metal fence."

"You take a world of pains," I said.

"Ah, Brother Hepworth," he rejoined, "Thee sees we love our garden."[6]

It was significant to Hepworth Dixon that the first building he came upon as he entered the New Lebanon Village, at its very gateway, was a great stone barn. "The granary is to a Shaker," he wrote, "what the Temple was to a Jew." Barns were always well built and equipped with the best machinery.

The stock, consisting of horses, cows, oxen, and sheep, were well housed in these large, immaculate barns. Hervey Elkins reported that the Shakers took "great pains to improve their breeds of domestic animals, particularly cattle and sheep."[7] The Enfield (New Hampshire) society, about which he was writing, transported Durham cattle from Kentucky for this purpose, and a superior strain of sheep from France, the latter costing "from two to five hundred dollars per head." Poultry and turkeys were also raised at New Lebanon, and at one time several colonies of bees were kept. No dogs were allowed, and "no kind of beasts, birds, fowls or fishes" were permitted "merely for the sake of show or fancy." Special orders regarding the care of beasts, "the natural creation," were likewise enforced. They were never to be neglected, nor "chastened or corrected in a passion."

Some of these orders have a quaint interest. For instance: "Different species of trees, or plants may not be engrafted or budded upon each other, as apples upon pears, quince, etc. peaches upon cherries, or contrary wise." "The different species of animals should also be kept distinct, each in their own order." "No fowls, may be set on the eggs of fowls of different kinds."[8]

Creameries were models of neatness and well ventilated: "We believe that in order to make butter that shall be free from every taint," a Shaker elder declared, "we must begin with the cow barns. They are perfectly ventilated." Great care was taken to provide fresh water for the hen houses and all farm buildings. All in all, Shaker farms, as Emerson noted, were "model" establishments influencing practice everywhere in their neighborhoods; farmers seeking the most effective methods and machinery often

sought the advice which the Shakers stood ready to give.

The scope of agricultural activities may be judged by the following account of produce and stock of the Church family in New Lebanon a few years before the Civil War:[9]

*Produce Raised on the Farm.*
Hay, tuns 118. Barley, 100 bushels. Oats, 375 bush. Corn & Cob, 219 bushels. Cucumber seed, 265 lbs. Onion seed, 747 lbs. Potatoes, 320 bushel. Wool unwashed, 380 lbs.

*Stock Kept.*
Oxen, 3 yoke. Steers, 2 yoke. Fatten oxen, 1 yoke. Fatten cows, 6 all butchered. Cows Milch, 20. Young Cattle, 15. Sheep, 80. Horses, 3.

*Produce of Orchards and Nurserys.*
Apples, 300 bushels. Pears, 12 bushels. Quinces, 24 bushels. Cherries, 18 bushels. Currants, 16 bushels. Grapes, 12 bushels. Strawberries, 21 bushels. Plumbs, 10 bushels.

*Fruit Sold.*
Apples, 67 bushels, 5 bbls. of sauce. Tomato, 72 gallons. 24 gls. Maple (?) Currants, 8 do. Quinces, 13 bushels.

*Preserves Made.*
Apples dried, none. Tomatoes, 100 gallons. Strawberries, 18 gallons. Cherries, 7 gallons preserved, 7 dried. Blackberries, 11 gals. Whortleberries, 3 gals. Grape jelly, 3 gals. Pears, 6 gals. Plums, 36 glls. Quince, 30 glls.

*Produce of Dairy.*
Cheese, 1131 lbs. Butter, 2538 lbs.

In 1860, more than 800 bushels of oats, 515 bushels of corn on the cob, and 6 tons of fodder corn were grown. In that year, the crop of eating apples amounted to 1,200 bushels, and cider apples to 400 bushels. Ten bushels of gooseberries and 84 bushels of pears were picked. In 1863, 40 bushels of currants were sold. Some mutton was marketed as early as 1810. In 1866, more than 5,200 pounds of beef were sold and more than 500 pounds of "fried tallow." Most of the butter and cheese at this time was consumed at home; in 1860, only 380 pounds of cheese were marketed, and in 1863, only 50 pounds of butter.

It will be noted that grain was not raised on a large scale even as late as 1858, and from the first, the Shakers were obliged to buy corn, wheat, rye, barley, and oats in great quantity from outside the limits of their own domains. Neither could the relatively small number of sheep supply the Believers with sufficient wool, nor their own cattle with sufficient hides or beef. When one considers how extensive were such industries as tanning, cloth manufacture, and the drying of sweet corn, it will readily be seen that the society could not supply sufficient raw materials for its own de-  51 mands, and the oft-repeated opinion that the Shakers were·sufficient unto themselves must be radically revised in this regard. Nevertheless they utilized their own resources as far as they were able, and hired "world's people" when labor shortage became acute.

The conduct of the farmer was subject to detailed regulation. It was required, for instance, that "when brethren and sisters are about the farm and pass through bars, or gates, they should always leave them closed, unless they find them evidently left open on purpose. And when brethren are about the farm, and find gates open, bars down, or fences broken down, they should put them in order, if consistent, if not, inform those set in order to take care of them, on their return home. All implements of labor, carts, waggons, sleighs, sleds, etc. should be put into their proper places, on Saturday night, and as far as consistent every night; and all of these things should be done in season to retire at the time appointed, if possible."[10]

Believing that variety of occupation broadened one's faculties and increased one's pleasure, they advocated "frequent shifts in duties ... to even the load," a practice "facilitated by the fact that nearly every adult male was quite conversant with almost all the tasks of the farm."[11] Although each department had a deacon in charge, the general practice was followed of allowing each man to do the work he liked best. Many a visitor remarked on the quiet tenor, the harmony of all the labors on the Shaker farms. "You see that the men who till these fields, who tend these gardens, who bind these sheaves, who train these vines, who plant these apple-trees, have been drawn into putting their love into the daily task; and you hear with no surprise that these toilers, ploughing and planting in their quaint garb, consider their labor on the soil as a part of their ritual, looking upon the earth as a strained and degraded sphere, which they have been called to redeem from corruption and restore to God."[12]

The repute which Shaker husbandry had in the world, as evidenced by Johnston and Dixon among others, was based largely, however, on the fact that the Believers specialized in two fields: the growing, packaging, and marketing of garden seeds, and the preparation of medicinal herbs for the pharmaceutical market. The products of their fields, orchards, and kitchens were well known locally. Their marketing practices were highly respected. But in the American world at large, and even abroad, it was the famous Shaker seeds and herbs which had a name and commanded a premium in an increasingly competitive market. Their seed business, an apologist for the sect recently wrote, "made some amends for celibacy by eventually disseminating Shaker integrity to all parts of the country."[13]

These two occupations were significant developments in American economic history:

1. In both fields, later important segments of American industry,
   the Shakers were pioneers.

2.  They combined, in one setting, operations of both field and shop.

3.  They were early examples in our history of large-scale enterprise, representing a step away from household to factory production.

4.  Yet the profit motive remained subservient to good work, the desire not to compete but to excel. "When a Shaker is put upon the soil, to beautify it by his tilth, the difference between his husbandry and that of a Gentile farmer, who is thinking solely of his profits, is likely to be great. While the Gentile is watching for his returns, the Shaker is intent upon his service."[14]

# The Garden Seed Industry

As in all Shaker industries, the beginning was small. The seed business originated about the same time, 1790-1800, in the two New York communities of New Lebanon and Watervliet, spreading then to the societies in New England. The Believers at Watervliet had a "family garden" as early as 1790, about two acres. "Joseph Turner supervised it, and began to raise a few seeds for sale."[15] Shortly afterward, the business was run by one Ebenezer Alden, who was to become the inventor of a "printing box" for hand printing of the seed bags. (The Shakers are said to have been the first to put up seeds in small paper envelopes.) From 1811, when the Watervliet Shakers raised about $300 worth of seeds, to 1840, at the height of the enterprise, the seed business was their chief industry.

In an old account book, "Seeds Raised at the Shaker Gardens,"[16] 1795 is given as the first year in which garden seeds were systematically grown at New Lebanon. Onion seed was the largest item—201 pounds—while scarcity beet, carrot, cucumber, and summer squash brought the year's total to 44 pounds, priced at $406. The following year, radish seed, two varieties of turnip, and three of cabbage were raised. The head gardener or seedsman in these early years was one Artemas Markham.

The record shows a slowly increasing business in these and other varieties of seeds. By 1800, the sales had passed the $1,000 mark. In 1805, 1,385¾ pounds of seeds were raised, selling for $1,240. Flax seed, which is not mentioned in the early garden seed book, was an important item—perhaps the largest selling commodity during the first decade or so of the century.[17]

At first, the seed business was confined to a local area. As time went on, the trips of seedsmen became more extended, not only to the "Northward," but to the "Eastward," the "Southward," and the "Westward," "until    53 in all parts of the country the Shaker Seed wagon and the shrewd, honest, sedate but kindly Shaker Brother, who sold the seeds, were familiar as the spring-time."[18] The important westward route through eastern and central New York was inaugurated by 1812 or earlier. In that year, 1,313 pounds of seeds were sold for $1,198. With the exception of the year 1818, the annual production after 1814 was in excess of 2,000 pounds, which provided an income of well over $2,000. In the first twenty-five years of the seed business at the Church family, 37,242 pounds of seeds were raised at a market value of $33,901.

Some difficulty was caused by the fact that almost every New York and New England society became engaged in this business, and as it prospered, each seed company extended its field of operations. As a result, societies naturally encroached upon one another's territory. In a letter dated Watervliet, December 26, 1822, Brother Morrell thus voices his complaint to Daniel Goodrich of Hancock:

... Being placed in this poor condition, we were obliged to seek ways and means to get our livelyhood and pretty soon commenced the business of raising garden-seeds. There being none among the other societys of believers at that time who thought it worth commencing, or at least were not under the necessity to do it. All this time we vended our Seeds throughout the State we live in. But our Lebanon Brethren in a few years perceiving it was becoming profitable and that we were not able to supply the call for Seeds commenced the business. This we had no objection too, because they first entered into this agreement not to sell any Seeds this side of the North river. But soon our Brethren in Hancock followed, and not only they but still our Brethren towards the east did likewise, so that in a short time the business become so extensive, that our Lebanon Brethren were under the necessity to cross the river (but not without our consent and full union first) The Brethren at Hancock soon followed, so that now through our liberality of giving in we are almost compeled to give ells and some pretty long ones too. Our Lebanon Brethren, on the north, on the South, on the east and on the west of us. And our Hancock Brethren a breadth through out whole state more than three hundred miles long so that at present we are confined to less than one fifth part of the state we live in and have no right to sell one seed in the state you live in nor any other state to the east of us. For the correctness of the above statement, see the limits proscribed to us. Beginning from this to White Hall, 72 miles north, Also from this to New Hartford 92 miles, a little south of northwest, from there to the east end of Lake Ontario, then down the St. Larance to Ogdensburg. A little patch in the northwest corner of our state, Look also at the number of inhabitants residing in those countrys limited to us to sell seeds in. Excepting we sell as many seeds in Albany and Troy as we can, and our Lebanon Brethren do so too at both of those places, we also sell a few at New York and some at Brooklyn and our Lebanon Brethren do likewise. I had almost like to forgot to state that we sold all the seeds we could in our limits proscribed to us, and you and our Lebanon Brethren sell 5 times as many seeds as we do and I believe it would not be much out of the way to say 7. . . .[19]

The gardeners often kept a journal of their daily occupations, and from these interesting sources much may be learned regarding the various problems and rewards of this important industry. One such "garden account" begins with miscellaneous remarks and observations on such matters as "cureing" corn, preserving beets, and growing onion seeds. A "trial of the vegetation of seeds" from 1829 to 1840 is carefully recorded. The following varieties were included: scarcity, scarlet radish, orange carrot, squash, ice top lettuce, mammoth lettuce, "parsnep," "hybrid turnep," "turnep beet," mangel beet, "E. C. cucumber," "D. W. cabbage," "E. D. lettuce," watermelon, Savoy cabbage, marrow-fat peas, rutabaga, and sage. In 1836, 150,000 seed bags were printed at New Lebanon, and in the five-year period 1836-1840, 930,400. These were printed on home presses in eight sizes known as pound bag size, bean size, beet size, onion size, cucumber size, cucumber long size, radish size, and lettuce size. Onion, lettuce, and cucumber seeds seem to have been the most popular at this time.

In 1836, Charles F. Crosman, the garden deacon at the New Lebanon Church family, issued for the first time a gardener's manual, at four to six cents each, "to enable our trading customers . . . to obtain some practical information relative to the raising and management of those valuable kitchen vegetables which are considered the most useful and important in a family." A printing of 16,000 provides an index of the scope of the business at that time.

According to the catalogue which prefaces the manual, the following kinds of seeds were being raised and put up in 1836:

> Asparagus (Giant), Bean (six varieties), Beet (six varieties), Cabbage (five varieties), Cauliflower (Early), Carrot (two varieties), Celery (White Solid), Corn (two varieties), Cucumber (four varieties), Lettuce (six varieties), Melon (three varieties), Mustard (two varieties), Onion (three varieties), Parsley (curled or double), Parsnip (two varieties), Peas (four varieties), Pepper (two varieties), Pepper Grass (Double), Radish (four varieties), Saffron (American), Sage (English), Salsify (or Vegetable Oyster), Savory (Summer), "Spinage" (Roundleaf), Squash (four varieties), Turnip (five varieties).

In 1843, a more complete manual was issued containing "Plain Instructions for the Selection, Preparation and Management of a Kitchen Garden." 55

The chapters deal with

The following entries are culled from a gardener's journal covering the period from 1840 to 1849.[20] The head gardeners or foremen during this time, in succession, were: John Allen, Franklin Barber, George Allen, Philemon Stewart. It will be noted that the seed bags were cut, folded, pasted, and printed by the Shakers themselves in their own seed shops. Certain devices were used to save labor, but the ever-present task of sorting over and throwing out old seeds that were returned by various consignees was a manual operation with no alleviation.

**1841.**  January    11. Thrash the celery.
                      12. Put up two cash orders for Poughkeepsie.
                      14. Put up the seeds for Hudson.
                      15. Put up the Pine Plain Seeds.
                      16. Finish off the two loads—plain labil and mark.

         February    6. The week past cleaning seeds at the tan house.
                         Repairing the machineary & making a new one
                         for the purpose of shaking our great ridle after
                         altering making braking & having a great deal

|            |           |     | of trouble we finally succede & our machine works well & we think if carefully used will prove to be a great improvement and save much hard labour. |
|------------|-----------|-----|---|
|            |           | 27. | Repairing the cutting block, printing press, etc. |
|            | March     | 13. | H. Bennet & John have commenced getting & picking up stuff for a new seed cupboard which is to be 16 feet long 8 high & 2 deep. |
|            |           | 26. | Franklin sows the hot bed. |
|            | June      | 1.  | Put up $150 worth of seeds in $5 and $10 boxes. |
|            | August    | 25. | 785 Advertisements received from Albany. |
| **1842.**  | January   | 31. | Printed and cut some bags: we cut enough to with those on hand to make a years stock, but the printing is not yet done. The spring to raise the types against the ball broke after using it about 3 days. . . . Have been lately looking over the types & setting up a new Bill or Catalogue adapted to the Southern demand. |
|            | March     | 5.  | There has been a new Beet machine made this winter & today we use it. Strip the white & turnip Beett. It works finely. |
|            | September | 19. | We have sorted the majority of the Old Seeds, torn open the poor papers, etc. they have sold better than for 3 years heretofore I think generally. |
|            | October   | 1.  | Finish boxing the Western Load. 224 Boxes am'ting at $3353.67. |
|            |           | 4.  | Aaron D. Bill starts off alone on the Western Journey intending to be back in 3 weeks. . . . Put up the Newburgh seeds 11 Boxes Amt. at $145.00. |

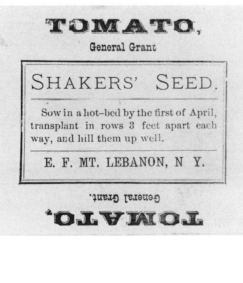

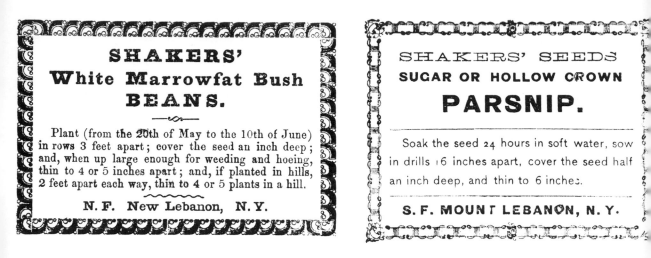

**1843.** February 24. We have concluded to have the prices of all papers of seeds at 6 cents. . . .

March 11. We have printed 850 Seed Bills the past week for the North Family. . . .

October 27. Geo. makes a set of Spools for packing-twine for this shop. F. casts a printing Ball & fixes for a little printing of bags. . . .

November 8. Smash and wash out the Tomato Seed.

10. Geo. throws out Old Seed from Cuba. . . .

December 18. F. & Geo. engaged in makeing a leather band or a belt for carrying the seed mill at the Tan House, weighing seed, etc.

**1844.** February 17. F. C. & S. puts up the Granville & Hudson loads.

23. Geo. lineing fans for faning seeds.

**1845.** September 24. Geo. Cleaning marking instruments makeing ink, etc.

October 16. Geo. St. & Sml finish Cleaning seeds for the west. . . . Joel Turner an old man almost 70 years old says he papers and paists 400 bags in a day.

31. P. Stewart calls the bill for us from about ½ past 6 oclock P. M. till 1 oclock at night boxing Seeds to a good jog.

November 1. We finish Boxing, nailing and laybilling the seeds for the *West*.

**1847.** January 9. Samuel W. says he has printed 30 Thousand [bags] in one day when the press worked well, and run steady.

25. I have been turning some Mallets, and grinding the knives we cut bags with.

The quoted entries have dealt principally with activities in the fall and winter, when the inside work was done. The gardeners or seedsmen were busy all year—fertilizing, cultivating, hoeing during the spring and summer, and threshing, cleaning, boxing, and labeling in the fall and winter. The Western Load, which covered a good section of New York State, was the important shipment of the year; the journalist uses capital letters for this entry, and upon the actual dispatch of this annual load, one can visualize the relief attendant on the consummation of an arduous task.

Production involved the services of many members, besides the seedsmen and gardeners, especially during the late fall when boxes of seeds were being prepared for shipment. During the year, the office deacons carried on the correspondence; teamsters and peddlers had charge of deliveries; carpenters made seed boxes; millers, the "seed mills"; and printers, the labels and catalogues. The sisterhood cut and pasted seed bags and "papers," sometimes as many as 286,200 in one year (1867), and in "hurrying times" helped with putting up seeds. Even the aged were usefully employed, as was the Shaker custom; in the gardener's manual, for example (see October 16, 1845, entry), Joel Turner, "an old man almost 70 years old," told a seedsman that he papered and pasted 400 bags a day.

Distribution was wholesale to the larger markets, on commission and with discounts ranging from 15 to 33 percent. In smaller communities, deliveries were made by one-horse wagon. In both cases, "dubils" were collected sometime after shipment, and unsold seeds returned to the community. Starting about 1812, the Western Load, through central and western New York, was the largest shipment. Other consignments went to New York, Baltimore, Philadelphia, as far south as Florida, to Canada, and even to dealers in Europe.

The Shakers were careful to sort and throw out old seeds, and not to mix their own product with any purchased, as at first, from the world. On April 13, 1819, the deacons and trustees at Hancock, New Lebanon, and Watervliet signed the following agreement:

> We, the undersigned, having for sometime past felt a concern, lest there should come loss upon the joint interest, and dishonor upon the gospel, by purchasing seeds of the world, and mixing them with ours for sale; and having duly considered the matter, we are confident that it is best to leave off the practice, and we do hereby covenant and agree that we will not, hereafter, put up, or sell, any seeds to the world which are not raised among believers. . . .

For some unexplained reason, the only exception was melon seeds!

Doubts of the wisdom of continuing the seed business occur as late as 1841. One "journalist" observes under the date of April 26: "It has    59 generally been thought that for some years past we have extended our seed business far beyond the medium to make it profitable for us and by reason of others as well as ourselves raising and selling so many seeds the market has become clide [?]—it appears to be almost useless to try to raise seeds expecting to sell them & get what they are worth. (Onion seed selling at ¢25. per lb. & but little sale for that or any other kinds—we are almost afraid we shall have to fling many of them away, for we have now upon hand I should think $10000 worth.)" There was talk of reducing the acreage devoted to seed gardens, and turning part of the space at least into kitchen gardens. Nevertheless, the seed business continued to show profits. The sisters of the First Order made 31,000 paper seed bags in 1845, and the following year they put up 40,000 bags of seeds. If the extent of the business can be measured by the number of cloth and paper bags made, the seed industry showed a perceptible increase rather than a decrease during the next twenty-five years:

*Table of Sisters' Work on Paper Seed Bags*

| 1846 | 24,700 | 1858 | 130,000 |
|---|---|---|---|
| 1847 | 6,000 | 1859 | 200,000 |
| 1848 | 206,000 | 1860 | 260,000 |
| 1849 | 69,000 | 1861 | 7,900 |
| 1850 | 6,500 | 1862 | 50,000 |
| 1851 | 36,000 | 1863 | 52,000 |
| 1852 | 64,000 | 1864 | 130,000 |
| 1853 | 102,000 | 1865 | 136,100 |
| 1854 | 104,000 | 1866 | 75,450 |
| 1855 | 110,000 | 1867 | 286,200 |
| 1856 | 101,500 | 1868 | 200,000 |
| 1857 | 30,000 | 1869 | 32,000 |
|  |  | 1870 | 255,000 |

Evidently the seed business at New Lebanon made a good recovery from the Civil War depression and weathered for a considerable period the pressure of outside competition. In 1868, the "list" of seeds raised in the Shaker gardens and on "out-farms" amounted to $7,196.10, and in 1870, a high total of $7,570.15 was recorded. This success may have been due partly to the fact that the Shakers came to resort to "worldly" methods of advertising. Brightly colored posters were distributed, and the seeds were put up in neatly labeled boxes and in gaily tinted little packages. The next decade or so after 1870 saw "many unlooked-for reverses" in the seed business, but the industry continued at Mount Lebanon until the late 1880s or early '90s.[21]

The garden seed business was as important to other families at New Lebanon as to the Church family. The herb and seed gardens at the Second family, for instance, covered a considerable acreage, and the large shop that came to be used for the manufacture of chairs was at one time the site of a thriving seed business. The early seed packages bore the initials or name of Daniel Hawkins and the initials of "S. F." for the Second family. The North family also carried on an extensive seed business.

# The Dried Sweet Corn and Dried Apple Industries

The business of drying sweet corn for the wholesale and retail market was started at New Lebanon in 1828 and continued throughout the century. At first the process consisted merely of boiling the cobs in great iron kettles, cutting the kernels off with hand knives, usually three-bladed affairs screwed to a vise, and then drying them in the sun on large boards. A drying house was erected in 1840. Large wheeled platforms ran out of this house so that the corn, spread thinly over them, could be exposed to the sun at will. It was then raked at intervals to insure even drying. This early process was imperfect, however, as the corn was apt to sour if not properly dried, and success was largely dependent upon the weather.

*Three-bladed device for cutting the kernels from sweet corn. The upright knife at the end scraped the cob clean.*

TRADE MARK.

**Directions for making SUCCOTASH!**

Take two parts corn and soak for five hours, then take one part White Beans. Parboil in plenty of water untill tender, pour off the water, add them to the corn and gently boil a few minutes, add butter and season to suit the taste.

**SWEET CORN FRITTERS.**

1 pint soaked corn, ½ teacupful of milk, ½ teacupful of flour, 3 table-spoonful of melted butter, ½ teaspoon black pepper, ½ teaspoon salt, 1 egg, beat and mix all together cook as griddle cakes.

An excellent style of using it.

*Device for quartering apples. The hole in the board is fitted with two blades crossed at right angles. The plunger forced the apple down on these knives and through the receptacle beneath the bench.*

At a later period, the process was mechanized by the introduction of steam-operated corn-cutting machines. The corn was delivered to the drying house in August and September by neighboring farmers; the Shakers themselves grew only a small portion of what was needed. The husked corn was weighed, and then the ears were separated into small square baskets, using only carefully selected ears. The Chatham (New York) *Courier* thus described the process:

> The baskets of corn are closely packed upon an elevator to the extent of nearly a ton, a rope is pulled, and the engine in the basement lowers them into a steam-box, where they are subjected to about six minutes of rather intense cooking. This accomplished, a bell rings, and they rise, pass the first floor, steaming from their bath, to the second floor. . . . The second floor is devoted to removing the corn from the cob. Here are three machines operated by steam, each capable of removing the corn from forty-five ears per minute. The machines are fed directly from the baskets, while the cobs shoot through an inclined tube into the carts, and are drawn away. . . . The corn falls into larger baskets, which are placed upon a car, and then rolled along a track which connects, by means of a long bridge, the building we have just left with the kiln. The corn is then placed in long shallow pans, and subjected to an even

heat from the roaring furnaces below. In this manner two kilns full are dried in twenty-four hours. The dried corn is then passed through a mill which winnows from it every particle of silk or husk which may be with it, and placed in a large bin. A tube passes from this to the lower story. A barrel is placed on the scales, a slide pulled in the conductor, and the barrel filled to a certain weight. It is then headed, marked, and is ready for shipment. In this manner they expect to fill twelve hundred barrels this season (1879). They also put up a fine shelf package for grocers' retail trade.[22]

In 1866, this commodity sold for $20 a barrel and constituted a prosperous industry at the Church and Second families. In October and November of that year, one account (to Levi Shaw, trustee at the North family) amounted to 59 barrels, or $1,180. Dried pumpkin was also sold at this time, the price ranging from $9 to $10 a barrel. Popcorn was sold for $4.50 a barrel. In the early 1880s, the severity of the competition in the dried sweet corn industry was such that the business was greatly reduced, but it continued to provide an economic return throughout the century.

The Shakers raised an extensive apple crop. (For the many ways in which these apples were used, see p. 126.) Many devices, such as one for quartering apples, were introduced by the Shakers. Apple-paring machines, set on frames, were made in some number, and at a later period purchased from the city and attached to homemade benches or chairs with improvised arms.

# Medicinal Herbs

The medicinal herb industry was as natural an outgrowth of the Shakers' early interest in gardening and agriculture as was the seed business. Each was a semi-agricultural occupation, a combination of garden and shop activity. It was only a step from farming to kitchen gardening, and but another step to herb gardening and the growing of select vegetables for their seeds. The Shakers were among the first in this country to see more than the obvious possibilities of gardening, and here, as in many other fields, their habitual genius for recognizing and developing economic opportunities is apparent. The use of herbs for domestic purposes, and eventually for sale, illustrates the capacity of the Shakers to free themselves from restrictive doctrine, to place "their economy on a scientific basis," and to make full use of native resources.

The passion of the people composing this sect for being useful, for doing useful things, and for making things useful is evidenced in these soil culture activities. It was consistent with their pragmatic philosophy that plants 63 should be utilized in every way possible. Some were useful for food, some for their medicinal qualities, some for seed production; in their roots and leaves, in their flowers and fruits, one or the other useful quality was present. This was true of larger shrubs and trees as well, and certain barks and leaves were sought not only for their value in medicinal preparations, but also for their usefulness in making dyes and in tanning leather.

The Shaker herb industry was an outgrowth, in part, of faith in botanic medicine. Although the question of health—physical and spiritual—concerned them from the beginning, the treatment of disease underwent many changes from the time of Mother Ann. In the first opening of the gospel, having separated themselves entirely from the world, "it was a peculiar trait" of the Believers' faith, Youngs wrote,

> not to rely much on outward means and remedies to remove
> diseases and infirmities. A learned physician was considered as very
> needless and unprofitable in general cases. It was recommended
> to rely more on the power of God, and on zeal and energy of spirit,
> than on the skill of a doctor.... The principle was adhered to in
> a good degree, and much infirmity was surmounted without
> medical aid; and indeed there were many real gifts of healing, in
> consequence of refusing natural means.[23]

"But the gift of healing by supernatural power," the Shaker historian conceded, "was too precious to be granted as a common favor, and as the body is subject to disease, it was indispensable that there should be some means for the relief of the afflicted." In time, therefore, an order was established of physicians or nurses, consisting of two males and two females, who had access to medical books and were allowed, in surgical cases, to consult with the world's doctors. There remained, however, a variety of opinions on the treatment of disease: "some have the most confidence in the old system of metallic drugs; others confine the medical art to the use of herbs; . . . and some again have great faith in Water-cure or Hydropathy."

In 1843, in response to a divine revelation, the use of tobacco, "strong drink," and swine's flesh was abandoned. Somewhat later, many families adopted the principles of vegetarianism. All along, great attention was given not only to diet, but to such matters as ventilation, lighting, the proper distribution of heat, refrigeration, and sanitation in general. And of course, to cleanliness.

In a catalogue of "medicinal plants, barks, roots, seeds, flowers and select powders" issued by the New Lebanon society about the middle of the last century, the claim is made that this industry was first established in 1800, "being the oldest of the kind in the country." Eldresses White and

Taylor also state that the Shakers were "the first in this country to introduce botanical medical practice, the first roots, herbs, vegetable extracts for medicinal purposes placed on the market having borne the Shaker stamp."[24] Prominent in the venture was Eliab Harlow (1762-1840), the first "physician" at New Lebanon, who had "commenced the vegetable or botanic practice of medicine about 1796, under the instruction of a Dr. Root, of Canaan, Connecticut." Associated with him, in early years of the industry, was Garrett Lawrence and later Barnabus Hinckley. The date 1800 is substantially correct. It should be noted, however, that although the gathering of herbs was practiced "from the first of the organization for the use of physicians at home . . . [only] very few were sold except for the purpose of purchasing medicine to be used instead of herbs." According to *The Manifesto*, the Believers did not begin to prepare herbs and roots for sale until 1820.

A careful examination of a collection of early ledgers kept by the trustees at New Lebanon bears out this statement. With the exception of rose water, no record of the sale of herbs or extracts occurs until the year 1821, when, on November 21st, an entry under "Articles Sold" reads: "for herbs . . . $1.15." On February 12, 1823, an entry of $21.50 is made "for Herbs & oils," and on April 2, one of $2.34 for "herbs & Extract."[25]

*The Manifesto* statement is further supported by an interview in 1852 between Edward Fowler of the New Lebanon society and a representative of *The American Journal of Pharmacy*. Fowler is quoted as saying: "It is about fifty years . . . since our Society first originated as a trade in this country the business of cultivating and preparing medicinal plants for the supply and convenience of apothecaries and druggists, and for about twenty years conducted it on a limited scale." According to this source, the business was not conducted on a very serious scale until about 1820, when "Drs. E. [Eliab] Harlow and G. [Garrett] K. Lawrence, of our society, the latter an excellent botanist, gave their attention to the business, and induced a more systematic arrangement, and scientific manner of conducting it, especially as to the seasons for collection, varieties, and methods of preparation."[26] Responding to the increased demand for medicinal herbs, and conscious of the fact that the drugs on the market were often spurious and adulterated, these botanists, about 1820, laid out "physic gardens," gardens specifically for medicinal herbs.

The industry prospered from the first, stimulated no doubt by the growing popularity of the so-called Thomsonian medical system, named for Samuel Thomson of Massachusetts (1769-1843), an itinerant herb doctor who advocated vegetable remedies and wrote *A New Guide To Health*, a best-seller in its day.

By 1830, herb catalogues were being issued, and the same year $2.50 was paid to Phineas Allen, a Pittsfield (Massachusetts) printer, for 4,700 labels. The fine reputation of the product was widespread even at this early 65

Double Distilled

𝔇𝔄𝔐𝔄𝔖𝔎
**Rose Water.**

Prepared at
Shaker Village, Mer. Co. N. H.

*THE MANUFACTURERS OF THIS MEDICINE*
Have been for fifty years the largest gatherers of Roots, Barks and Herbs in the World. Their Botanical Gardens are the most extensive in America. Very costive persons should use the Operating Pills in connection with the Syrup.

MOTHER SEIGEL'S
A CURE FOR IMPURITIES OF THE BLOOD
CURATIVE SYRUP
OPERATING PILLS
A CURE FOR DYSPEPSIA & LIVER COMPLAINTS
EXTRACT OF AMERICAN ROOTS

This Bottle contains the active medicinal virtues of more than one pound of Roots, Barks, and Herbs, in a very concentrated form. Although the bottle is small, it *contains more doses* than any other medicine in the market at the same price.

date. On October 18, 1831, a box of herbs valued at $30.68¾ ("subject to 25 pr. ct. dis.") was sent to Paris, and on October 25th, 13 boxes of medicinal herbs were delivered "on board Ship Hannibal in the port of New York" consigned to Charles Whitlaw, "Botanist of London, England." This order amounted to $895.65. In this year (1831), "about 4,000 lbs. of roots and herbs were sent to the market." By 1836, production had increased to 6,000 pounds, and in 1849, to 16,500 pounds.[27]

In the early years of the industry, wild herbs constituted the main sources of supply. With its serious development arose the cultivation of medicinal plants. It is difficult to state just what plants or herbs were grown first. The gradually increasing demand for Shaker herbs and extracts made it necessary to rely upon outside growers for large quantities of different herbs, roots, etc. As early as 1826, we find the Shakers buying from outside sources such items as red rose, sweet marjoram, cicuta extract, saffron, and lobelia.

When Benson Lossing, the artist-historian, visited New Lebanon in 1857, he was conducted through the herb shops by Brother Edward Fowler, who was then in charge of the business. The press, Fowler told him, had the power of 300 tons and turned out each day about 250 pounds of herbs and 600 pounds of roots. In 1855, the output (4,000 pounds in 1831, 6,000 in 1836, and 16,500 in 1849) had increased to 75 tons. Ten persons were ordinarily employed in the business, with sometimes twice that many. Fowler thus described the herb houses:

> The drying and storing of so many plants requires much space, and
> several buildings are occupied wholly or in part for this purpose;
> the principal and central one of which is a neat structure about
> 120 feet long by 38 feet wide, two stories high with a well-lighted
> basement and airy garret. The basement is devoted to the pressing,
> grinding and other heavy work, whilst at one end the steam boiler

is placed. The first story is used for packing, papering, sorting, printing and storing the products, whilst the second story and loft are used exclusively for drying and storing. Being well-lighted and airy, these rooms are well fitted for the purpose. Racks of hurdles are conveniently placed along the center on which the herbs previously garbled are put to dry, which is rapidly accomplished by the free circulation of air that is maintained throughout. The sides of the second story room are arranged with large and tight bins, in which the plants are put as soon as they are properly desiccated, until removed for pressing.[28]

In *Harper's New Monthly Magazine,* Lossing explained the method of cracking, steaming, and pressing roots and herbs he had seen in use at New Lebanon.

In one corner is a large boiler, into which the herbs and roots are placed and steam introduced. From this boiler the steamed herbs are conveyed to grated cylinders, and subjected to immense pressure. The juices thus expressed are then put into copper pans, inclosed in iron jackets, in such manner that steam is introduced between the jackets and the pans, and the liquid boiled down to the proper consistency for use. Some juices, in order to avoid the destruction or modification of their medical properties, are conveyed to an upper room, and there boiled in a huge copper *vacuum pan,* from which, as its name implies, the air has been exhausted. This allows the liquid to boil at a much lower temperature than it would in the open air.[29]

*Power-driven double press used to compress herbs at the Niskeyuna Shaker community.*

The dried roots were reduced to an "impalpable powder" in an adjoining room. They were first crushed under two revolving granite disks, and then ground into fine powder in a mill made of two upper stones and a nether stone of granite. The upper stones revolved on a central shaft and at the same time turned on their own axes, forming a double action.

The addition of such machinery as a steam boiler and a globular-shaped copper vacuum pan for drying the herbs was a further impetus to the herb industry. Three double-presses, similar, no doubt, to the one used at Niskeyuna and capable of pressing 100 pounds daily, were then being used. *The Manifesto* records the amount of herbs pressed in 1850 as being "not less than 21,000 lbs." besides about 7,000 pounds of extract. In 1852, a new steam engine and other additional machinery were bought; the next year 42,000 pounds of roots, herbs, and barks were pressed, and 7,500 pounds of extracts produced.

The vacuum process was apparently the Shakers' own invention. Propagating medicinal plants "long before such cultivation became widely spread in the United States," they "also devised the famous system for taking down medicinal extracts 'in vacuo' and their vacuum apparatus was a model for the great medicine industry of today."[30]

There is some controversy over who invented and first used the vacuum process, the Shakers or the Tilden Company in near-by New Lebanon, which was organized in 1847-48. The Shakers claimed that they had "adopted the vacuum pan as a necessary item by the recommendation of several members of the New York College of Pharmacy, whom we consulted on the occasion."[31] The Tilden Company, however, stated that "while our manufactory was in process of erection, members from the family of M. Fowler [Shakers] visited our works, and knew we were engaging in the manufacture of extracts by a 'new process' because they saw the apparatus, and made inquiries in regard to it and our manipulations. . . ."[32] There is another story that the secret leaked out when an apostate from the society, who was familiar with the process, was taken into the employ of the Tildens. In support of the Shaker claim it should be noted that in 1853, Gail Borden, hearing of the Shakers' method for drying herbs in a "low vacuum" vessel, visited the society, and using their equipment, perfected his formula for condensed milk, patented in 1856.

The comprehensive nature of the industry at mid-century is evidenced by the declaration on the cover page of an undated catalogue issued about this time: "Catalogue of Medicinal Plants, Barks, Roots, Seeds, Flowers and Select Powders; With their Therapeutic Qualities and Botanical Names; also Pure Vegetable Extracts, Prepared in Vacuo, Ointments, Inspissated Juices, Essential Oils, Double Distilled and Fragrant Waters, Etc. Etc. Raised, Prepared and Put Up in the Most Careful Manner, by the United Society of Shakers in New Lebanon, N.Y." The title concludes with the verse:

> A blade of grass—a simple flower
> Culled from the dewy lea;
> These, these shall speak with touching power,
> Of change and health to thee.

The "physics gardens" at New Lebanon occupied at this period about 50 acres, which were given over chiefly to the cultivation of hyoscyamus, belladonna, taraxacum, aconite, poppy, lettuce, sage, summer savory, marjoram, dock, burdock, valerian, and horehound. Extract of taraxacum was the chief product. Conium, hyoscyamus, and belladonna classed next. About 50 minor varieties of plants were also raised. "Nearly 200 varieties of indigenous plants were collected, and 30 or 40 other varieties were brought from the South and West and from Europe."[33]

The extract business in particular was stimulated by reorganization and improvements, and in the period 1861-1862 more than 100 different varieties, both solid and fluid, were being manufactured. These were usually put up in five-pound or one-pound bottles, but in some cases one-half-pound, one-fourth-pound, and one-eighth-pound and ounce sizes were used. Total production in 1861 amounted to 3,588 pounds of solid extract and 5,544 gallons of fluid extract. In 1862, 6,478 pounds of solid extract were prepared, and in 1864, 16,450 pounds of extracts were "dressed." Between 1860 and    69

1867, the yearly output of powders or pulverized roots and herbs averaged over 7,000 pounds. Ointments and such preparations as oil of wormwood, rose water and Norwood's tincture also showed an increased production.

A fragmentary but intimate glimpse of the herb business at New Lebanon around the Civil War era is presented by one of the Shaker sisters, Sister Marcia Bullard, who wrote as follows:

Forty years ago it was contrary to the "orders" which governed our lives to cultivate useless flowers, but, fortunately for those of us who loved them, there are many plants which are beautiful as well as useful. We always had extensive poppy beds and early in the morning, before the sun had risen, the white-capped sisters could be seen stooping among the scarlet blossoms to slit those pods from which the petals had just fallen. Again after sundown they came out with little knives to scrape off the dried juice. This crude opium was sold at a large price and its production was one of the most lucrative as well as the most picturesque of our industries.

The rose bushes were planted along the sides of the road which ran through our village and were greatly admired by the passersby, but it was strongly impressed upon us that a rose was useful, not ornamental. It was not intended to please us by its color or its odor, its mission was to be made into rosewater, and if we thought of it in any other way we were making an idol of it and thereby imperiling our souls. In order that we might not be tempted to fasten a rose upon our dress or to put it into water to keep, the rule was that the flower should be plucked with no stem at all. We had only crimson roses, as they were supposed to make stronger rosewater than the paler varieties. This rosewater was sold, of course, and was used in the community to flavor apple pies. It was also kept in store at the infirmary, and although in those days no sick person was allowed to have a fresh flower to cheer him, he was welcome to a liberal supply of rosewater with which to bathe his aching head.

Then there were the herbs of many kinds. Lobelia, pennyroyal, spearmint, peppermint, catnip, wintergreen, thoroughwort, sarsaparilla and dandelion grew wild in the surrounding fields. When it was time to gather them an elderly brother would take a great wagonload of children, armed with tow sheets, to the pastures. Here they would pick the appointed herb—each one had its own day, that there might be no danger of mixing—and, when their sheets were full, drive solemnly home again. In addition to that which grew wild we cultivated an immense amount of dandelion, dried the root and sold it as "chicory." The witch hazel branches were too tough for women and children to handle, so the brethren cut them and brought them into the herb shop where the sisters made them into hamamelis. We had big beds of sage, thorn apple, belladonna, marigolds and camomile, as well as of yellow

*Label-printing press from the Niskeyuna settlement.*

THE HERB-HOUSE, MOUNT LEBANON.

dock, of which we raised great quantities to sell to the manufacturers of well-known "sarsaparilla." We also made a sarsaparilla of our own and various ointments. In the herb shop the herbs were dried and then pressed into packages by machinery, labeled and sold outside. Lovage root we exported both plain and sugared and the wild flagroot we gathered and sugared too. On the whole there was no pleasanter work than that in the "medical garden" and "herb shop."[34]

Lucrative medicinal herb industries were developed in several other communities, notably Watervliet, Harvard, the two Enfields, New Gloucester, Canterbury, and Union Village, Ohio. All issued catalogues in the 1840s and '50s, when the industry was at its peak. Among more prominent botanists was Thomas Corbett of Canterbury, New Hampshire, who, at the request of leaders of the society, took up the study of medicinal herbs about 1813. In cooperation with Dr. Dixi Crosby, professor of surgery at Dartmouth, he worked out the formula for Corbett's Compound Concentrated Syrup of Sarsaparilla, which won a medal at the Philadelphia Centennial in 1876. It has been said that the Shaker sarsaparilla was the forerunner of our modern soft drinks.

One is constantly struck by the paradox of a people so mystical in their faith being so practical in their work. Was it compensation? Or was it because they "put their minds" to it? Characteristic of the sect was the

71

sentiment of Elisha Myrick, the herbalist at Harvard, in reviewing his year's labors:

> The earth has generously repaid man for his toil—nature gives abundantly to those who ask aright—to ask aright we must ask in the Language of Science the only language she can understand—we must first know her laws before we can obey them—and we can never know these laws except by deep study and constant application.

## Bottles, Jars and Labels.

The reputation of the Shakers for self-sufficiency has been such that they have been credited with making almost every article found in their homes and shops. This is true in particular regarding the fine glassware and earthenware found in the "nurse-shops," dwelling houses, and herb buildings. This ware was never manufactured, however, as far as the writer has learned, by a Shaker society. The quantities of bottles, jars, jugs, vials, and demijohns needed for the herb industry and other uses were purchased from a variety of sources.

As in the seed business, the labels required for the papers and jars of herbs and extracts were at first printed on presses constructed by some ingenious Shaker mechanic. As time went on and the fame of Shaker medicines became widespread, the business managers of the industry found it expedient to have the printing done by regular commercial printers and electrotypists.

## Sisters' Work in the Herb Industry.

The major part of the laborious and routine labor connected with the medicinal herb industry, such work as cleaning roots, picking and "picking over" flowers and plants, cutting sage, cleaning bottles, cutting and printing labels, papering powders and herbs, and "dressing" or putting up extracts and ointments, was done by the sisters. They also made the ointments. The herb houses were situated in the Second Order section of the Church family at New Lebanon, and most of this work was done by the Second Order sisters. The deaconesses assigned certain sisters to the occupation of picking and cleaning herbs, flowers, and roots; a record was kept of the number of days so spent, and the Order was reimbursed by the family deacons at the rate of twenty cents a day.

The first record of the sisters' part in this important industry occurs in 1841.[35] In 1847, the Second Order sisters cleaned 4,500 pounds of roots, and in 1848, 9,327 pounds. By 1850, they were engaged in putting up "elm flour" and "composition flour" in two-ounce packages; in the twenty-year period 1850-1870 more than 30,000 pounds of these preparations were papered. The manufacture of ointments by the sisters dates from 1852. In the next twenty years, 5,550 pounds were made and dressed. The various extracts made by the Shaker chemists or "botanists" were being put up for the market by the sisters in 1855, and in the next fifteen years a total of more than 75,000 pounds were prepared. Norwood's Tincture of Veratrum, one of the principal medicines produced, was first put up in 1859, when 143 bottles were dressed. The next year, a thousand bottles were prepared, and in the six years between 1865 and 1871, when the record ends, 1,349 gross (bottles?) were dressed by the Second Order sisterhood for the pharmaceutic market. The deaconesses' accounts show several miscellaneous activities in which the sisters were at one time or another engaged. In 1853, 576 bottles of "sweet herbs" were dressed, and in 1860, three gross of verbena. Rose water was distilled from 1861 on, 35 gallons in that year, 20 in 1862, 25 in 1864, 82 in 1865, 55 in 1866, and so on. In 1861, 118 herb sheets, used in the collection of herbs, were made, and these were supplied as needed. The picking and drying of poppies and marigolds occupied much time. In 1870, 12,564 bottles were cleaned to be filled with Norwood's Tincture, and in 1871, 14,079 bottles. The extent of the herb or extract business at this time may be gauged by the fact that in 1870 the Second Order sisters cut more than a million labels.

## The Medical Department.

It has been noted that herbs were first used as medicines or in exchange for medicines. The progress of the society soon necessitated the organization of a medical department or "order of physicians," run by two males and two females. The first nurse shops were constructed soon after the organization of the society. Eliab Harlow and Isaac Crouch were the first physicians at New Lebanon; later, as we have noted, Garrett Lawrence served with Harlow in this capacity, and at a still later period the medical responsibilities were undertaken by Barnabus Hinckley. Sisters were assigned to the infirmary as nurses.

The Shakers at New Lebanon, Canterbury, and elsewhere made early use of electric current for therapeutic purposes. Sometime in the 1820s, if not earlier, several "static" machines were invented. These consisted of large glass cylinders which revolved against a chamois rubbing pad producing a frictional electricity, which was applied for curative purposes to afflicted parts of the body. The first reference to such machines is found in an old medical register, under the date of April 17, 1827, when five dollars was charged to Olivar and William Hull for the use of "an electrical cylinder."[36] In Elizabeth Lovegrove's journal, the following entry occurs on March 31, 1837: "Elder Sister remains feeble but it relieved some of her cough by the vaper bath and electricity." On April 2nd of the same year, it is recorded that "Elder Sister . . . is not much better, we keep her in and continue shocking her." On June 9th, one of the elder sisters fell down and hurt her side. Skunk cabbage leaves were applied and tea was prepared  73 made of Johnswort and peppergrass seed. The nurses also resorted to "shocking rubbing and bleeding her."[37]

In such large communities as those developed by the Shakers, there was naturally a certain amount of sickness, especially among the older members, as well as the expected quota of accidents in the shops and on the farms. In the main, however, they were a healthy, temperate people, leading out-of-door lives, subject to few of the worries that harassed the usual wage-earners, maintaining regular hours in sleeping, eating, and working, living under the most sanitary conditions, and achieving as a group an enviable record for longevity.

*The longevity of the Shakers received a great deal of atten-tion in the nineteenth century. The life expectancy among Believers—over a decade longer than that of the world's people—is not surprising when the Believers' temperate lifestyle is considered: moderation in all activities, whole-some diet, regular exercise, excellent sanitary conditions, and freedom from stress.*

# The Mechanical Arts

"Variety in harmony is the desideratum." This aphorism by a Shaker elder, Oliver Prentiss, expresses the ideal of all Shaker work, but particularly the mechanical arts. We use the term to include all occupations carried on in the tan houses, mills, and shops, chiefly by brethren. From the earliest years of the order, the Shakers had the reputation of being highly versed in the mechanical arts. The mechanical arts became imbued with that progressive spirit which characterized the whole system of Shakerism during these early decades of vitality and development. Seldom did the visitor fail to notice how farming and industrial operations were accelerated by all manner of skillful means and devices, how the labor of the household was lightened by labor-saving machinery fashioned in the Shaker shops, and how efficiently sanitary systems had been constructed. In the water power that drove all the shop machinery, in the machines themselves, in the many farming and manufacturing operations, and in the constant constructive activity which permeated the material life of the sect, the hand of the skilled mechanic is ever amazingly apparent.

The versatility of skills possessed by many individuals in the Shaker order is astonishing. Two examples may suffice. When Henry Blinn, at the age of fourteen, was indentured at Canterbury in 1838, his first work was sawing staves for pails. Then he was transferred to the farm, and for a short period to the blacksmith shop. He was subsequently placed under the deaconship of Thomas Holt, who had charge of the carding mill and the stove, tinware, and cut nail industry, eventually rising to the management of the mill. At the age of nineteen, he qualified as an instructor of children, a position he held for eight years. During this period he taught his charges how to braid whiplashes, began the study of printing and binding, and took his turn as night watchman and helper at harvest time. In time he became an elder, and then a member of the Canterbury–Enfield ministry. Even his ministerial duties and writing did not prevent him from learning and practicing other occupations, such as dentistry and bee-keeping.

Another elder, Giles Avery of the New Lebanon Church family, also served, as was the custom, a long apprenticeship in hand labor before he was considered qualified for spiritual leadership. Avery's manual employment consisted of carpentry, plastering, plumbing, digging foundations,

*Elder Henry Blinn of Canterbury and Enfield was proficient in thirteen or fourteen widely divergent trades. His many occupations included blacksmith, writer, teacher, dentist, and bee-keeper.*

sawing stone, repairing buildings, making wagons, joinery, making dippers, and constructing cisterns and orcharding. "How similar to colonization in a new country, communal association is," he wrote in his autobiography, "that members of a community should be willing to turn a hand in any needed direction in order to render their best service in building up and sustaining the cause."

# Tanning

Tanning, an industry followed in most of the communities, provides a good example of how the introduction of improved apparatus for tanning, rolling, and splitting the leather resulted in a more productive industry. A small building for grinding bark and finishing leather was in use the first year the society was organized. For twenty years, the bark was ground by horse power on a circular stone. Early in the nineteenth century, the business was facilitated by the introduction of a cast-iron bark mill operated by water power. In 1807, the tan house was enlarged and machines added for rolling the leather. Between 1805 and 1810, shipments of calfskins, "sheap" skins, "lam" skins, foxskins, horsehides, sole leather, "ruffuse" (refuse) leather, white leather, upper leather, harness leather, etc., were being sent to neighboring and distant markets. The business was of such dimensions that the Shakers were not able to raise all the hides they needed, and these were bought from farmers and cattle dealers in the neighborhood or near-by towns and cities.

Twenty years later, with the greatly increased demand for hides and leather, more buildings were erected and the vats increased to thirty-two. Ledgers covering the period from 1810 to 1830 are crammed with leather sales and the conclusion is self-evident that at this time tanning was among the most active occupations at the Church family. The total account of stock work in 1835 was as follows[1]:

| | |
|---|---|
| 199 | Sole leather hides |
| 95 | Upper leather hides |
| 12 | Harness leather hides |
| 25 | Horse hides |
| 468 | Calfskins |
| 452 | Sheepskins |
| 90 | Woodchuck and Cat skins |
| 26 | Deer skins (dressed wash leather) |

In 1836, the account was as follows:

| | |
|---|---|
| 82 | Slaughter Sole leather hides |
| 38 | Spanish Sole leather hides |
| 69 | Slaughter Upper leather hides |
| 55 | Patany Upper leather hides |
| 5 | Harness leather hides |
| 22 | Horse hides dressed whip leather |
| 3 | Horse hides tand |
| Total 274 | hides |

| | |
|---|---|
| 600 | Calfskins tand |
| 280 | Sheepskins tand |

| | | |
|---|---|---|
| 22 | Do | dressed white |
| 20 | Do | dressed wash leather |
| 4 | Do | tand with wool on |
| Total 326 | Sheepskins | |
| 5 | Dog skins tand with the hair on | |
| 59 | Woodchuck skins tand | |
| 5 | Calfskins tand | |
| 20 | Deerskins dressed | |

In 1834, "the hides ... were softened in a common fulling mill, but in 1840 a wheel or cylinder was used and considered a great improvement." In 1844, a total of 539 hides and 1,010 skins were prepared. As the sales increased, "the old process of tanning leather in cold vats was by far too slow to suit the sellers and buyers of this fast age, and a steam boiler was introduced in 1850 for heating the vats and leaches. . . . " As long as there was adequate man-power in the community, the business was able to compete successfully with the world.

The tannery at the Church family did a steady amount of business for the other families, and this was charged on a yearly account. Yearly bills for tanning in 1833 were: to Charles Bushnell, $91; to Daniel J. Hawkins, $77.75; to Aaron Bill, $25; and to Joseph Allen, $49.25.[2]

There were many by-products and "by-activities" connected with the tan-yard. On February 4th, for instance, a 54-gallon cask of neat's-foot oil was prepared. On the 6th, "F. S." made a pair of mittens and tapped and

heeled a pair of "splatter dashers." On the 12th, "J. W. made a new leather apron and fixed his old beeming apron"; and Peter Long bought 62 deerskins for 57 cents apiece. After the skins were shaved, the hair was sold; on August 19th, it is recorded that 89 bushels of hair were loaded "into sacks for Anderson the hair merchant." "Sig" (urine) was extensively employed in blackening leather, and the surplus was sold. In Benjamin Lyon's journal (see page 83) there are many references to the sale of this tanning ingredient: December 26, 1839, seven barrels were sold in Pittsfield for $5.83—one item among many.

The tanning business was continued at New Lebanon almost uninterruptedly until late in the century. Tanneries were also maintained in other Shaker communities, notably those at Watervliet, Canterbury, Alfred, and Hancock.

## Manufactures in Leather.

Leather from the tan house was used in several community industries: the manufacture of bridles, saddles, saddlebags, and harness, and the making of shoes and mittens. Horsewhips were also made at New Lebanon from an early date, for home use and for sale. The horse hides for the lashes were dressed at the tannery and the lashes cut and braided by the brethren and boys.

The business in saddles and saddlebags was not of long duration, but the extensive use of the one-horse wagon in the early decades of the last century gave an impetus to the occupation of making and repairing harness, and this industry continued over a much longer period. Leather boots and shoes, or shoes with linen cloth tops, were made for the use of the Believers themselves, and often for others, until well into the nineteenth century. In most of the societies, a certain amount of bookbinding was done, not only for printed publications, but for the manuscript song and copy books commonly used in the early years of the sect.

*On the opposite page is the original shoemaker's shop at the Second family in New Lebanon. The typical early cobbler's bench had a double-paneled lid that protected the cabinet and, as is shown here, also served as a work tray. The cobbler made lasts to fit the foot of every member in the family; these were kept in racks above the bench. The candlestands were necessary in every shop since so much work was done in the early morning and late evening.*

*Cloth shoes with leather soles were made for the Believers themselves and often for the world's people until well into the nineteenth century. In the earliest regulations of the sect, it was "contrary to order to have right and left shoes" or "to pare the heels of the shoes under."*

*A wrought-iron latch made around 1830 in the Hancock community.*

# The Blacksmith and Machine Shops

The Shaker blacksmith was a mechanic, "a universal chore-man." Except possibly for a few years before the society at New Lebanon was organized, the blacksmith's shop was more akin to a machine shop, and with the institution of power-driven machinery became even less like the "smithies" of popular fancy. The contribution of these workers in metal to the revenues of the embryonic order was second to none. Their skill was constantly being drafted into the service of the farm and shop, their products were sold in the early trustees' offices, and they did jobbing for the farmers and gentry of the surrounding country.

The versatility of these early smiths was remarkable. They could turn their hands to almost anything required in hardware or wagon-making, and they were called upon to repair all sorts of tools and machinery. They forged and mended chains; wrought and cut saddle nails, sheathing nails, wagon nails, spikes, brads and copper nails; set horseshoes; shod sleighs; made knife blades and all kinds of shop and garden tools; mended "chizzels," augers, frying pans, ox-yokes, shovels, plow-irons; made rings, staples, hasps, picks, bails, iron and steel candlesticks, gate hangings, latches, "ketches," chest hinges, keys, axes, saws, scythes, and butcher knives; constructed wagons and wagon boxes; sharpened drag teeth; "ironed" neck-yokes; made clothiers' shears; and turned out "sundry brass ware." Hoes were manufactured in some quantity as early as 1789 and sold for 5 shillings, 4 pence apiece. In 1806, there was still a demand for these tools, the price at this time having advanced to 8 shillings. Turning tools were

80

also made in 1789. A set of wagon boxes sold at this date for 12 shillings. Cut nails, ten penny, sold in 1790 for a shilling a pound, wrought nails for slightly more. A pair of "nailers shears" was sold July 17, 1790, for 3 pounds, 12 shillings. Two pairs of grinding shears were sold in 1806 for 24 pounds. "Taylor's shears" were marketed at this date for 16 and 18 shillings; in 1810, two pair of tailor's shears sold for $3.24. The first kitchen "arches" may have been made at outside furnaces (the Church paid $12.70 in 1807 for arch irons at the Dalton "furnice"), but these were also made at the Shaker blacksmith shops, and we find such items listed as a frying arch which was sold in 1824 to the North family for the sum of $12.

A certain amount of farm and shop machinery was also manufactured by the Shaker blacksmiths and machinists, the whole process, pattern-making, casting, framing, and so on, being carried through as an independent project. In 1793, Benjamin Bruce invented and made a machine for setting card-teeth. A trip hammer was made in 1800, and in 1828, the first foot lathe for turning and drilling. Machines for mortising and dovetailing, for making wooden shoe-pegs in quantity, for filling herb packages, for gumming saws, and for facilitating numbers of other operations formerly done by hand, were also devised at an early date.

Hundreds of knives were used in the herb business for cutting roots, stems, and barks. At first these were all made in the blacksmith's and wood-turner's shops; at a later date, the blades were purchased and fitted into the homemade handles. Countless tools were also produced.

The business of making wrought and cut nails was "for several years . . . a source of considerable income. These wrought nails were used in the coarser work while building, until the year 1812 when they were superseded by the cut nails [the Shakers may have been the first to make cut nails]. Wrought nails were also used as early as 1780 for shingling and lathing, but with the introduction of cut nails, soon after the organization of the Community, the wrought nails passed out of use. The machinery for cut

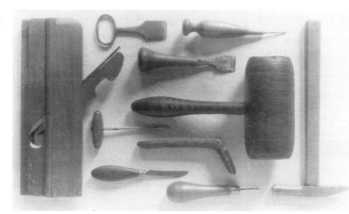

Collection of small tools used in various occupations, including two chisel-edged instruments used in making buttonholes in garments, two awl-like bodkins, a maple mallet, an L-shaped tool used in pressing bonnet pleats, a paring knife and a knife for cutting herbs and roots, a sister's hammer, a gimlet, and a molding plane.

nails and the work of forming the heads by a hard hammer, employed not less than twelve persons and yielded a very profitable income."[3] The manufacture of cut nails was "closed" in 1830.

Tinsmithing was an allied trade. At New Lebanon, Watervliet, and other societies, most of the tinware used in the kitchens, gardens, and shops was made in the community shops: measures, watering pots, funnels, sugar scoops, shaving cups, match safes, needle cases, boxes, pans, dust pans, bread and cake tins, and so forth.

## Machine Shop Work.
The machine shop at the Church family was equipped with several machine lathes propelled by water power over a huge wheel. The shop was located on the mountain side, and considerable energy was generated by this method. Iron work of all kinds was turned out at this factory. Here the pattern makers worked, and here many of the mechanical devices were constructed that were used by the Shakers in their manifold activities. Also, wagon-making and the manufacture of wagon parts presumably were carried on at this place. One of the black-smith's shops was reorganized in 1846 by the installment of water power for driving the great trip hammer made earlier in the century; this shop was equipped also with machine lathes and various mechanical devices for making machine parts.

Jobbing was done for other Shaker families and for outsiders. In 1838, "Work done at Machine Shop for others" was reported by the trustees to amount to $164.81—not a large revenue, but one of the many contributions advancing the common fund. A few entries for 1839 in "A Journal of Domestic Events Kept by Benjamin Lyon" will illustrate some of the activities at the machine shop. [4] Lyon was a capable mechanic, and we must overlook his literary shortcomings.

82

*The Shakers made beautiful tinware for widely divergent uses. Teapots, oil cans (for filling kerosene lamps), measures, and baking tins were among the more popular items.*

| | |
|---|---|
| January 1. | Tuesday work to the Mashine shop at boreing waggon hubs for the Second faimely. |
| January 5. | Saterday go to the Mashine shop saw some timber for a fraim to drive spoks. |
| January 25. | Friday ... doe a little in the shop make some patruns to cast Waggon boxes.... |
| February 1. | Friday work some at mortising hubs for the First Orders one horse waggon help Amos Bishop some about sawing waggon fellews [fellies]. |
| February 23. | Saterday work some in the shop go to the Mill & get some Iron Staves for the Plaster Mill cary them to the Smith shop to repare go to the Second famely get some molding sand to cast a scrue box for the mill. |
| May 24. | Friday work in the shop at a pare of Thils [thills] for a one horse Waggon etc. |
| July 11. | Thursday go to the mashine shop saw out dipper rims. |
| December 3. | Tuesday I go to the Mashine Shop & grind some joiner tools. |
| December 8. | Saterday I do chores take the Candle mashine & wheal it down to the first Order.... |
| December 13. | Friday I doe chores to the Mashine Shop & grind axes & knives to be in radeness to kill the hogs next week. |

83

Miscellaneous activities are also recorded in the trustees' accounts. In 1835, for instance, a charge to Daniel Hawkins included work in turning gudgeons, boring segments, and hanging and checking balance wheels. Iron castings formed an appreciable item.

Lyon's record of "domestic events" illustrates well the variety of occupations to which a mechanic, or any other workman for that matter, was obliged under the Shaker system to devote his time and talents. The machine shop occupied only a portion of this brother's schedule. He carried grist to the mill, put up corn for the hogs, mended floors, drove merchandise in from surrounding towns, cut and split wood and sawed boards, helped the sisters pick over apples and "put up" apple sauce, worked occasionally at the tan house and "gardening house," plowed and harrowed, hauled manure, assisted in the cooper's shop, periodically drove the "coalts" to turn the washmill, and did endless cleaning up chores. It was the widespread application of this spirit that more than anything else was responsible for the long continued success of the Shaker experiment in communistic living.

# Miscellaneous Trades—Milling, Carpentry, Jobbing, Shingle- and Brick-making

The early Shakers wanted to be self-sufficient, independent of the world. They grew most of their own food, manufactured most of their clothing, and provided the essential means for their own shelter. Yet it should be noted that the principle of self-sufficiency was not carried to an extreme. A good society, they held, was not an impoverished society. They believed in obedience and chastity, but never took vows of poverty. The criterion was use. That which was useful to health of mind and body was right; they renounced only the superfluous. Joseph Meacham and the first elders of the United Society wisely adopted the policy of maintaining friendly business relationships with the "world." At a time when Shakerism was widely misunderstood and condemned, it would have added to the difficulties of developing a sound institutional life if the Shakers had rigidly cut themselves off from buying from outside sources. Their asceticism did not go that far. From the outset, they bought from and sold freely to the world's markets, and no misunderstanding existed on the economic level such as characterized the world's attitude to the Shakers' religious doctrines. Merchants and tradesmen were glad to have the Shakers' business, and found it was to their advantage to handle Shaker goods.

At first, in 1789, the New Lebanon Shakers carried their grain to one William Norton's to be ground "without taking Tole and the Tole to be paid for in Leather and Nails." The old stone gristmill of the Church family was erected in 1824; the date appears in end-irons under the north gable.

Before this, the gristing was probably done in a smaller mill. The first record found of this industry appears on September 14, 1824, when a charge of $64.44 was made to Joseph Allen for grinding grain. Grain was sold to farmers and dealers direct from the mill after this date, and several entries in the trustees' accounts testify to a steady income from this source. On April 15, 1839, for instance, appears the entry, "Grain from the mill, $24.98," and on July 30th, "Rec'd from the mill, $13.00."[5] The mill was at first run by water power on an over-shot wheel. After a time, however, even with the artificial diversion of several streams of water, this method was found to be inadequate to furnish power during dry seasons, and one of the first turbine devices used in this section of the country was installed.

The sawmills and carpentry shops were among the busiest places in the industrious villages. The fact that the society at New Lebanon boasted of six such mills by 1839 is evidence of a particularly active occupation. These mills were equipped with buzz or cylinder saws (said to be a Shaker invention) as early as 1813. From an early date the Church family did a large business in wood-turning and in planing and matching timber. In 1835, work done for one Thomas Bowman in "plaining and matching 7482 feet floor plank" amounted to $56.11½, and the same year similar work was done for families in the same society.

Shingle- and brick-making and stone-sawing were at one time active industries, and shingles and bricks were often made on orders from the world's people. As early as 1789 (December 22), we find an item noting the sale of 5,000 shingles. Numbers of old shingle-benches attest to the labors of the early carpenters. Bricks were also manufactured at the East family brickyard as early as 1789, although they were seldom employed in the Shakers' own buildings until later. Operations at the brickyard continued until 1840 or after.

*Early bench used in making shingles or staves.*

*The layout of Shaker villages was planned with communal as well as individual needs in mind. Similarly, every unit of space within the dwelling was utilized in the most functional manner possible—built-in cupboards and drawers were one solution much in evidence in Shaker dwellings.*

Eventually, the gristmills supplied them with flour and meal, as well as some surplus capital. The fulling mills removed the grease from their woolen cloth. They quarried and sawed stone for the foundations of their buildings; they molded and baked the clay for their many brick buildings, and they made the shingles for the roofs. Seldom was it necessary to buy materials. All the building skills—carpentry, masonry, plumbing, etc.—were available within the family or society. Inventions and labor-saving devices facilitated the work.

# Brooms and Brushes

It is appropriate, in view of the Shakers' concern for cleanliness and neatness, that one of their chief industries should have been the manufacture of brooms and brushes; the broom, in fact, has been referred to as a fitting emblem or symbol of Shakerism. "Its manufacture," writes Elder Goepper's interviewer, "is one of their favorite industries, and they have more ways of making it useful than are known to the outside world. They never disgrace it by making it stand behind the door, as if it were responsible for the untidy litter about the house. The Shaker broom is always hung up against the wall when not in use. They put a clean white cotton hood on some of their brooms, and when thus equipped use them to dry-polish their smooth hard wood floors and to remove the last trace of dust from the hard and shining surface."[6]

No Shaker industry was perhaps as widespread as the making of brooms: brooms, broom handles, and brushes (shoe, clothes, scrubbing, dustpan, whisk, etc.) were made and sold in most of the Shaker societies. Not only did almost every society engage in this manufacture, but it was common to almost every family within certain societies. This was the case at New Lebanon. The South family, the Canaan families, the North family, the East family, as well as the Church-center families, all followed this occupation. These groups sold to one another as occasion demanded, but each had its own markets and maintained its own business relationships.

The Shakers at Watervliet are credited with being the first colony to raise broom corn and manufacture brooms. This was in 1798. It is also claimed that Theodore Bates of this community invented the so-called flat broom as contrasted with the earlier round broom and brush.

By 1805 at the latest (this seems to have been the time that broom corn was first grown on a serious scale in western New England and New York and the date coincides with that given by Alice Morse Earle[7] for the first systematic raising of broom corn for use in broom manufacture), the broom industry at New Lebanon was in full swing, and brooms and brushes were being delivered to Albany, Boston, and Hudson as well as to such near-by towns as Cheshire and Lanesboro. The business of turning broom handles for other families and societies was also under way by 1805, and probably several years earlier.

By 1808, brooms were selling at from 30 to 50 cents apiece, and brushes at about 20 cents. One lot of 32 brooms was delivered in Albany in September 1809 for about 16 cents apiece. In 1810, five "splinter" brooms sold for a total of 70 cents, and two long-handled brooms for $1.12½. By 1811, both round and flat brooms were being made, as well as a variety of brushes. In September of that year, nine horse brushes sold for $8.46, 12 large shoe brushes for $4.86, and 11 small shoe brushes for $3.30.

A steady business in making brooms and brushes was maintained by several families at New Lebanon throughout the century. The stores bought from and sold to each other according to the trends of supply and demand. Brushes were made principally in the south of the village, and these, especially the shoe brushes, invariably bore the "D. H." impression on the handle which indicated they had passed the inspection of Daniel J. Hawkins, senior trustee. In the period 1820-1830, brooms were listed at a nearly standard price of 30 cents apiece. Thirty dozen round brooms, for instance, were sold on one occasion for $112.50.

The broom and brush industry was still in a prosperous condition at the Church in 1861. In that year, 170 dozen brooms were made, and in 1862, 95 dozen brooms and 18 dozen brushes. The manufacture of brushes was discontinued shortly after this period, but brooms were made until quite late in the century. A number of entries occur which reveal that a great deal of the raw material for the broom and brush industry was bought

*Below, a brush vise used by the Church or Center family at New Lebanon.*

*On the right, various Shaker brushes.*

from outside sources. Some broom corn, however, was raised at home, and such items occur as the purchase in 1831 of 96 bushels of broom corn seed for $14.40.

As in other occupations, techniques improved with experience and demand. Broom handles were made of soft maple timber and were turned in a common foot-lathe. The first apparatus used for tying the corn on the handle was quite simple, "merely a wheel and shaft," the broom twine being wound around the shaft. "The rim of the wheel was arranged with pins, and operated by the feet."[8] The broom was made "by holding the handle in one hand and applying the brush with the other while winding."[9] A few years later, the process was improved by "the addition of a bench to the roller, in a frame fastened to the bench, with a rag-wheel to hold the cord, when wound upon the roller with [a] short crank as before. The manufacture of two dozen of brooms per day, well made, was considered an exploit, quite equal to the same of six or eight dozen at the present day."[10] At first, the seed was removed from the brush by a crude machine consisting of a wheel fitted with irregularly projecting spikes and turned by hand. The earliest broom and brush vises were Shaker-made.

Later in the century, "Shaker broom-winders" were sold under that name by commercial houses. By mid-century, the name "Shaker" had become a guarantee of quality, not only with brooms, seeds, and herbs, but with other products of the order. "Stoves of the Shaker Improvement" were bring advertised by foundries in Albany in the 1820s, and later, as we shall see, mercantile houses were promoting such products as washing machines, mangles, and chairs.

# Miscellaneous Manufactures

In addition to the basic industries of farming, gardening, apple and corn drying, tanning, blacksmithing, milling, preparing herbs, raising seeds, and making brooms and brushes, the Shakers turned their attention, even at the beginning of their history as an organized society, to the manufacture of many articles needed in the daily tasks of our early national life. While the sisters were occupied with their domestic duties and their own industrial pursuits (see later sections), the shops of the brethren were hives of activity. Besides those manifold products turned out for the immediate use of the community itself, the New Lebanon shops engaged in the manufacture of a long list of articles for the outside market. As early as 1789, the Shakers made whips and whiplashes, pails, tubs and keelers, dippers, cheese hoops, casks, barrels, churns, firkins, dry measures, hand cards, brass and pewter buttons, shoe buckles, stock and knee buckles, harness buckles, candles, clothiers' shears, hoes and miscellaneous ironware. By the turn of the 89 century or soon after, they were also manufacturing spinning wheels and reels, and the famous oval boxes; and by 1810, if not before, such products as smoking pipes, sieves, riddles, and various types of baskets. Mops were also made at an early period. If one adds to these basic and secondary or subsidiary industries such trades and occupations as brick-making and bricklaying, shingle-making, fulling, masonry, carpentry, cabinet-making, quarrying and stone-sawing, fence building, wagon-making, hydraulic engineering, wire-making, tool-making, tinsmithing, tailoring, carding, and clock repairing, besides the many industries carried on in the home, shop, and field by the sisters of the order, it can hardly be said, as critics have implied, that the range of their industries was "not great."[11]

The products of their shops made a considerable contribution to the welfare of the society, even though production was limited in certain cases and at certain periods.

Although coopering, joinery, and carpentry were allied occupations often pursued by the same artisans, it seems that at New Lebanon, at least, the first became a specialized craft under a skilled brother, Nicholas Bennett, and later, Henry Markham. The product included pails, tubs, churns, casks, barrels, firkins, keelers, dry measures, and wooden bowls.

**Coopers' Ware:** Pails, Tubs, Churns, Casks, Barrels, and Firkins. Among the first covenanters at New Lebanon there must have been one or more individuals skilled in the trade of coopering, and an active business along these lines was established immediately after the gathering of the community. Entries of "sundry coopers' ware" are not uncommon in 1789; by 1790, the ware was generally listed in more specific terms. For twenty-five years, there was a steady output of pails, tubs, churns, casks, barrels, and firkins. *The Manifesto* reports that this business did not flourish for long—one reason being the scarcity of lumber.[12] These products were still being sold in 1820, however, and when a new brethren's shop was built at the Church family in 1826, one room was reserved as a cooper's shop. Pails and tubs were sold in some quantity as late as 1830-1832. Production probably did not stop until late in the last century, for the community itself constantly needed such articles as butter and lard firkins, apple barrels, wash and dye tubs, keelers, churns, and seed pails. A date on the bottom of one of the latter indicates that seed pails at least were being made as late as 1874.

Tubs and pails were usually made in three sizes, although sometimes odd sizes were produced for special purposes. Tubs were often sold in nests of three. The first pails were manufactured with what were known as "wood-loops." Later they were bound with band-iron, and this type sold for a slightly higher price. The handles and bails were usually of wood.

*Collection of coopers' ware. The wooden-bound pail on the end of the bench (right) was a milk or "calf" pail. Next to it is a salt or sugar pail; a similar type, but without the cover, was used for water. Leaning against the wall is a shallow tub or keeler used in washing dishes or small clothes. Two dippers are also shown, one of which is in a spit box. The handled measure was often used for shavings. On the floor, right to left: apple sauce bucket; flour, meal, or grain pail; chopping or mixing bowl; seed pail; and another apple sauce bucket.*

Beef barrels, "Pott ash" barrels, and meat barrels were sold as early as 1789. Flaxseed casks sold for four shillings apiece at this date, and firkins from four to six shillings. In 1789, a total of 132 casks were sold to one person—Jeremiah Landon. On May 8, 1790, a churn was sold for five shillings, sixpence; by 1806, the standard price was thirteen shillings. In 1809, with the advent of the new coinage, the price was around $2.75.

**Dippers.** The manufacture of wooden dippers was entered upon at the outset, and continued for a half century or more. They were made of ash and maple, and were often sold, like tubs, in nests of three. The first dipper item occurs on June 16, 1789; this sold for one shilling, fourpence.

Piggins were also used in the Shaker home, but apparently this type of dipper was never made for sale.

**Oval Boxes.** No product of the Shaker wood-working shops possesses greater charm than the multi-sized oval boxes which were made throughout the last century, and were made early in this century by the Second family at Mount Lebanon and at Sabbathday Lake. All kinds of boxes for all kinds of uses were manufactured, but the oval box was a successful refinement

of the more common form, and its novelty and usefulness had a wide appeal.

General utility boxes, usually round, were made in the colonial period, but the Shaker boxes, made in a graceful oval shape, were, like other products, an improvement in form and craftsmanship over their prototypes. For practical purposes, boxes can be crudely fashioned receptacles. When they are made with such finesse as the Shakers gave them, with snugly fitting covers, graceful "fingers" lapping around the side, and yellow, dark red, or green stains, one feels that the objective transcends mere utilitarianism.

As with many other products, improved methods of manufacture were adopted as time went on. "At first the rims were cut from the log in a common saw mill. . . . In 1830 a buzz saw did the work of cutting out the rims."[13] Two years later, the rims and tops, which had been planed by hand, were also planed by machinery. The "fingers" also, which had been hand-cut at first, were later machine-cut. The automatic element in such early machinery, however, was largely absent, and it is wrong to consider such articles as oval boxes, sieves, tubs, pails, etc., as machine-made products. The "machine" was nothing more than a refined tool, and each box or sieve had to pass through the hands of the individual craftsman, process by process.

The rims of these boxes were usually made of maple; the tops and bottoms, of pine. It was common to sell them in nests, a nest consisting at first of twelve boxes, then of nine, and at a later date, of seven and

five. In the trustees' accounts, they were not referred to as "oval boxes" until 1833.

In 1805, two "neasts" of boxes sold for $3.33. Thirteen shillings was the standard price for a nest.

By 1834, oval boxes were sold by number. The largest sizes, Nos. 1, 2, 3, 4, and 5, were the most popular. The introduction of improved methods of manufacture evidently increased the business, for large quantities were being sold by 1834 and 1835. For the next thirty years or more, the output was steady.

"Fancy oval covered wooden boxes" were made at the Second family from an early period, and in an undated leaflet, a pyramid of eleven boxes graduated in size is illustrated, the whole forming one full nest which sold for $5. The price varied from the smallest boxes (No. 11) which sold for $3 a dozen to the largest (No. 1) which were listed at $9 a dozen.

**Buckles.** At the time the society at New Lebanon was organized, it was still the custom of the country to wear stocks, knee breeches, and buckled shoes. Steel and brass buckles were manufactured by the Shakers as early as 1789, and for a short period constituted a remunerative industry. With the advent of a different style of dress, the business languished.

**Buttons.** Jacket, coat, and sleeve buttons were also made at the outset of communal organization. Some were of polished brass or pewter, while    93

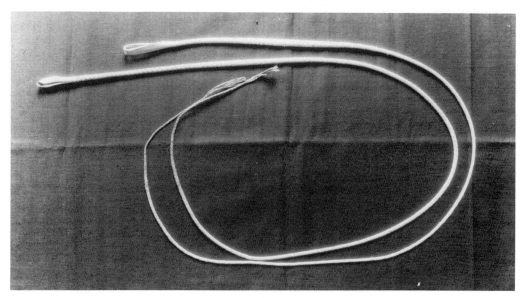

*Braided whiplashes made at New Lebanon and Niskeyuna.*

others were horn molds covered with cloth. The sleeve buttons were made in two parts attached by a chain. These buttons were used for the brethren's garments, but there was also some outside sale. For a number of years after 1825, a small business was also conducted in bone and ivory buttons.

**Whips and Whiplashes.** The manufacture of horsewhips and whip-lashes also dates from the beginning of the settlement. This business was continued at New Lebanon for forty years or more. Sales were not infrequent in 1830 and after, but the whips and lashes sold at this period were purchased from the Watervliet settlement, which evidently had taken over the industry from its sister colony. The lashes were made of horsehides dressed at the tannery and then cut and braided by the brethren, and often by the younger boys. The stocks were turned in the wood-working shop. William Whiting was one of the chief manufacturers at New Lebanon.

**Cheese Hoops and Dry Measures.** Cheese hoops or rings were used in pressing the curds after they had drained in the open-weave cheese baskets. The hoop was lined with cheesecloth, and after being filled with the curds, was placed in the press, which was screwed down at intervals until the cheese was hard. The Shakers made their own presses and cheese baskets.

Dry measures as well as cheese hoops were made of tough, hard wood, generally ash. At Hancock, measures were made either with or without covers, a difference which probably accounts for the terms "sealed" and "unsealed." Occasionally they were fitted with handles.

94

A small business was done at an early date in cheese hoops and dry measures. The former were sold in 1789 for eight pence. By 1809, the price was about 30 cents. In 1790, a half-bushel measure listed at three shillings, fourpence. In 1806, a "Seat of Meashers" could be obtained for ten shillings. Three measures sold for 75 cents in 1809, and two for 37 cents in 1813. By 1833, one could buy four small measures for 50 cents, a peck measure for 40 cents, and a half-bushel measure for 56 cents. These were often sold in nests, and at Hancock it was usually specified on the books whether they were "sealed" or "unsealed." Unsealed half-bushels were bought from Hancock for 36 cents apiece, sealed half-bushels for 44 cents apiece.

## Wool Cards, Wheels, and Reels.

Only a few years after the founding of the sect at New Lebanon, two industries were established which proved for a time to be sources of considerable revenue. These were the manufacture of hand and machine cards and the making of hair and wire sieves.

Hand cards were first made in 1793, and for some twelve or fifteen years, their manufacture was a lively industry. *The Manifesto* states: "During the continuation of the business, all the available help of the First family was secured. Even the farmers and teamsters would eagerly catch every

*Shaker reels. The one at the left, from Sabbathday Lake, was known as a "snap-reel." The long wooden trigger makes a snapping sound when the wheel has made 40 revolutions, thereby standardizing at two bouts the length of the yarn wound into the skein. The clock reel at the right measures a single bout at 20 revolutions.*

95

*On the right, a Shaker spinning wheel, sometimes called a wool or great wheel, from the New Lebanon community.*

spare opportunity to assist in the setting of the card teeth. All the family were very much interested in the work, and their mornings and evenings and even the few minutes while waiting for their meals were utilized in this employment."[14] Early in the next century, a Church family brother, Nicholas Bennett, invented a "machine" for pricking the leather, and in 1809, another machine, for shearing cloth, was invented. Subsequently, teeth-setting machines, the invention of the Englishman Arthur Scholfield, were adopted. With the advent of teeth-setting machines about the year 1815, this hand work was necessarily abandoned. The wire used for the teeth was at first "drawn" in the brethren's shops. During the War of 1812, this occupation was again resumed for a short time.

Wool-carding machines were introduced into near-by towns about 1800, and for the next few years the Shakers sent their wool away to be carded into rolls. They soon began to do their own work, however, a carding machine having been purchased from Pittsfield in the year 1809.

The next year, $478.06 was spent for "cards for a Large machine," 10,000 card nails were bought, and $23.84 expended for dyestuff. This or another machine was sold to one Libeas (?) Barton on May 20, 1811, for $280.00, together with 71½ feet of "twiled" cards at $178.75. The Church evidently still possessed a machine, for wool cards were being sold in some quantity from 1810 to 1814, and in lesser quantity for some years afterward. In 1814 appears "a bill of work for carding machine," indicating that the Church order apparently supplied materials and work for another card house at the New Lebanon community. This second machine may have taken over the bulk of the community's business. In 1816, bands were sold, presumably for this same machine.

Spinning wheels and plain and clock reels were made early in the last century if not before. In 1812, the society purchased a spinning jenny consisting of 24 spindles, and the home need for spinning wheels was supplied by this machine. Another such spinner was bought in 1821. Spinning wheels were still manufactured for the market, however, as late as the 1830s. Twenty shillings was the normal price. In 1818, seven wheels were sold for $21 and in 1831, three "great Spinning Wheels" were sold for $7.50. Wheel parts, such as the benches and whorls, were also supplied. Reels were made during the same period. One was sold on September 13, 1805, for 12 shillings. In 1809, the price was $2, a quotation which was standard as late as 1831. A "quilwheel" ($3) is listed under date of April 19, 1819.

**Sieves.**   For a long period, an important industry at New Lebanon consisted of the manufacture of wire and hair sieves and riddles (coarse sieves). These were designed principally for household use, for sifting flour, straining, etc., but they had other uses, and many were said to have been sold for pharmaceutical and chemical purposes. Wheat riddles were also made in some quantity, and seed riddles were a necessity in the garden seed industry. The business at first was not confined to any one family, but about 1830 it was taken over by the South and Second families, and the Church family bought from them to redistribute to its own market.

The earliest record falls in the year 1810.[15] On September 18th, "sives and brushes" amounting to $18.09 were sold. A sample of account entries for the following year is given below:

| 1811. | Aug. 8. | To 1 Sive | $ .58 |
|---|---|---|---|
| | Sept. 24. | To 12 Small Sives | 3.84 |
| | | 6 Smaller Sives | 1.20 |
| | | 12 large Sives | 8.70 |

*Three-legged sieve-binder with collection of sieves, sieve rims, and riddles. The two large heavy-wire sieves or riddles were used in the seed business. The handled cover of the sieve-binder has a lead rim to increase pressure.*

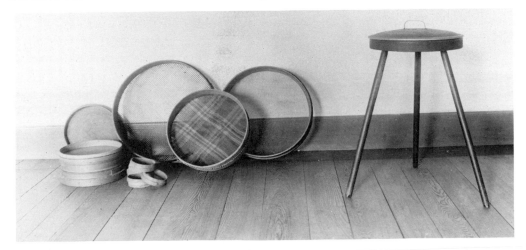

By 1821, sieves are specified as being made of either wire or hair. Horses' manes and cows' tails were used for the latter and woven on special looms by the sisters into the round ash frames. This woven mesh was stretched between the two parts of the sieve, tightened and bound, or sewed on the outside, on a "sieve-binder." On June 4th of that year, 16 of these "hare" sieves were sold for $7, and "½ doz. waer sives" for $3.50.

Under the superintendence of Daniel Hawkins, leading trustee of the South and Second families, this business had become well established by 1830.

**Baskets.** In a letter written in 1856, Amelia Murray, an English traveler to the states, referred to the "delicate baskets" made by the Shakers, "in the manufacture of which the line of beauty has unconsciously introduced itself." These were the "fancy baskets" of white poplar, first woven in 1813. For a number of years a new design was put out annually: "cap" baskets (covered and uncovered), knife, spoon, sugar bowl, box, hexagon, round, "cat head," "kitten head," saucer, tub (in six sizes), fruit, demijohn, flask, cushion, card, fancy, knitting, brush, work, twine, boat (for scissors), and so forth. The wooden forms on which they were woven were carved by George Wickersham.

The weaving of small, fancy baskets of poplar wood belongs in the category of the sisters' occupations. The Shakers also made larger baskets of split black ash for the many uses of the farm and home, and a small but consistent business was carried on from early in the last century until about the time of the Civil War, and perhaps for a longer period. In the early days, traveling groups of Indians made and sold baskets to the Shakers.

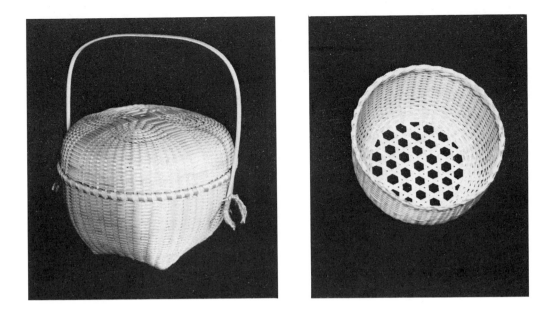

Several of these have been found in the settlements, decorated in quaintly formal patterns with berry juice.

Shaker basketware is characterized by an almost unending variety of patterns. Large, shallow ones, sometimes called "conscience baskets" because of their generous size, were used in the weave-rooms and washhouses. Egg baskets were finely woven, sturdy little affairs, like deep nests. Special sizes were adapted to cherry, grape, or plum picking, larger and stronger ones for heavier fruits. Winnowing baskets were used on the farm. Cheese baskets of large, open weave, whitened by the draining of whey and constant scrubbing, were found in many a Shaker dairy. Immense baskets of varying capacity were used for holding herbs, roots, and barks. Chip baskets, often lined with leather, were used by the sisters for carrying chips or fire kindling. Poplar fancywork or knitting baskets were made in all sizes and shapes. Thousands of general utility baskets, difficult to classify, were also woven in the Shaker societies. A few prices will show how cheaply these beautifully constructed articles were placed on the market[16]:

| 1809. | Nov. 7. | To 4 Baskets | | $2.00 |
| 1811. | Sept. 23. | To 3 Baskets | | 1.50 |
| 1831. | April 29. | To 1 Basket @ 8/ | 1 do @ 4/ | 1.50 |
| 1833. | June 1. | To 1 large Chease Basket | | 1.00 |
| | July 4. | To 1 Tool Basket | | .75 |
| 1835. | June 6. | To 12 Baskets @ 2/6 | | |
| | | 24 " @ 1 | | |
| | | 12 Palm Leaf Baskets | | 9.42 |
| 1855. | Aug. 6. | To 10 small baskets @ 10¢ | | 1.00 |
| | | 6 " @16¢ | | .90 |
| | | 6 long " | | 1.25 |
| | | 6 round " | | 2.00 |

After the Civil War, the ministry at Mount Lebanon "labor[ed] at basket-making in the intervals of their travels and ministrations, and [had] a separate little 'shop' for this purpose near the church."[17]

**Pipes.** At the East family in New Lebanon, there were natural deposits of red clay which were early utilized for making bricks, and this section of the community became commonly known as "the brickyard." It may have been due to the ready supply of such clay that the Shakers became engaged in the manufacture of pipe bowls and stems soon after the beginning of the last century. Smoking was a common habit, even among the Believers themselves in these early days, and there was no moral or hygienic reason why the manufacture of pipes should not have been carried on. The Millennial Laws, revised in 1845, contain many specifications covering the careful use of pipes to prevent fires, and it was not until after the Civil War that smoking was definitely repudiated as an obnoxious habit.

The bowls were made of both red and white clay. The wooden stems were ordinarily made in two lengths, ten and fifteen inches. The first record appears in 1809, when "some pipes" were sold for $1.62.[18] In 1810, such items appear as "2½ doz. pipes . . . $1.40," "30 doz. pipes . . . $18.73," and "80 doz. pipes . . . $40.00." In 1814, pipe "boals" were sold in quantity for a penny apiece, and the stems for three cents each. Pipes were being sold by the Church family as late as 1853; in a gardener's diary, under date of November 23, 1843, is the entry: "B. M. after pipe stem timber below the sap woods."[19] It is probable, however, that the Watervliet colony was the chief source of supply at this later period. By 1835, pipe bowls were being purchased in large orders from Frederick Wicker, the Watervliet trustee, and although the stems may have been and probably were still made at New Lebanon, the center of the industry had shifted to the other settlement. Wicker received $8 a thousand for both red and white bowls.

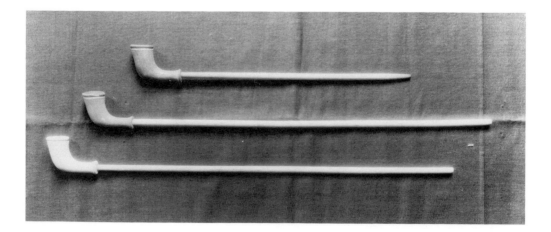

**Pens.** A small industry in making steel, brass, and silver pens was carried on by the Shakers at New Lebanon and Watervliet for a number of years, and they have been credited with being the originators of the metal pens. A letter written in 1878 by G. A. Lomas to the editor of *Scientific American* was claimed by this Watervliet brother to have been written with a silver pen, "one slit," made in that village in 1819. "Two or three years previous to the use of silver for pens," this letter continues, "our people used brass plate for their manufacture, but soon found silver preferable. Some of our people, now living, sold these pens in the year 1820 for 25 cents, and disposed of all that could be made at that price. The machinery for rolling the brass and silver plate was a home invention; also the shears for cutting the pens. . . . At the above date (1819) the inventor writes: 'I now have my new shears, with which I have cut 292 pens in 14 minutes; this is doing it with dispatch!' The metal used was melted silver coins; and at one time the worker says, 'I melted up $55.00 or $60.00 of silver money.'"[20] The pen handles were made of wood and tin and were so made that the pen could be closed "telescopically."

It is not known who this inventor was. We know, however, that Freegift Wells made pens at Watervliet, and that Isaac Youngs engaged for a time in the same occupation at New Lebanon. In the Church family accounts, the first record of a sale of silver pens is in 1825.[21] On August 27th of that year, one was sold for 31 cents. On June 18, 1829, two dozen silver pens were sold for $3.50. In 1831, the price was two shillings, old currency.

Most of the pens sold at New Lebanon were obtained from Watervliet. In 1826, two dozen silver pens were bought from Frederick Wicker for $5; in 1827, six dozen for $15; in 1828, one-half gross of "cased silver pens" for $15 and eight dozen "black handled" silver pens for $14. The Church was purchasing from this source as late as 1835, when four dozen silver pens were bought for $7.

## Miscellaneous Products.

A survey of the occupations followed in all the eighteen Shaker societies would include a number of small shop industries, some of them dependent on available skills present in a given family or community.

A few other items of small manufacture should be mentioned before this section is closed. Certain ones, like scythe snaths or handles, seem to have been made for a time. Round wooden spittoons, or "spit-boxes" as they were called, were made chiefly for the use of the family, but some were sold to other communes or to outside markets. An item in 1839 shows that they brought about 25 cents apiece. Sugar boxes were being sold in nests by 1830, the price varying around 80 cents a nest. Horn combs were sold by Charles Bushnell of the North family in 1835 for $1 a dozen. Horn was also used in the repairing of umbrellas and occasionally in making escutcheons. Spool stands were made in several sizes, and sold in 1838 for from 50 to 80 cents apiece. Spool boxes were bought largely from the Watervliet colony, and swifts from Hancock, where swift-making was a thriving industry in about 1830. "Nail dishes" listed in 1835 for a dollar a dozen. Candlewicking was sold in this year for 25 cents a pound.

Floor mops were made at an early period in many societies, and they were sold until well after the middle of the last century. These were made of tow, cotton, and wool. In the 1840s, the mop industry was concentrated at the Canaan Lower (or South) family. Tow mops sold for about $2.25 a dozen, cotton mops for about $3 a dozen, and "thrum" and wool mops for about $4 a dozen. The handles were turned at the Church family for a penny apiece. As late as 1867, brooms and brushes continued to be the chief industry at the Canaan family.

# The Clothier Shops

The Shakers went a long way in supplying their own needs from their own shops. This spirit of self-dependence is nowhere better illustrated than in the complete system of raising their own flax and wool, weaving their own cloth, and making their own clothes. A tailoring shop was instituted at the very beginning of the New Lebanon commune. This was managed by David Slosson, an experienced tailor, who was one of the first converts to the faith. Slosson had several apprentices under his charge, and these in turn became proficient in the art of making clothes; later, certain individuals were sent to other societies to help in the organization of similar shops.

Few if any printed rules governed the occupation until about 1825, when the clothier shop was reorganized and a greater measure of standardization was given to the processes. However, differing tastes, improved methods, constant experimentation with dyes, shifting costs, etc., made such desired standardization difficult, and forty years later, in a "Circular to Believers Concerning Dress," the ministry was still attempting, in the name of economy and uniformity, to regulate Shaker costume.

These early tailoring establishments not only supplied coats, vests, breeches, stocks, surtouts, and hats for the brethren of the order, but also made clothes for outsiders.

The business of scouring flannel and of fulling and dressing cloth was carried on in the clothier shops and fulling mills during the first half of the last century, and provided constant employment for several brethren. The fulling of cloth was a process distinct from and antecedent to the dressing or glossing of the material. When woolen cloth came from the loom, it was apt to be saturated with the grease or oil applied to the yarn before it was woven. Sometimes the warp had been strengthened by treating it with a starch sizing. The fullers often used "fullers earth" as an absorbing agent to clean off this oil or sizing. Such cleansing was the first step in the finishing of cloth. Following this, the cloth was shrunk and thickened in the fulling mills by immersing it in hot soapy water and beating it with "paddles" or heavy stocks, rubbing it together, or pressing it between rollers. Cloth was dressed by inserting it between hot iron rollers. A close relationship was necessarily maintained between the sisters' weave rooms and these fulling shops. Cloth was dressed for other families in the community and often for the "world's people." Diaper and other cloth was sold in

103

*Straw hat for summer wear, and wooden form for brethren's fur or felt hats.*

1809 and regularly afterwards. Cotton and worsted cloth, shirting, drab cotton, worsted and flannel were being marketed in 1828, diaper and cotton shirting in 1837, and horse blankets in 1839. In 1835, the Church shops scoured quantities of flannel for the North family at the rate of two cents a yard, besides fulling and dressing large amounts of cloth.

Coordinate with the clothing industry was that of "hatting," or the making of felt, colt's fur, and wool hats. For five years after 1787, it was managed at the parent order by Reuben Hosford, an experienced hatter, who made fur and wool hats for his own and other societies and the world at large. Hundreds were sold in the first few years of the community's existence. In 1792, he was sent to organize the business at Hancock, which then became the center of the industry. Nine shillings was the usual price for a colt's fur hat in 1789. A colt's fur and wool hat cost ten shillings, a "caster" (beaver) hat, one pound and twelve shillings. Felt hats were listed at eleven graded prices depending on the size. "Hatter's jacks" were sold in 1811 at the rate of $4.50 for 6½ pairs, and one item reads as high as $20.25.[1] By 1828, "fine wool hats" were sold for $1.75 apiece, and fur hats as high as $6. Later in the century, after the Civil War, the Mount Lebanon Shakers made hats, mittens, and leggings from coon's fur, wool, and silk. Straw hats were also made.

Eventually the Lebanon tailors and hatters confined their attention to making men's clothes and hats. The cutting and fitting of sisters' clothes became the function of the tailoresses. A more comprehensive insight into the work of the clothiers may be gained from a description of the kind of garments first worn by the brethren, and of the changing styles of later periods. The following authentic account was written in 1858, evidently by one of the New Lebanon tailors.[2]

104

# Garments

The early Believers accepted the simple, plain form of dress that prevailed among the common people of the world, and laid down no rules that should govern the Societies in this respect. The first American converts were extremely varied in the form, color and quality of their garments, but as they became more associated and united they inclined more to a uniformity, and were influenced largely by the manners of the first Elders.

After the organizing of the Church the uniformity of dress became a matter of much more consequence, and they adopted for the Sabbath, a dark blue coat, with a cape that came up to the neck, and lay upon the shoulders. Cuffs to the sleeves were six inches long. Pockets were cut at the waist and a large lid covered the horizontal pocket. The front edge of the coat was nearly straight, having some six or eight buttons of an inch in diameter, and button-holes three inches long. One half of these were for ornament and no place was cut through the cloth. On the back of the coat, at the lower extremity of each side seam, was a large double fold or plait, taking about three inches of cloth and folded twice. At the waist, on the back, was a large "square stitching" three or four inches long, and about one fourth as wide and a button at the head of each fold, and another button at the bottom of the skirt, which came a few inches below the knee.

The vest was from the same cloth, the waist falling a little below the natural waist. The skirts were about seven or eight inches long. In front these were cut off to an angle of about forty-five degrees, from a point at the lower button. In the back, the skirt was divided into two sections, which overlapped each other one or more inches. The whole of the vest was made from the same piece of cloth. If the front was broadcloth the back would be of the same quality. A row of twelve buttons were arranged in front, and large pocket lids were set to the waist line.

The lower garment, especially for the Sabbath and for journeys, was black-lasting breeches which ended a little below the knee, these being supplemented by long black stockings. A row of four buttons ornamented the suit at the knee, while the breeches and stockings were secured in their proper places by a strap and a large brass buckle just below the knee in the front.

As the sleeves of the shirts were made large and very long, a blue silk ribbon, under the name of "sleeve tie" was fastened around the arm just above the elbow to secure them in place when the coat was laid aside.

The covering for the neck was called a "Stock." This was made of some very stiff material about two and one half or three inches wide and covered with white or blue silk, and fastened by a buckle on the back of the neck. The white stocks were generally worn on the Sabbath and were considered a part of the uniform, while the blue were for more common use.

In 1810 the white stocks gave place to white cotton, linen, or silk neckerchiefs which are used more or less at the present date [1858]. The wearing of stocks was the general custom of the day and many of the portraits painted at that time will give a much clearer impression of the style.

The hats were made of fur or wool, with low crowns, about four inches high and brims five or more inches wide. These generally were colored black. The form of the hat has undergone some slight changes during the past forty years, and the crown now measures about five inches deep and the brim four or four and one half inches. The children generally wear caps.

The shoes were made of calf-skin and fastened with straps and show buckles.

The foregoing was generally termed the "Sunday Suit," and was preserved in the Society as quite necessary for several years.

For more common use, trowsers generally were worn, especially when engaged in manual labor, but the cloth was of a poorer quality and colored with a cheap dye. Surtouts and great coats were made for those who needed extra garments while on their journeys. The same provision was made for boots, overshoes, socks and mittens. Gloves were seldom seen.

This form of dress continued in use, without change till the year 1805. The Society was now resting on a more permanent foundation, and had been blessed with an experience of some eighteen years. From the first the Believers had been studying the advantages to be derived from the principle of Christian economy and utility, in all that pertained to a life in the Community.

At this date, the breeches and long stockings were laid aside on the Sabbath and the plain trowsers were substituted in their place. For several years, however, after this proposed change, individuals might occasionally be seen, who were on a journey, dressed as formerly, with long stockings, and with highly polished knee and shoe buckles.

In 1806 blue coats and vests began to give place to the steel-mixed, and this latter was adopted as the uniform color. Among the reasons for discontinuing the "blue" was partly on account of the expense of the Indigo, and the labor of making the garments. Trowsers for winter use were made of woolen cloth or of serge. For summer Sabbath uniform, the trowsers were of linen or checked cotton, blue and white. Garments for manual labor were generally of tow cloth.

Another radical change was made in 1810 when the gray was laid aside and the coats and vests were made of drab-colored cloth. The

form of the coat was also changed quite essentially. The double folds of the skirt were set aside, and a single fold adopted. The front edge was cut more circling, and fell back at the bottom of the skirt, some four inches. The pocket lids of the coats and vests instead of being cut with two scallops and leaving a point in the center, were cut with a curve on the lower, parallel with the upper edge.

A collar of about one and one-half inches wide, was added to the coat. This was made upright. Over this was a cape that extended to the edge of the shoulder. All the buttons and button-holes were now omitted, and for the fastenings of the coat in front, two or three pairs of "hooks and eyes" were substituted.

The vests were cut shorter in front, and the skirts reduced to correspond more closely with the height of the person, which made the medium length about seven inches.

By adopting the use of suspenders a slight change was made in the form of the trowsers, which had been, to this date, so formed at the waist as to hold themselves in place without any other aid.

Shoe buckles were laid aside, and strings of leather or cloth were used instead.

For several years the trowsers for uniform on the Sabbath in summer were colored with nutgall, but in 1820 these gave place to garments made of cotton, striped blue and white.

In 1832, the drab vest, which had been largely in use since 1810, was partially displaced by the introduction of a fine blue. While this color was generally used in the summer, the drab was retained for use in the winter. Blue seems to have been a favorite color for summer, and in 1854 they obtained a delicate, fine article of light blue, that was of foreign manufacture.

For winter use the blue was laid aside in 1840 and drab was established as the uniform color for vests, and continued to be used till 1854, when blue was again introduced.

From 1813 to 1840 the surtouts and great coats were made of drab-colored cloth, manufactured by the Society, then a finer quality of cloth was purchased and used till 1847, when a steel-mixed again was introduced.

The pressure of outside competition was more and more keenly felt as the century advanced. About 1866, Elder Giles Avery of the central ministry wrote that the manufacture of cloth had seldom been a source of profit, and advised that the factory of the New Lebanon society, "be not rebuilt."

Until it was cheaper to buy cloth and clothes from the world (about 1852), no Shaker industry was more self-sufficient than the clothing. For a long time, beginning in 1787, shoes were made by Isaac Crouch, Hezekiah Phelps, and others. Palm-leaf and rye or oat straw bonnets, for sale as well as home use, were made from the 1820s until the Civil War period.   107

Steel and brass buckles (see page 93) for stocks, knee breeches, and shoes, and jacket, coat, and sleeve buttons (see page 93) of brass, pewter, bone, or ivory, were manufactured for many years after 1789. The weave and clothing shops produced not only clothes, but necessary items such as sheets, blankets, cloth shoes, carpeting, chair "mats," cloth seed bags, meal bags, "bread clothes," towels. One of the principal customers for horse blankets was P. T. Barnum's circus.

In conversation with two Shakers at Busro, Indiana, Donald MacDonald, a member of Robert Owen's party when the English socialist visited America in 1824, was shown a black silk handkerchief "of their own making, which he was wearing around his neck. . . . Some of the longer established societies, he said, made silks of a very superior description." Drab-colored silk neckerchiefs, woven from silk produced in the Kentucky societies, were being used by the Shakers as early as 1818, and in the '20s and '30s were made for sale. If no other evidence existed, these lovely creations would belie any charge that the Believers were averse to color.

*The brethren's garments were simple, practical, and—*
*whatever the occasion, the season, or the availability of*
*material—uniform in style, color, and quality of fabric.*

# Occupations of the Shaker Sisters

The emancipation of women from a position of social inferiority and the investment of the Deity with feminine as well as masculine virtues were fundamental principles in the Shaker theology. Ann Lee was convinced that by granting equal rights to women one of the chief evils of the existing

*The sisters' garments were plain in style, devoid of orna-mentation. The* Millennial Laws *forbade Believers from wearing any garments superfluously trimmed, "which would have a tendency to feed the pride and vanity of man." The short outdoor wraps shown here were common in the late nineteenth century.*

social order would be corrected. Although she felt that such equality would be hastened by the liberation of women from the bondage of the marriage relation, a concept which was widely condemned by "worldly" critics, the ends she sought were nevertheless praiseworthy. The institution of Shakerism deserves acclaim on this account alone—that in it from the first, women were coequal with men in all the privileges and responsibilities of leadership and labor. The Shaker government was dual in every department, and women were as free as the men to speak in meeting or to write for publication. Under the management of various deaconesses, the sisters carried on occupations and industries of their own quite independently from the brethren, although they labored for a common cause.

Their accounts were kept separately. The matter is thus explained in Seth Wells's "Importance of keeping correct Book Accounts"[1]:

> Tho' the Sisters have but little to do in the business of
> commerce; yet, being willing & desirous to do their part & bear

*The girls' clothes room was kept in perfect order since the sisters were "under special injunction to take good care of all things, with which they are entrusted, and to see that no loss comes through their neglect."*

their portion towards supporting the temporal interest of the Church or family in which they live & let their works be known, they are allowed to keep a Book account of the incomes of their own separate earnings & the expense of purchases made for their particular use. This is done by the Deaconesses at the Office. Of course, the money brought in by their own exclusive labors, is at their disposal, out of which they can make purchases of such articles as they need, exclusive of the general purchases made for the use of the family. Yet all these receipts and purchases are entered on the Book of Incomes and expenditures kept by the Deacons; so that the whole amount of the receipts and expenses of the family, both of the Brethren & Sisters, are regularly entered on book, & show at one view, what the real incomes & expenditures of the family are from year to year. This is the order & practice in the Church & Second Family at New Lebanon, & should be done in every family that feels an interest in keeping the order of the Gospel & supporting the united interest of the Family.

Much of the time of the Shaker sisters was occupied by such domestic tasks as washing, ironing, cooking, cleaning, mending, "schooling" and taking care of the many girls who were placed in the care of the society. When one considers the size of the dwellings, the number of men, women, and children living the communal life, and the almost religious emphasis placed on order and cleanliness, it can be seen that household occupations represented no small undertaking. The work was carefully organized, however, and through routine a high standard of efficiency was maintained.

*The behavior of the Believers was strictly regulated; at mealtimes, detailed table monitors emphasized economy and good manners.*

The system of rotation in such duties as those of the kitchen kept the necessary routine from being over-arduous.

It was the custom among the Shakers to charge certain sisters with the responsibility of caring for and educating the girls taken into the society, and certain brethren with a like oversight of the boys. The "common branches" were taught at New Lebanon, even though somewhat irregularly, from the outset of organization. In 1808 or soon after, evening schools were established, attendance at which, however, was voluntary and the sessions rather intermittent in character. It was not until 1815 that the Shaker school was settled on a firmer basis, and in 1817 a public school on the Lancastrian plan was formed for the benefit of all the children. The girls were taught for a period of four months in the summer, and the boys for a similar period (November to March) in the winter.

A schoolhouse was built at the Church family in 1839. From the first the Shaker schools were inspected by district officials and conformed to the general school laws of the district and state. Each family at New Lebanon sent its own children to the school at the Church family, and tuition was charged to respective family deacons at the end of the year.

The *Millennial Laws* are quite specific about the schooling of the children.

> **1.** Children of different families among Believers gathered into order, should not be schooled together, if it can reasonably be avoided.

**2.** Girls school should be kept in the summer, and boys school in the winter, and they should never be schooled together.

**3.** Spelling, Reading, Writing, Composition, English Grammar, Arithmetic, Mensuration, The Science of Agriculture, Agricultural Chemistry, a small portion of History and Geography, Architecture, Moral Science, Good Manners, and True Religion, are sufficient as general studies for children among Believers.

**4.** No member but those appointed by the Ministry may study Physic, Pharmacy, Anatomy, Surgery, Law, Chemistry, etc. etc. And Phrenology, Mythology, Mesmerism, and such sciences as are foreign from Believers duty, may not be studied at all by Believers. The Ministry and Elders must be the proper judges, how far any of the studies allowable, may be prosecuted.

5. Those who teach school, shall devote their time to teaching their scholars, and not to studying themselves, further than is necessary to enable them to do their duty in teaching; but they should have a good understanding of all the branches they are required to teach.

6. The Bible should be read in schools, and the New Testament made use of as one of the general reading books. Children should be taught the History of the Rise and Progress of Believers, and the names of the founders of our society.

7. Picture books, with large flourished and extravagant pictures in them may not be used by Believers.

8. In connection with other school studies the children should be taught to sing.

9. Children should be kept in an order by themselves, where it can be done consistently. And as a general rule, boys should remain in the children's order, until sixteen years of age, and girls until fourteen.

10. No one but such caretakers as are appointed, should interfere in the dictation of children.

11. Children should never be made equals and playmates of, by those who are older. All should be sociable with children, but not familiar.

The Shaker sisters and younger girls also helped the brethren, especially in the herb and seed business. They printed the labels used on the herb packages and papers, and the gathering and "picking over" of the herbs and roots gave many sisters constant employment. The paper and cloth bags used in the seed business were also made in the sisters' shops. The final stages in the preparation of the renowned Shaker apple sauce and maple sugar were in their province, and their assistance in shelling the corn used in the dried sweet corn industry was invaluable.

Certain industries, spinning and weaving in particular, were taken over entirely by the sisterhood, the work being carried on at the washhouse or laundry. The tailoresses made and mended the sisters' clothes. In the sisters' shops were made the palm-leaf bonnets, poplar baskets, table mats, knitwear, Shaker cloaks, floor mops, and a long list of other fancy and useful articles.

Dairy products also yielded a steady income. The sisters did the milking and made the butter and cheese, and in the great kitchens, barrels and barrels of apple sauce and pickles were put up each year. Tomato catsup and various preserves were also sold in large quantity, and wines found

a ready market.

*Above, a sister weaving a strip of carpeting.*

*Left, Sister Sadie Neale is shown engrossed in weaving, one of her many activities at New Lebanon until her death at age ninety-eight.*

# Weaving and the Manufacturing of Cloth

New Lebanon was organized some time before the so-called "homespun" industries had given way to manufacturing establishments. Women who joined the society were often experienced in those many domestic arts practiced in colonial homes, and it was natural that they should continue to spin yarn, weave and dye cloth, dip candles, and engage in the countless occupations which made small industrial units of the homes of that period. In a very true sense, the early Shaker community was just an enlarged colonial household.

Looms were constructed or used at the very outset, as were many other devices and tools employed in the manufacture of cloth—"great" wheels, reels, swifts, skarns, flax foot-wheels, "pleasant spinners," and hatchels. Carding and spinning and the weaving of woolen, cotton, and cotton-wool cloth were done exclusively by the sisters, who also for several years hatcheled all the flax used in making linen cloth. Until 1809, when a machine was invented for the purpose, the cloth was cut with shears made by the Shaker blacksmiths. A mill for carding wool was built, as we have noted, at an early date, and a clothier's mill was constructed where fabrics were dyed. The looms were in constant use until about 1853, when the compara- 115 tive cheapness of mill cloth made it seem uneconomical for the Believers to rely wholly upon their own product. For a long time after this, however, these looms were not wholly idle, and material for shag chair mats, toweling, serge trousers, linen frocking, worsted gowns, cotton handkerchiefs, carpets, spreads, etc., continued to be woven in the community.

Before the writer are two weavers' records which date from the 1830s. One is "A Weaver's Memorandum; or An Account of Weaving, etc. Kept by Hannah Treadway. D. 1833 & 34."[2] The other is a yearly account of weaving from 1835 to 1865; the recorder was Sister Joanna Kitchell.[3] The memorandum serves as a guide to the technique of weaving. In the first part is reckoned the number of runs, yards, "overplus of quarters," and "remainder in half knots," depending upon the number of biers, bouts, and threads resulting from the number of spools used in warping, the table ranging from ten to forty-four spools.

Joanna Kitchell's record reveals what an all-inclusive program of work the early Shaker weavers set for themselves. In 1835, a total of 1,205 yards of cloth was woven for frocks, surtouts, flannel shirts, habits, trousers,

*Weaving, spinning, hatcheling, dyeing, and other sisters' occupations were all carried on in the commodious wash-house or laundry. In the weaving room, material had to be carefully woven according to given specifications.*

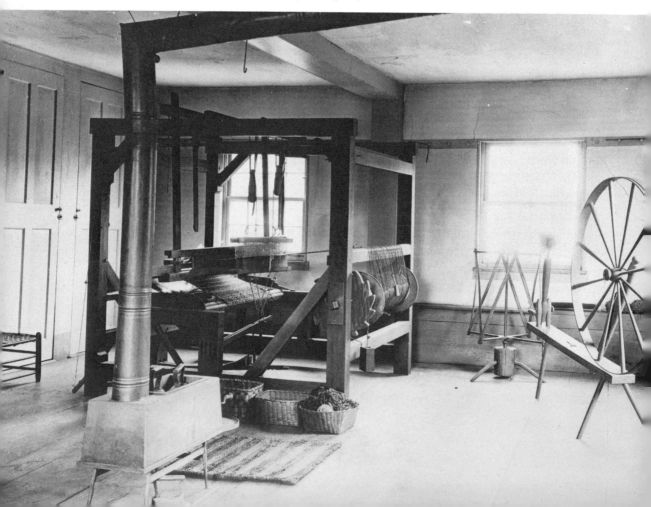

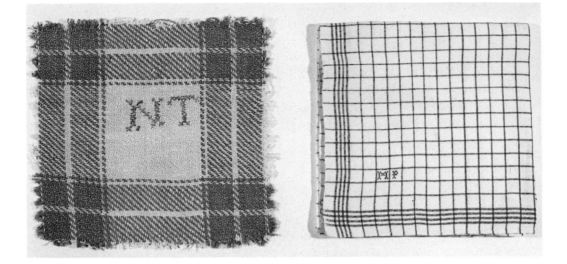

drawers, bags, garden sheets, serge, worsted serge for shoes, drugget gowns, drugget linings, drugget trousers, worsted trousers, worsted gowns, cotton and worsted jackets, jacket linings, worsted linings, and wash aprons. In 1836, 1,337 yards were woven for many of the above purposes, besides such additional uses as tow and linen frocks, barn frocks, boys' trousers, coarse flannel, linen ironing clothes, cotton and wool blankets, and narrow cotton and wool sheets. In 1837, 78 yards of horse blankets (wool with a cotton warp) were woven on the same loom, and 99 yards of checked linen "pocket handkerchiefs." In this year is the first mention of the characteristic red and blue cotton and worsted cloth which was used so commonly in Shaker dresses.

From 1841 to 1851, a total of 24,234 yards of material was woven. Serge, worsted, flannel, cotton, linen, and drugget cloth constituted the main product. Hundreds of yards of blanketing, carpeting, toweling, bagging, shirting, lining, and frocking were also woven. Whether these figures stand for the total cloth production of the family or for the output of Sister Joanna's loom alone is not clear in the original manuscript.

A noticeable decrease in production appears about this time. While the annual output varied from 1,500 to 2,000 yards before 1851, it was less than 1,000 yards after this date, decreasing to 581 yards in 1861. The revival of the chair industry at the South and Second families is reflected in the weaving of the shag chair mats, which commenced in 1858 and continued until the journal's close in 1865, and in the few penciled items in another hand which carry the record to 1874. More carpeting was woven in these later years, as well as cotton cloth for handkerchiefs. In 1865, cotton-wool was still being woven in quantity; flannel cloth for gowns, drugget for trousers and jackets, fulled cloth for boys' frocking, and linen for trousers also kept the old looms from being idle.

117

# The Sisters' Sewing Shops

The cloth used for the brethren's and sisters' clothing was woven on order from the tailors and tailoresses. Certain materials had definite uses and had to be woven to given specification: for instance, frocking for the smaller boys was woven with fewer biers than that for the older boys. The width of the material was governed by its use. The actual making of the sisters' garments was done in the sewing or tailoring shops, just as the brethren's clothes were made in the clothiers' shops. The cloth was cut, pieced, and sewed on the long counters which were made for every sewing or tailoring room, while much of the finer work was done at the smaller sewing desks or cabinets. When a garment was completed, the initials of the one for whom it was made were worked into the fabric, and this person was henceforth responsible for its proper care. Other fabrics, such as towels, bags, cloth shoes, etc., were similarly marked. To each brother was assigned a sister who washed, ironed, and mended his clothes, and exercised "a general sisterly oversight" over his "temporal needs."

Paper labels printed on a Shaker press were also used on hats, bonnets, surplus boxes, or drawers of clothing, and the like. In 1856, a "mall" of such labels was sent by a well-wisher, signing her name "E," to the office sisters. The cover is thus inscribed:

> Dear Sisters at the Office, all,
> Will you receive this present mall,
> The best I have I give to you,
> And sure, I hope it well to do,
> In marking clothes and jars and pot;
> And other notions you have got.
> And should you wish for any more,
> Just write a list and hand it o'er!
> E.

The pages contain labels for such articles as drugget trousers, "summer footins," winter footings, winter shirts, fine shirts, summer shirts, drugget gowns, pocket handkerchiefs, "wollen stockings," "wollen shirts," winter coats, summer coats, socks, shoes, silk handkerchiefs, "wollen mitings," "wollen gloves," leather gloves, "leather mitings," cotton worsted gowns, worsted gowns, light colored gowns, drab gowns, blue gowns, and worsted trousers.

The dress adopted by the Shaker sisters varied in style with different periods. The same process of standardization that brought uniformity to the brethren's apparel applied to garments of the other sex. *The Manifesto* thus describes the various forms of dress worn by the sisters[4]:

Many persons wore short gowns with short sleeves [over their dresses] . . . of light-colored, striped cotton. The stripes went around the sleeves, but lengthwise on the body of the dress. The waist extended to the hips, while the dress reached a few inches below the knees. For more common use the short gowns reached only some eight or ten inches below the waist.

Over the dress in front, was worn a checked apron, about one and one-half yards wide, cut circling at the top and gathered to about two feet in width. A white binding of an inch went across the upper edge which terminated in white tape-strings that were tied in front with a double bow. These aprons were an inch shorter than the dress or about

*Believers Emma and Sadie Neale, sisters from Williams-town, Massachusetts, were Shakers for more than ninety years. Both were dedicated to their religion and active within the New Lebanon order. Sister Sadie was orchard deaconess, teacher, and postmistress; Emma became a trustee of the Church family.*

two inches from the floor. Homespun linen was largely used till the year 1800, when the Sisters learned to card and spin fine cotton, and were able to manufacture their own dresses, aprons and kerchiefs.

The extended dress, or dress worn under the short gown, was generally black and fell to within one inch of the floor. After several years the black was partially laid aside and garments of blue were introduced. In 1811, the long outer dresses were adopted for summer and winter use, by all classes.

Black silk shoulder kerchiefs were worn for many years, when they gave place to fine, white lawn or linen, that were manufactured in the Society. In 1818 drab colored silk neck kerchiefs were used. Subsequently, some very beautiful silk kerchiefs were made by the Believers in the western and southern states.

For winter use the dress reached quite to the floor. These were made with two box plaits in the rear part of the skirt, and from these single plaits, of one-half inch in width, extended to a line from under the arm, where they met the plaits from the front part of the dress. The waist of these dresses extended several inches below the natural waist, and ended in a point on the back. Under the dress was a bodice, agreeably to the prevailing custom. These were abandoned in 1811. The sleeves ended just below the elbow, and were supplemented by plaited cuffs.

Blue and white checked aprons were largely used and blue cotton neck kerchiefs; these last were finished with two or three white borders, about three-eighths wide and one-half inch apart.

On the head the Sisters wore a fine lawn or linen cap. They were formed by plaiting and gathering, to adjust them to the head. These were trimmed in front with a border of open-work, one inch wide. Tape was passed through the back hem of the cap, and brought forward, then over the head, and returned to terminate in a box knot behind.

Muslin was used in the Society in 1806 and made into caps, and also into kerchiefs. Collars with a cape attached were worn in 1810, but previous to this date the neck kerchief only was used. Girls on accepting a head-dress have generally arranged the hair under a net woven for that purpose. The form of the caps changed quite essentially in 1819. A border in front of about three inches in width, made of leno, was attached to the cap and considered very beneficial.

As those who entered the Society wore high heeled shoes, the custom was continued for a great many years. The uppers were generally made of cloth, while the heels were formed from blocks of wood and neatly covered with leather. The shoes were secured to the feet by straps and shoe-buckles.

In 1787 a hat braided of straw and styled a "Chip Hat" was
generally worn by the women of the country and continued in use till

1805. It was covered, inside and out, with black silk. The crown was about one inch deep, covered with a band of silk of the same width, which was formed of fine plaits across the band. Silk ribbons were attached to the crown and brought down over the brim and tied in the rear of the neck. The brim of the hat was not less than six inches wide. From Chip Hats, the change was made to simple bonnets, similar to those worn by the Friends or Quakers. These were made of pasteboard and covered with light colored silk. The crown was made wholly of cloth and fitted to the head by plaiting, but were made without capes.[e]

In 1827, the bonnets were made of palm leaf, and trimmed with a small silk cape and ribbons.

The sisters were responsible for a definite allowance of wearing apparel. An order dated May 10, 1840, gave to "Females under 26" at the First Order, New Lebanon: 2 outside gowns, 2 worsted gowns, 3 common winter gowns, 1 white gown, 2 cotton and worsted gowns, 2 light colored gowns, 2 cloaks, 2 winter petticoats, 3 summer petticoats, 1 white petticoat, 2 "good checkt aprons," 2 good winter aprons, 6 kitchen aprons, 9 shifts, 3 palm bonnets, 1 pair of "nice" leather shoes, 1 pair of wash shoes, 6 pairs of cloth shoes, 2 pairs of socks, 16 pairs of stockings, 10 common neckerchiefs, 8 white neckerchiefs, 16 caps, 12 collars, 3 pairs of undersleeves, 8 underjackets, 2 white handkerchiefs, 2 fine checked handkerchiefs, and common handkerchiefs "as many as needful." Females under twenty received a smaller quantity of clothing. The following articles were forbidden: checked collars, silk cushions, silk shoe or bag strings, silk bonnet strings for every day, frills or ruffles on bonnets, pearly collar buttons, green aprons, bombazine aprons, clasp garters, and "bought striped gowns with wider stripes than the good Church Order stripes."

# Palm-leaf and Straw Bonnets

The manufacture of palm-leaf and straw bonnets was an important Shaker industry, at New Lebanon and other societies, from the late 1820s until the Civil War period. The price varied slightly above and below $1. Children's bonnets sold for about $5 a dozen. In the journal kept by the deaconesses at the office of the Church family, an itemized account of bonnet sales is given covering a period from April 1836 to June 1837. In this time, 1,866 bonnets were sold to other societies and to the world, the account amounting to $1,963.71. On October 27, 1838, a shipment of bonnets to New York and Philadelphia amounted to $528.95.

The following brief description of the early bonnet industry was written by one of the Mount Lebanon sisters:

> The palm leaf was purchased from Cuba. It was first sized and dampened. The longest leaves were used for warp, and the shorter pieces for filling or woof. These were tied into hand looms to pieces

*Hannah Wilson (left), a member of the Upper Canaan family, with Sister Margaret (last name unknown) of the same family.*

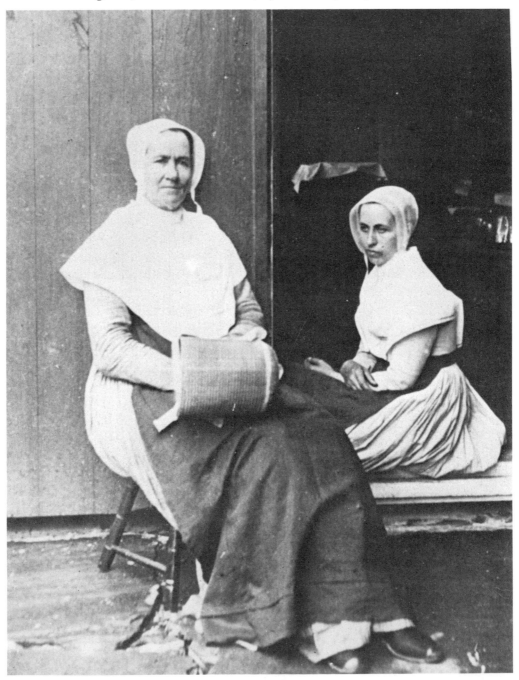

of thread previously placed through a harness and reed. Then the weaver would tie the loose end of palm leaf to the apron rod of the loom and proceed to weave with short strands threaded through a wooden needle. When completed the woven pieces were known as "chips." In a much smaller loom were woven the braids. These were of two widths: one, one-half inch wide, was called the crown braid and the other, an inch in width, the fore braid.

The chip was then treated to a flame of burning alcohol to singe off the fiber roughened by the sizing machine. Each "chip" was then varnished on one side, and a thin cloth pasted on the reverse side. Each "chip" made one front piece and crown piece; the pliable wire was sewed around the crown and front edge. The back edge of the front piece was securely sewed to the crown and the narrow ½ inch braid was sewed over the crown to cover the joining; the wider braid was doubled and bound over the front edge of the bonnet.

These bonnets were not commercialized after the Civil War, but they were worn by the Shakers themselves. Most of the later ones were made of rye or oat straw.[5]

Bonnets were made in graded sizes, 5's and 6's for the children, and 7's, 8's, 9's, and 10's for the sisters. These sizes were regulated by cutting out the bonnet parts on paper, wood, or sheet iron patterns, and then piecing them together over wood forms or molds.

The effect of the Civil War on the bonnet industry was instantaneous. At the Church family, New Lebanon, 533 were sold in 1859, 470 in 1860, and 238 in 1861. The next year only a dozen were made. That some bonnets

were made for sale after the war is evident, however, from a schedule of prices on bonnets set by the office deaconess at Mount Lebanon, 1869. According to this schedule, straw bonnets were worth "from three to five dollars when trimming is furnished by ourselves." Palm bonnets were priced from $2 to $2.50.

# Kitchen and Dairy Industries

Shaker apple sauce was as well known in antebellum days in New England and New York as the Shaker bonnets, seeds, brooms, or herb extracts. Apples were raised extensively by the Believers and large consignments were also received from the neighboring farms. "Paring bees" were held several times a week in the fall. The sisters trimmed and cored the fruit while the brethren ran the paring machines. The apples were then desiccated in the drying house; a large stove on the ground floor furnished heat, and the apples were stirred until dry in large bins located in the floor above. When cool they were packed away in barrels to be made later into apple sauce. Inferior fruit was turned into vinegar, or cider to be used in making the cider apple sauce. Sauce, presumably apple sauce, was being distributed at Hudson and other centers as early as 1814. Apple sauce and dried apples were sold by the barrel in the 1830s and perhaps earlier, and for fifty years

this was an important industry. In 1848, 36 gallons of apple butter were prepared, and this product appears in the deaconesses' accounts for several years afterward. In 1855, apple sauce was sold for the equivalent of four shillings a gallon; in 1856, the price was $12 a barrel. Cider and vinegar were made in the 1820s and for many years afterward. In 1828, cider was sold for $1 a barrel and vinegar for $3 a barrel.

About the middle of the last century, a lucrative maple syrup industry was developed which continued for many years. In 1853, the sales were so numerous that a separate section of the trustees' accounts was devoted to this business. Entries appear amounting to $130, $136, $201, $250, etc. By 1860 at least, the product was being advertised the year round in certain

*The everyday kitchen duties were carefully organized and rotated systematically to prevent the routine from becoming over-arduous; however, seasonal activities—the preparation of wines, sauces, jellies, preserves, and maple sugar cakes (as in the picture)—drew the sisters together in groups of concentrated effort.*

newspapers. The making of maple sugar cakes, sometimes filled with butternuts, was begun at a slightly later date, but developed into an active household occupation about the time of the Civil War.[6]

A large grove of maples was located near the New Lebanon village. "The camp was on a side hill about two miles from the settlement," Sister Marcia recalled, "and here the great sheet iron kettles were arranged one above another and connected with pipes and faucets so that the boiling sap could easily be run from one to the other. In the early spring, a detachment of sisters went out and washed all the buckets before they were hung upon the trees. The sap was first boiled down by the brethren at camp and then brought in on the ox sleds to the 'sugar shop,' where the sisters took charge of it. Shaker syrup is remarkably fine because it is clarified by the addition of milk, one quart to twelve gallons of syrup. . . . The syrup was stored in two-gallon jugs, sealed with resin, and one of these jugs was opened each Sunday morning for the family breakfast. In fact, the syrup was entirely for home consumption, though the sisters made quantities of little scalloped sugar cakes for sale, some plain, some with nuts. . . ."[7]

The preparation of wines, sauces, jellies, and preserves constituted another industrious household occupation during this same period. A package of labels, some dating before and some after 1861, shows that the following wines were made: blackberry, cherry, elderberry, grape, white currant, red currant, and apple. Metheglin was also put up, as well as a tonic known as wild cherry bitters. The first mention of wine occurs in 1859, when ten gallons were concocted by the office sisters. Two barrels were sold in 1860, and about the same annual quantity in the next few years.

Quince, peach, cranberry, raspberry, citron, pear, grape, pineapple, strawberry, "plumb," and tomato sauce were prepared by the sisters for home use and for sale. Currant, apple, raspberry, and many other kinds of jellies were put up in quart containers which sold for the equivalent of eight shillings each; cherry, plum, crab apple, cranberry, and quince preserves were sold for four shillings a quart.[8]

A considerable business was also done in cucumber pickles and tomato catsup. Pickles were sold as early as 1811, and after 1818, such entries are not uncommon. The sisters of the Second Order put up 6½ barrels of pickles in 1840, and in the period 1840-1855, more than 100 barrels were sold. This business continued until 1870 or after. In 1848, the First Order sisters prepared 43 dozen bottles of tomato catsup, and tomato sauce was sold in large quantities, by the bottle and by the gallon.

Dairy products were a household staple and also provided a steady although not large income. The sisters did the milking, except in stormy weather, and prepared the butter and cheese, the surplus of which was marketed after the family needs had been met. Cheeses were sold as early as 1810, the price at that time being four for $17.04. In 1841, 200 pounds of cheese were made by the First Order sisters at the Church, and in the next fifteen years, these sisters had manufactured 5,433 pounds. The current price in 1854 was the equivalent of one shilling a pound.

Other related industries added to the family's revenues. In 1841, the First Order sisters sold 100 pounds of sausages. Ten years later, strawberries were cultivated and marketed in some quantity. In 1853, currants were sold by the bushel; 24 bushels in 1853, 21 bushels in 1854, and so on. Gooseberries were also raised, and in 1865, five barrels of dried elderberries were put up. By 1860, a poultry business had been inaugurated: 160 fowls were "picked" by the First Order sisters in this year, and 70 turkeys and chickens by the Second Order. From 1863 on, the office sisters sold in their store quantities of preserved or sugared sweet flag root, sugared butternut meats, and sugared lemon and orange peel.[9]

# Boxes and Baskets, Knitwear and Miscellaneous Products of the Sisters' Shops

Besides the numerous occupations and industries already mentioned, the Shaker sisters engaged in the manufacture of many forms of wearing appar-

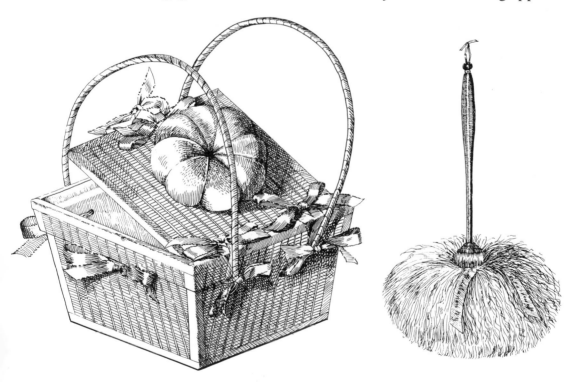

el and articles which appealed to the nineteenth-century gift-seeker and housewife. The young women learned to sew and knit at an early age, and the aged busied themselves with such handicraft after they were unable to perform other occupations. For no one did the day's work end with the evening meal; the brethren had their outside chores, and the sisters

and young people went to the dwelling workrooms to spin yarn, knit socks and gloves, braid rugs, or make pincushions. A ready sale was assured of this varied fancywork since visitors were frequent at the Shaker settlements. One of the chief diversions of sojourners at the fashionable Lebanon Springs near New Lebanon was to call at the Shaker shops and purchase mementos of their visit, and the income derived from such patrons appreciably swelled the total resources of the society.

The writer does not know just when the two stores operated by the New Lebanon families were first established. The trustees' office and store were built in 1827, but fancy goods may have been sold before this date. Needlework, basketry, table mat, fan, and duster making, and other similar occupations were carried on extensively in the second and third quarters of the last century. Certain occupations, such as whiplash braiding, "picking over" herbs, mop and mat making, and basket weaving, engaged the time of the sisterhood at an even earlier period.

The sale work done by the children and "caretakers" was listed separately. In 1860, they made 229 face braids, 1,254 cushion linings, 109 cloth seed bags, 27,226 paper seed bags, and performed forty-eight days' work on yarn, hair, etc. In 1861, they lined 449 round cushions and 1,600 square cushions, made 110 tomato cushions, 48 wings and feather dusters, braided 167 yards of palm-leaf braid, picked dandelion seed for three weeks, "besides going to school." The children also hemmed and shagged, picked out walnut and butternut meats, footed stockings, made brushes and velvet cushions, cut labels, picked flowers, besides helping their elders in many other occupations.

# Dyeing

The bleaching and dyeing of cotton, linen, and wool were complementary occupations which engaged the whole time of several Shaker sisters. In the very early days of the settlement, dyeing was done not only for the family itself, but for outsiders and other societies. Such items occur as that for June 9, 1790, when yarn was dyed for Israel Talcott to the amount of two shillings. Indigo was then the common dyestuff. Later, such dyes were used as logwood, copperas, camwood, madder, red tartar, and fustic; the first three were bought by the barrel and redistributed to other families and societies. Sumac leaves were also employed. The most common native vegetable dyes were hemlock and butternut. These the Shakers prepared themselves.

From 1837 to 1855, a journal was kept at the Church family in New Lebanon by Elizabeth Lovegrove and another sister whose name was not     131 recorded. In 1840, Sister Elizabeth was assigned, "as clay in the hands of the potter," to work at the washhouse, where she became so interested in the various operations involved in preparing raw flax and wool for weaving that she kept a memorandum of the activities in which she and her companions engaged. The journal reveals a very complex industry that was far from being standardized and that was replete with experimental procedures.[10]

The work began each year in the month of April, when the flax and tow yarn were boiled and colored, the flax bucked and hatcheled, and the winter's wool sorted, picked over, and washed. Dyeing was one of the principal occupations. The diary continues:

May 1840

> This month we commenced bleaching and whitning our cotton cloth, had about one thousand yards for the family and one hundred for the Office.

25. They began to shear the sheep.
> This week we coloured about 60 yards of cotton cloth in hot butternut dye for frocks and trowsers, and 60 yards for linings.

28. Commence combing white worsted.

June

> The first week in this month we put the butternut bark to soak.

6. finish combing the white worsted, had 36 lbs.

> We put the wool into the butternut dye about the middle of the 2nd week in June and finished colouring butternut the 14th of July.

> We finished combing the 29th of July.

> The following disposition of the wool for 1840 was made:

Memorandum of worsted.
11   lbs. for stockings, grey and some white
36   for linings and fine crape white
9    for common crape Butternut
6    for Cloak head linings do fine
15½ fine worsted trowsers butternut
9    for linings for blue jackets, to fill on cotton
20   for Serge trowsers
12   for drugget trowsers
7½ for fine drugget gowns
7    for quality & sewing thread
6    for backings

*Above, opposite page, a corner of the washhouse, showing a unique stove for heating irons.*

*Opposite, a typical ironing room in the washhouse. Flat-irons rest on ridges along the sloping sides of the stove.*

Fifty-two pounds of wool were coloured blue, and ten pounds coloured black for boys frocks.
By reason of a scarsity of water we had to send all the rest of our wool to be carded among the world this season.

We finish spinning the 29th of August.

We finish the wash house work colouring scouring boiling out yarn etc October 9th and the writer took a tour [turn?] in the kitchen.

In the succeeding years, much the same routine was followed. A hot or cold butternut solution was the common dyeing medium. Carpeting and shagging were colored in a red and green dye. "Little girls gowns" were often colored in an old red dye. In 1844, 66 runs of cotton yarn were colored "hemlock" for little girls' gowns. Worsted linings were dyed drab. Horse blankets, carpets, and shagging were sometimes colored blue with "pussly" (purslane). Yarn was dyed blue for pocket handkerchiefs, footings, linings, window curtains, gowns, trousers, jackets, and thread.

A few scattered items are selected from Sister Elizabeth's journal to give a more intimate insight into the operations of the washhouse:

| | | | |
|---|---|---|---|
| **1844.** | July | 29. | The Wool is all greased. |
| | Aug. | 5. | Boil the cloth for sheeting; put out 5 pieces of shirting to whiten. |
| | Aug. | 12. | Scour the first piece of butternut worsted. |
| | Sept. | 20. | We colour 3 runs of yellow yarn for the office. |
| | Oct. | 2. | Fix and boil in lye a quantity of yarn. |
| **1845.** | May | 12. | On account of a failure in the quality of the bleaching salts, all the coarse cloth except 64 yards has been whitened in the sun & wind. . . . |
| | May | 25. | We finish 75 runs of yarn in the blue dye that is partly coloured in hemlock dye. |
| | | 27, 28. | Two hired men shear the sheep. 210 in number. |
| | June | 5. | Wash the wool to color butternut, and put the linen cloth in whey. |
| | July | 8. | Commenced coloring copperas by the directions given at Harvard, but it looks very bad. |
| **1846.** | April | 17. | We finish carding tow. We have had 17 carders beside the girls. . . . Our mop spiners this week have spun 100 mops. |
| | April | 20. | Commence shrinking cloth and continue boiling yarn. |
| | | 29. | We have had a new reel made to rinse bleached cloth. |
| | May | 12. | Dye seems quite too strong of Potash. |

|       |       | 13. Only dip twice and conclude not to try to work the dye till it is in better order. |
|-------|-------|--------|
|       | June  | 26. Several days previous to this we have put some lye in one tub of butternut dye but we cannot yet determine whether it does much good or not. |
|       | Aug.  | 21. Elizabeth Munson from the 2nd family came to assist us in coloring with camwood. |
| 1847. | April | 19. go to washing and put down our first yarn to buck in the red rinsing tub. |
|       | June  | 1. We wash the wool to color blue. After scalding in the Liquor 20 min. we wash in warm suds, then rinse in cold waters. |
|       | June  | 17. We receive a pair of new Combing tongs made by Arby. |
|       | Aug.  | 23. Prepare for coloring, logwood green. |
|       | Sept. | 1. Coloured red for horse blankets with Nicwood and red wood, putting the yarn and chips in the kettle together, but long before we got cleaned up we promised ourselves never to do so again. |
| 1848. | June  | 1. Iron the rest of the cloth and color some copperas yarn to finish a piece of kitchen gowns. |
|       |       | 8. Wash the Wool to color blue & drab. Commense at 5 oc. A.M. & Finish 7 oc. P.M. |
|       |       | 17. Finish combing white & grey worsted. |
|       |       | 19. Commence coloring conjurations. |
|       | Aug.  | 31. Finish coloring and clean the dye house. |
|       | Sept. | 5. Make some composition of sumac & copperas for darkening colors. |
| 1849. | June  | 13. We commenced greasing worsted with lamp oil, very unpleasant, comb a little to try the grease. |
|       | Aug.  | 10. Color red and green, and filling for Ironing Blankets compound blue. |
|       |       | 28. We madder our red yarn. |

The diary records the sale at this time (1840 and after) of such products as checked pocket handkerchiefs, diaper, serge, drugget, horse blankets, strainers, crepe, and mop fabric.

Elsewhere it is remarked that the Shakers did not believe in bright colors or ornamentation of any kind. Their cloth was dyed in subdued colors. Rugs and carpetings were sometimes more positive in tone, but the feeling of restraint is evident even in these weavings. It is interesting to note that if there was a forced repression of that natural delight in exuberant color which is characteristic of the normal human emotions, this religious censorship did not always function. During the period when the Shakers inclined to spiritualism and its attendant visions and trances (1837-1847), "gifts" or revelations from the spirit world were common. All such inhibitions on the longing for bright ornaments and colorful garments are removed in the vision of the "heavenly dresses" promised to the faithful in the City of Peace (Hancock) by the spirits of Mother Ann and Father William. The brethren were to receive "beautiful fine Trowsers, as white as snow; these resemble a garment of purity, with many shining stars thereon. The buttons of a sky blue color, and the appearance of them like glass. A Jacket of a sky blue color also, with gold Buttons thereon, and on these buttons are wrought in fine needlework, many elegant and pretty flowers, of different colors. A fine white silk handkerchief, bordered with gold, to tie about the neck . . . A coat of heavenly brightness, of twelve different colors, which can not be compared to any natural beauties . . . A pair of heavenly shoes, perfectly white . . . A fine furr hat, of a silver color." The sisters' garments were to consist of a gown "of heavenly brightness" and of "12 very beautiful colors." "A pair of silver color shoes . . . A fine muslin cap, with beautiful triming, also a pretty collar and handkerchief for the neck . . . A Bonnet of silver color, trimed with white ribbon, also a pair of blue silk gloves."[11]

*The sisters' dyeing room. Although, as a rule, the Believers used very subdued colors, the dyeing process itself was replete with experimentation as Elizabeth Lovegrove's journal reveals.*

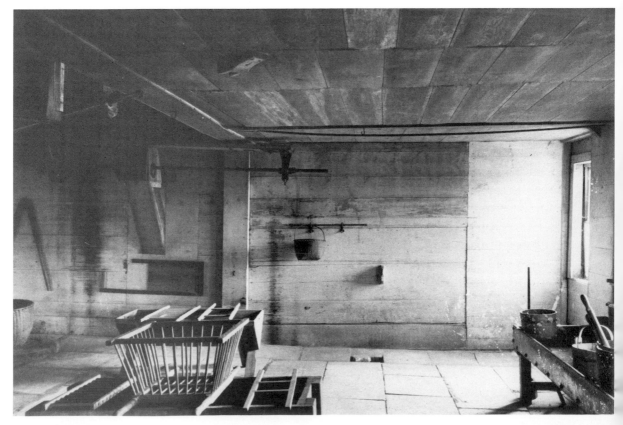

# Shaker Culture
# and Craftsmanship

Thus far the Shakers have been viewed primarily as scientific agriculturists and industrialists. It has been pointed out that the sect was notable for its extreme industry and for the variety and high quality of its soil and shop productions. A portrait of Shakerism, considered from an occupational point of view, is not well-balanced or complete, however, if emphasis is not placed upon the spirit of fine workmanship which pervaded this industrial life and elevated it into a kind of guild enterprise where nothing but faultless craftsmanship was tolerated. As a prelude to an exposition of the chair industry, it will be well to review those factors in the social and religious culture of the society which actuated such ideals of craftsmanship and gave distinction to their utilitarian arts. Chairs were made for the market, and a study of this industry is pertinent to the present theme; what is said here is necessary also to an understanding of all Shaker furniture, architecture, and decoration, and will likewise serve to give a more just appreciation of the entire occupational panorama.

A people who had withdrawn themselves from the world, as did the Believers in Christ's Second Appearing, relinquishing all personal claim to what they had accumulated and owned, renouncing all vanities and worldly ambitions, often breaking family and home ties before entering into this spiritual and communal fellowship, must before long have developed a more or less definite culture.

The early Shakers were a pioneering people. Their immediate task was to sustain their institution in the interests of survival. They were conscious of a particular destiny, an aloofness from the world, a kinship with a divine plan, a fellowship of interests, but this consciousness was not at first refined into more than a general plan of how to live. The situation was not unlike that of the early New England religious towns; in order to advance their religious welfare they had to spend long days, long months, and long years in clearing and cultivating land, building dwellings and shops and barns, laying out roads, raising cattle and horses, weaving cloth, grinding corn, and inaugurating the complex agricultural and industrial life that was necessary to insure economic independence and expansion. Under such conditions, there was no leisure for the intellectual or artistic expressions of 137 a secure civilization. Their first expositions of doctrine were not elaborated until early in the last century, nor were their laws and orders coded until nearly fifty years after the first Believers settled in America.

The key to the early temporal activities of the Shakers is given in Elder Giles Avery's dictum: "The most important uses must necessarily engage [the] attention, time and strength." The comparison is drawn with "the pioneer settlers in a new country." Protection against "hunger, cold and nakedness" came first, and time spent in such labors as "the culture of flowers" or the construction of "the merely ornamental in dress or architecture" was time misused.[1]

Elder Frederick Evans, one of the chief spokesmen of the order from 1830 until nearly the end of the century, voices the same principle as it affected styles of architecture. The Shaker buildings are well-proportioned but plain structures, bare of design. "The beautiful," he once told the historian Nordhoff, "is absurd and abnormal. It has no business with us. The divine man has no right to waste money upon what you would call beauty, in his house or daily life, while there are people living in misery." In building, the chief objects were light, an "equal distribution of heat," a "general care for protection and comfort," and other factors which pertain to "health and long life." Carpets and picture frames gathered dust, and

pictures were useless. Although flowers were beautiful, their true beauty lay in their usefulness.[2]

This philosophy of usefulness runs through all Shaker literature. Lamson reported: "This people are strict utilitarians. In all they do, the first inquiry is, 'will it be useful?' Everything therefore about their buildings, fences, etc., is plain."[3]

The same thought is found in Wells's remarks on education: "This life is short at the longest, and ought not to be spent in acquiring any kind of knowledge which can not be put to a good use." It was not the aim of the Shaker school system to make scholars, but to give the young people "as much letter learning as may be put to propper use, and fit them for business in the Society of Believers ... to give propper exercise to their mental faculties, & turn those faculties into the propper channel of usefulness for their own benefit & the benefit of their Brethren & Sisters."[4]

The correlate of this insistence upon literal usefulness was the rejection of what the Shakers liked to call "superfluities." Superfluities were as sinful as monopolies. Ornament was not only useless and "external," but impeded the spirit. Instrumental music was not employed in the early days of the sect. Like the Quakers, they repudiated also the idea of "steepled houses, with their costly cushioned pews, stained windows, and elaborate ornaments to attract the worldly minded, when the means for so doing were wrung out of the hard earnings of the poor laboring man and woman."[5] Shaker meetinghouses were plain but distinctive structures.

In the *Millennial Laws*, first formulated in 1821, a section was specifically devoted to such superfluities. These orders show in what detail the daily life of the Believers was regulated:

1. Fancy articles of any kind, or articles which are superfluously finished, trimmed or ornamented, are not suitable for Believers, and may not be used or purchased; among which are the following; also some other articles which are deemed improper, to be in the Church, and may not be brought in, except by special liberty of the Ministry.

2. Silver pencils, silver tooth picks, gold pencils, or pens, silver spoons, silver thimbles, (but thimbles may be lined with silver,) gold or silver watches, brass knobs or handles of any size or kind. Three bladed knives, knife handles with writing or picturing on them, bone or horn handled knives, except for pocket knives, bone or horn spools, superfluous whips, marbled tin ware, superfluous paper boxes of any kind, gay silk handkerchiefs for sisters use:—Checked handkerchiefs made by the world, may not be bought for sisters use, except head handkerchiefs. Lace for cap borders, superfluous suspenders of any kind. Writing desks may not be used by common members, unless they have much public

139

*Visitors' benches in the New Lebanon meetinghouse, built in 1822-24.*

*An early meetinghouse built by the Niskeyuna Shakers in 1791. Now destroyed.*

writing to do. But writing desks may be used as far as it is thought proper by the Lead.

3.  The following articles are also deemed improper, viz. Superfluously finished, or flowery painted clocks, Bureaus, and Looking glasses, also superfluously painted or fancy shaped sleighs, or carriages, superfluously trimmed Harness, and many other articles too numerous to mention.

4.  The forementioned things are at present, utterly forbidden, but if the Ministry see fit to bring in any among the forementioned articles, which are not superfluously wrought, the order prohibiting the use of such article or articles is thereby repealed.

5.  Believers may not in any case or circumstance, manufacture for sale, any article or articles, which are superfluously wrought, and which would have a tendency to feed the pride and vanity of man, or such as would not be admissible to use among themselves, on account of their superfluity.

The religious strain so pronounced in all the Shakers thought and did is not absent in such pragmatism. Their goods were dedicated to God; the whole estate of the society was a consecrated possession, and the members had solemnly avowed in their covenant that they were "debtors to God in relation to Each other, and all men, to improve our time and Tallents in this Life, in that manner in which we might be most useful." In the Shaker mind the right use of time implied not only the application of energy to useful enterprises, but such related factors as economy of time, materials, and methods; constant industriousness; the maintenance of strict order, neatness, and cleanliness; and devotion to the doctrine of that simplicity in speech, dress, and craftsmanship which was not only consistent with, but which also advanced the cause of sanctified living.[6]

Few have ever visited a Shaker community without being impressed by such industry, such order and cleanliness. In his defense of the Shakers before the General Assembly of the State of Kentucky in January 1831, Robert Wickliffe proclaimed that "in architecture and neatness, [they] are exceeded by no people upon the earth." Their villages and towns, he added, "bear testimony everywhere of their skill in the mechanic and manufacturing arts. The whole society live in unexampled neatness, if not elegance—not a pauper among them—all alike independent. . . . Who has visited one of the Shaker villages, that has not experienced emotions of delight at the peaceful, harmonious, but industrious movements of the villagers?"[7] Hayward, surveying the towns and villages of New England in 1839, reported that the Shakers "have become a proverb for industry, justice and benevolence." In another place, he notes: "They manufacture many articles for sale, which are remarkable for neatness and durability."[8] One of the keenest and most sympathetic observers of Shaker life and culture, Hepworth Dixon, gives us the following picture of New Lebanon:

> No Dutch town has a neater aspect, no Moravian hamlet a softer hush. The streets are quiet; for here you have no grog-shop, no

beer-house, no lock-up, no pound; of the dozen edifices rising about you—workrooms, barns, tabernacle, stables, kitchens, schools, and dormitories—not one is either foul or noisy; and every building, whatever may be its use, has something of the air of a chapel. The paint is all fresh; the planks are all bright; the windows are all clean. A white sheen is on everything; a happy quiet reigns around. Even in what is seen of the eye and heard of the ear, Mount Lebanon strikes you as a place where it is always Sunday. The walls appear as though they had been built only yesterday; a perfume, as from many unguents, floats down the lane; and the curtains and window blinds are of spotless white. Everything in the hamlet looks and smells like household things which have been long laid up in lavender and roseleaves.[9]

On entering a Shaker dwelling (at Shirley), William Dean Howells wrote, "The first impression of all is cleanliness, with a suggestion of bareness which is not inconsistent, however, with comfort, and which comes chiefly from the aspect of the unpapered walls, the scrubbed floors hidden only by rugs and strips of carpeting, and the plain flat finish of the wood-work."[10]

Shakerism, as well as other communistic systems, has often been indicted on the score that its severely regulated organization was not favorable to individual development and that its culture was so limited as to place restrictions upon individual growth and variation. While tending to "the development of some high qualities of character, such as obedience, resignation, loyalty, earnestness," and of "the talents which are exercised in mechanical invention," the system tended, in the opinion of Hinds, "to produce two distinctly marked classes; and that while one of them—the governing class, which holds the temporal and spiritual keys—has more than an average amount of shrewd good sense and thinking capacity, the other—the governed class, composed of the rank-and-file—does not compare favorably with the first in culture and general intelligence." Hinds noted, however, that important changes were taking place in the "internal character of Shakerism" and that "its leaders are more liberal and more tolerant than they were a quarter of a century ago. . . . It is also obvious that there is a growing party of progressives among the Shakers—men and women who, while firmly adhering to all that is deemed essential in the system, think it desirable that all non-essentials that stand in the way of genuine progress and culture should be modified or abolished."[11] The matter is put thus by one of the Shakers themselves:

> The arts and sciences, in a future day, will flourish under the patronage of those living the highest life, the Shaker life. Heretofore the work of drawing the lines between flesh and spirit has been so great that there has been no time to give to any other thought but that of watching all the avenues to keep out the evils that might

143

enter and destroy the good that has been gained.
In the new heavens and new earth, all that is pure and elevating
in art and the sciences will be understood and appreciated.[12]

Although undoubtedly there is truth in Hinds's criticism and in the fact that there was opportunity for such an extension of liberalism, it should be recalled that the system always allowed for the conservation and development of native talent. The skills possessed by the newcomer in the society almost universally found a useful place in the varied economic life of the village. Minors were apprenticed to their elders in the home, shop, or field. As no member was bound to remain in the order against his or her will, compulsion generally played a minor role in the cultural-economic scheme. It is true that education was narrowly utilitarian, and that literary opportunity was confined chiefly to books on religion—a situation reflecting the early overemphasis on doctrine. A keen theoretical as well as practical interest in the mechanical and agricultural sciences was apparent, however, at an early date, and books and periodicals of this nature were consulted by the brethren working in these fields. The Shaker system was founded primarily upon agriculture and horticulture; it was a progressive agrarianism, and it was Shaker policy and pride to keep abreast of the times. No obstruction to the betterment of his skill was placed in the way of the agriculturist, the herbalist, or the shop mechanic. The cause of Shakerism was the great drive, and in this cause there was a place for individualism as well as collectivism. Throughout the history of the sect an interesting balance seems to have been maintained between the policy of rigid insistence upon obedience to leadership and the more enlightened principles of encouraging self-development and self-expression.

It is not surprising that certain elements in this culture of the Shakers—their high valuation of utility in all forms, their regard for order and cleanliness, their insistence on regulation, their prejudice against all ornament and superfluity, their glorification of labor and fine, durable workmanship of any kind, the union of an earnest, consecrated spirit with a considerable amount of shrewd but honest business acumen, and an alertness in the application of the sciences—should be reflected in the various phases of their occupational life and in the quality of their manufactures. Whether their industrial products were made for their own consumption (most of their furniture, for instance), or for the world's markets, certain qualities are present. The product invariably functioned well. A high standard—one is almost tempted to say a religious, and certainly an ethical standard of merit—was set and nothing less praiseworthy was allowed to go forth as representative of Shaker workmanship.[13]

# Craftsmanship
# in Wood

No study of the Shaker economy would be complete without reference to the subject of joinery, and particularly to the widely known chair industry. The finest craftsmanship of the Shakers was expended on their furniture. In the products of the joiners' shops, certain basic values in the culture found concrete expression; usefulness above all else, no excessiveness in either line or mass, restraint always, strength, proportion—the most assiduous care that the essential function of the piece should be insured. Inspired and guided by a passionate devotion to the life of the spirit, the society's chair and furniture makers wrought into their work a sincerity freed from all dross and marked by a great humility. In these labors, the artistic coincided with the religious conscience, and in the end we find utilitarianism raised into the realm of undeniable charm and a quiet and pure beauty.

In one of Isaac Youngs's records of the New Lebanon Church, "joinering" and carpentry are considered under one category. William Safford, Park Avery, Daniel Hilt, Richard Treat, and others, in building the first houses and shops of the parent order, probably were also responsible for their furnishings. As we have noted, Shaker mechanics were often artisans as well, workmen with versatile skills. For this reason, and because Shaker doctrine discouraged individualism—although leaving the workmen relatively free to practice their trade—we know little, beyond their names, of the craftsmen themselves. What counts was their joint production, its scope and its distinctive quality. Except for chairs, and a few accessories such as clocks and lap desks, furniture was made for domestic use.

In the *Illustrated catalogue of Shaker chairs, foot benches, floor mats, etc.* (Albany, 1874), it is claimed that the Believers were "pioneers" in the chair industry and "perhaps the very first to engage in the business after the establishment of the independence of the country."[1] How the business originated is not known; perhaps, among the first converts there was a craftsman, one or more, with experience in this particular field.

The chairs were widely distributed by 1850, and many persons who are unaware that the Shakers made all their household furniture are familiar at least with the quaint slat-backs with their seats of varied colored webs. The prototype of the Shaker chair was the common slat-back which dated

146

from early colonial times. The strength and simplicity of this design appealed to the first cabinet-makers of the sect, under whose touch, however, the frequent crudities of those earlier chairs were refined and their utility greatly

increased. A lightness was given to the frames without sacrificing strength, and their chrome yellow, red, or natural finish gave them a charm which was heightened by the addition of colorful woven seats. Because of this lightness and the simple turnings of all members, even the first chairs made are readily recognizable as a Shaker product. The arms of these early chairs were crudely and poorly patterned, a defect which must have soon been

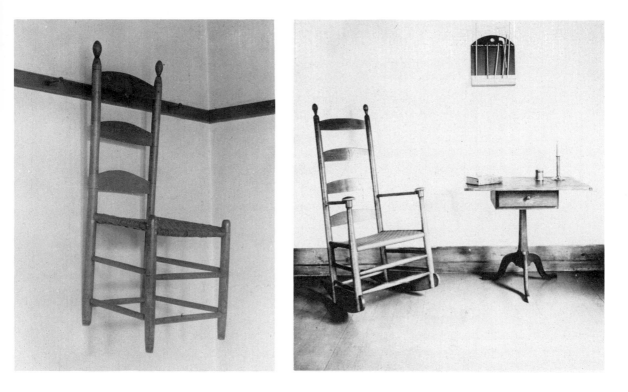

remedied, as few specimens of this type are known. A turned collar on the base of the posts also characterized this experimental stage. The armrests of the typical Shaker armchair are delicate but strong strips terminating in a modest scroll or fitting around and doweled into front posts which are crested by the so-called mushroom turning. Ordinarily, the armchair was a rocker having four slats. The frame was usually constructed entirely of native maple, grained wood sometimes being employed; later, other woods, such as birch, cherry, and butternut, were used, with cherry sometimes employed in the slats. The back posts always terminated in various shaped finials, sometimes of a simple, always of a graceful pattern.

At an undetermined date, probably in the first quarter of the last century if not earlier, a large percentage of the common Shaker three-slat sidechairs became equipped by some ingenious mechanic with the famous "ball-and-socket" device at the base of the rear posts, an example of the many instances in which the active Shaker mind improved on the status quo. This device consisted of a wooden ball fastened into the back posts by a leather thong knotted at one end and fixed into the post by a wooden dowel. By this arrangement one could tilt back or rock in one of these sidechairs without danger of slipping; the wear on carpets or the marring of floors was likewise prevented. In what community these "tilting" chairs originated is not known. They were made in the New Hampshire and Massachusetts settlements as well as at New Lebanon and Watervliet. Not only were these slat-backs an aesthetic improvement over the early country types, but they were made to fit every need of shop and home. The Shakers were among the first in this country to equip chairs with rockers. These were designed principally for the comfort of invalids and the aged. The rockers were short and gracefully cut in profile in the same manner as the arms, or as the legs of candle stands. Heavier rockers of the "sled" type were sometimes used for the brethren's chairs.

Chairs made for the market conformed more closely to a standard than those constructed for the varied uses of the shop and home. These latter were often characterized by interesting functional deviations from the norm. Several types prevailed, however, even in the comparatively small quantity consigned to early markets, and in all these forms the same note of delicacy combined with strength was maintained; whether intended for relaxation or some occupational need, each one may be identified as a product of Shaker craftsmanship. Not content with one pattern, the Shakers produced chairs for special uses; wagon chairs, one- and two-slat dining chairs, revolving chairs or stools (the forerunner of our swivel chairs?), invalid's chairs, high shop or counter chairs, slipper chairs, sewing rockers, and a variety of "foot benches."

It has been noted that the Shakers claimed to be pioneers in the chair business. A statement in *The Manifesto* places the first date of manufacture at New Lebanon in the year 1776, but the fact is not documented.[2] The earliest reliable evidence appears in the daybook of Joseph Bennett, Jr. On October 21, 1789, it is recorded in this book that three chairs were sold to one Elizah Slosson for eleven shillings.[3]

About 1852, the business was concentrated and reorganized at the Second

*A page from the centennial catalogue of Shaker chairs,*
*written in 1876.*

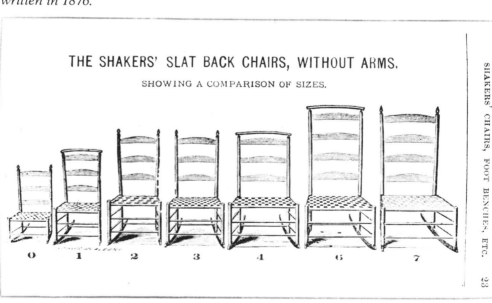

THE SHAKERS' SLAT BACK CHAIRS, WITHOUT ARMS.

SHOWING A COMPARISON OF SIZES.

0    1    2    3    4    6    7

SHAKERS' CHAIRS, FOOT BENCHES, ETC.

23

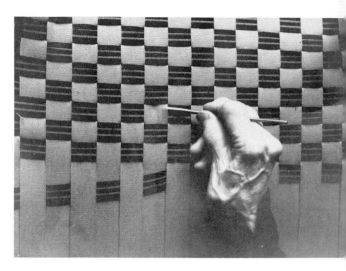

*Eldress Sarah Collins, a member of the South family, New Lebanon, was engaged in the Shaker chair industry for over sixty years. Highly skilled in her work, she is shown here weaving the tape seat of a chair.*

and South families in New Lebanon. A broadside dated 185- and signed by Jesse Lewis and D. C. Brainard of the Second family lists the kinds of chairs and prices prevailing in the mid-century:

| | |
|---|---|
| Large size armed rocking chair Frame | $3.25 |
| Medium size | 3.00 |
| Small      do | 2.75 |
| Dining     do | 2.00 |
| Easy       do | 2.00 |
| Common or kitchen | 1.00 |
| Childrens' | .75 |
| Splint Seat for Arm Chair | .50 |
|     do      do      do      Common | .38 |
|     do      do      do      Childrens' | .35 |
| Tape seat for the above | |
|     named varieties of Chairs | 1.00 |
| For Rockers | .50 |
|     do Button joint TILTS | .25 |
| Cushions Extra, at fair prices | |

Soon chairs appeared on the market in standard numbered sizes, with an applied gold transfer trademark to protect the society from imitations. Catalogues were first issued in 1874 and the chairs first exhibited publicly at the Philadelphia Centennial two years later. The catalogue printed on this occasion is interesting in that it included a number of Shaker hymns, a token of the belief that Shaker industry had its foundation in a religious faith.

# Shaker Inventions
and Improvements

At first, it seems, the Shakers were cautious about introducing inventions, or any "conveniences" into the society. In a memorandum dated New Lebanon, November 23, 1802, the ministry circularized the following covenant:

> Where as all the Deacons and Elders of the Church in this Place
> Together with the Ministry feel Sensible that the Church has gone
> too far in Building and in Labouring for outward Conveanence and
> Invention and that the Sensation is greatly Darkened thereby—we
> therefore Covenant together to be of one heart and one mind not
> to Promote tollerate or Incourage any more of these things until
> there is a gift in union. . . .[1]

If any brother or sister felt it to be right to bring in an invention not then in the Church, he or she had to signify the request in writing, whereupon the matter would be considered first by Elder David Meacham, then by the elders and eldresses, and finally by the ministry. After six months, a decision would be made.

As the economy expanded, however, the society became less scrupulous and eventually welcomed improvements, either its own or those originating in the world. One of Joseph Meacham's "way-marks," they may have recalled, was on this very subject:

> We have a Right to use or improve the Inventions of man so far
> as is useful and necessary but not to Vain Glory or anything
> superfluous . . . order and Conveniency and deacency in things
> Temporal is also becoming the Church so far as may be for the
> Honour of the Testimony and their own and others good. . . .[2]

The following list, which amplifies the one in *The Community Industries of the Shakers,* is drawn from various sources, printed and in manuscript, including reports of the Commissioner of Patents. In principle, the Shakers did not believe in patents, feeling that patent money savored of monopoly and violated the Golden Rule. It would be wrong, they held, "for the people of God to take advantage of their fellow creatures by securing patent rights and speculating thereon, as the children of the world generally do."[3] They found by experience, however, that sometimes that was the only way to protect their economic rights. Elder Robert Wagan was obliged to seek trademark protection for his chairs. Labels were also attached to Shaker brooms to guarantee their origin.[4] Even in the early years of the movement we find the initials D. M. (for David Meacham) printed as a trademark on herb and seed labels. The Shakers were always scrupulous about paying for concessions from the original patentees of various mechanical devices.

**1793** "Machine" for setting teeth in hand cards. Invented by Benjamin Bruce of New Lebanon. Bruce was also credited with later inventing a machine "for cutting and bending machine card teeth and punching the leather for setting."

**180-** Machine for pricking leather in wool cards. Invention of Nicholas Bennett, New Lebanon.

**1808** "The first electrical machine made in the Church was put in operation. It is designed to be used for medical purposes."[5]

**1813** Circular saw and circular "buzz." ("Of thin soft sheet iron, six inches in diameter . . . for cutting the hardest steel with the ease of tallow.") Said to have been invented by Freegift Wells of Watervliet and in operation at least by 1817. "The Shakers consider the discovery too useful to be monopolized by a patent," Wells wrote, "and consented to my giving it publicity as public property." In *Niles' Weekly Register* is the following comment: "The Shakers, at their village in Watervliet, near Albany, have this invention in very excellent use and great perfection. In a saw mill there, they have a set of machinery on this principle, erected at a very trifling expense, which, for cutting stuff for window sash, grooving floor plank, gaging clap-boards, etc. with one man and a boy to attend it, will perform the labor of thirty men."[6] In the "Records of the [New Lebanon] Church 1780–1855," the writer, I. N. Youngs, states, "Our society here have used matching works, in form of a circular saw, ever since about the year 1813." Tradition ascribes the invention of the circular saw, as well as cut nails and a method of making false teeth, to Sister Tabitha (Sarah) Babbitt of the Harvard Community (d. 1858, aged 74).

**1815** A threshing machine. New Lebanon?

**1816** "Hair caps." (For brethren who were bald.) New Lebanon.

**1819** Steel candlesticks. Made by Aaron Bill, New Lebanon.

Brass and silver pens. First cut by Isaac N. Youngs. "The machinery for rolling the brass and silver plate and the shears for cutting the pens were home inventions."

**1822** Fire engine and hose cart. Designed and built by Thomas Corbett of Canterbury. In a letter from one Nathan Smith, Concord, New Hampshire, August 15, 1822, to Professor Parker Cleaveland, Bowdoin College, Brunswick, Maine, Smith wrote: "I have visited the Society at Canterbury and seen an Engine for extinguishing fire which I thought very good and Was informed that it would throw water 20 feet further than the best Engine at Concord which cost over 400 dollars. This Engine was made by the Shakers & they have informed me that they could make another on the same plan & size for 300 dollars. If the College should conclude to get an Engine I think it would be best to engage the Shakers to make it . . . you may depend on its being faithfully made in every part of it."[7]

**1828** Machinery for matching boards invented by Henry Bennett and Amos Bishop. These brethren "used vertical rollers to keep the lumber straight and ropes and windlass to propel the same over circular saws, first making a groove, then a tongue."[8] The Bennett-Bishop machine was probably an improvement over the "matching works" of 1813.

**1829** An "atmospheric steam-engine." Patent granted on July 27, 1829, to J. Mead and A. B. Kitchell, Lebanon, Ohio. (Union Village brethren?)

**1831** The hydraulic water system at Pleasant Hill, Kentucky, built in 1831, was, according to a Dr. Ham, "purportedly the first water works in Kentucky." The Shakers were pioneers in the field of "water mechanics." Elder Matthew B. Carter of Ohio invented a governor for an over-shot waterwheel. A turbine waterwheel was invented by George Wickersham of New Lebanon, and a screw propeller by Thomas Wells of Watervliet. (Dates not given.) It is said that the first waterwheel ever made with controlling gates to hold it at a given horsepower was invented by the Shakers.

**1831** On June 2, 1831, Stephen Munson and Jonathan Wood of New Lebanon paid $150 to William Cobb of Norwich and Jacob Coller of Northfield for "the full and exclusive right and liberty" to use one of the revolving timber planes patented by David N. Smith in 1826. (A typical example of paying for patent rights.)

**1834** An instrument for cutting spectacle glass. Improvement of Isaac N. Youngs.

**1834** (or before). At Union Village, Ohio, machinery for sawing out staves for churns "with a wide hoopsaw then for jointing with a buzz saw, then for matching—after this they are set up and turned outside and in by machinery which is driven by horse power on an inclined wheel the motion of which is governed by a regulator."[9]

**1836** "Truss for hernia." Patent awarded February 17, 1836, to William Adair, Pleasant Hill, Kentucky.

**1836** An improved sun dial. By I. N. Youngs.
About this same time, the ingenious Youngs perfected what he called a tone-o-meter for setting the pitch for Shaker songs.

**1837** Bee hive. On November 10, 1837, D. A. Buckingham of Watervliet paid Russell Loomis, Jr., agent of patentee (John M. Weeks) five dollars for the right of "making and constructing said improved Hive for his own use and not otherwise." (Another example of paying for patent rights.)

**1837** A silk reeling machine was invented by Abner Bedell and Thomas Taylor at Union Village.
Brother Abner also made a loom for weaving palm-leaf bonnets.

**1843** A cultivator was made by Charles Sizer, New Lebanon.

**1844** An improved planing machine by Luther Copley, Hiram Rude, and others at New Lebanon. (The Shakers encountered some legal difficulty in using planing machines patented by others. An item under date of 1851 in the official records of the New Lebanon Church speaks about a "contention in law about Woodworth's patent" of a planing machine. One Gibson, presumably the holder of the patent rights, was trying to force the Shakers to pay him a percentage of everything made by the machine.)

**1846** "Temple for looms, self-acting." Patent granted February 10, 1846, to Arnold Palmer, New Lebanon.

**1849** An improved hydro-extractor, patented November 13, 1849, by M. C. Bryant, was manufactured and sold at Canterbury, together with recipes for making soap, etc.

At a later period, that society made for sale an improved mangle operated by a screw.

**1851**    Machine for sorting broom corn. On January 1, 1851, Lorenzo D. Grosvenor, Shaker Village (Harvard), Massachusetts, was granted a patent for his invention of a machine for "assorting" broom corn. The same year, on September 23, he was given another patent for "machines for stripping seed from broom corn."

**1852**    Metallic ball-and-socket device for chairs. Patent (number 8771) to George O. Donnell, New Lebanon. "I have invented [he wrote] a new and improved mode of preventing the wear and tear of carpets and the marring of floors, caused by the corners of the back posts of chairs as they take their natural motion of rocking backward and forward. . . ."

**1853**    In 1853, Gail Borden heard of the Shakers' low-vacuum vessel, a globular-shaped copper vacuum pan for drying herbs. On a visit to New Lebanon, using Shaker equipment, he perfected his formula for condensed milk, patented in 1856.

**1853?**    Machine for making oak staves or shooks for molasses hogsheads. Invented by Hewitt Chandler at Sabbathday Lake (New Gloucester), Maine, and manufactured in the Great Mill (built in 1853). The shooks were exported to the West Indies. Chandler also invented and sold an improved mowing machine. According to the Metric Bureau in Boston the first metric dry measures to be manufactured in the United States—in ten sizes from a decilitre to a hectolitre—were made in this Great Mill. Sieve rims were also made according to the metric system.

**1856**    An improved bit and brace. Patent granted August 26 to Daniel N. Baird (Daniel W. Baird?) of North Union, Ohio. Baird was also credited with perfecting Babbitt metal and inventing an automatic spring and a rotary harrow.
Other North Union inventions were a stove-cover lifter by Sewell G. Thayer, and the common clothes pin.
The Shaker wood stoves were an improvement over the box stoves of colonial times. In one type, the so-called "double-decker," radiation was increased by an upper chamber mounted on the lower one.
A "summer covering" for a flat iron stove was invented by George W. Wickersham of New Lebanon.

**1856** Julius Riedel of Pleasant Hill, Kentucky, was granted a patent (September 9) for "cartridges."

**1858** One of the best-known Shaker inventions was the washing machine, or "wash mill," a patent for which was granted to David Parker of Canterbury. This "mill" had been "perfected" at an earlier date by Nicholas Bennett of New Lebanon, who subsequently assigned it to Parker. There is also a record in the Patent Office of a patent issued on January 16, 1829, to one Amos Larcom, Watervliet, New York, for a washing machine, but whether Larcom was a Shaker is not determined. The Improved Shaker Washing Machine was awarded a gold medal at the Philadelphia Centennial Exposition on December 19, 1876. It was recommended "in unqualified terms" by the proprietors of the Revere House, the Tremont, and the American House in Boston; the St. Nicholas in New York; the Girard House in Philadelphia; Willard's Hotel, Washington; and "the managers of numerous large benevolent and manufacturing establishments throughout the land."[10]

Prior to the Civil War, the Canterbury Shakers were also selling "patent cheese vats," which may have been first devised at New Lebanon.

An improved windmill was also invented at Canterbury, as well as a revolving oven, the invention of Eldress Emeline Hart.

**1859** Fence post. To Philemon Stewart, New Lebanon, assignor to Auchampaugh Brothers, New Lebanon, New York, a patent (dated March 1) for cast-iron fence post.

**1861** To P. Cauhaupe (a Shaker?), New Lebanon, for the invention "Making capsules of copaiva." Date of grant, December 24,

*Model of wash mill or washing machine patented, sold, and used by the Shakers. The model is operated by a handle causing the dashers to move back and forth in the six tubs. Wires or cables attached to the scaffolding reduced friction on the sliding frame to which the dashers were attached. In use, the "mill" was run by water power.*

*"Self-acting" cheese press from New Lebanon, showing cheese hoop and block. The lever raises the circular plate, automatically exerting pressure on the curds within the hoop. From South family, New Lebanon.*

1861. Copaiva was a nauseous South American (Brazilian) balsam used in infections of the mucous membrane.

**1861**    Ploughs. To J. J. Rodman, South Union, Kentucky, on February 26, a patent for ploughs.

**1862**    To Robert Shepard (place not given), a patent for a "land leveler."

**1864**    A new and improved waterwheel. By H. K. Annis of Enfield, New Hampshire.

**1866**    U.S. patent to David Parker, Canterbury, New Hampshire (April 10, 1866) for an "Improved method of preserving and drying sweet corn on the cob." Also, to Parker (n.d.) patents for Corbett's Shakers' Compound and Shaker Sarsaparilla Lozenges.

**1869**    Chimney cap, the invention of Elijah Myrick at Harvard, Massachusetts (letters patent No. 90,380, dated May 25, 1869).

**1870**    Sash balance and lock. In the 1870s, Sanford J. Russell of South Union, Kentucky, was selling the Shaker Sash Balance which he had patented, also "a new device for securing ventilation, the Shakers' Window Sash Lock." Russell also invented a device which pared, cored, and quartered apples.

**1875**    A green-corn cutting machine, patented February 23, by William J. Potter, Mount Lebanon, New York, was exhibited at the Philadelphia Centennial the following year.

**1877** Improvement in washing machines. Patent awarded to Nicholas Briggs and Elijah H. Knowles of Shaker Village, New Hampshire.

**1901** One of the last Shaker patents was obtained on September 20, by E. J. Neale & Co., Mount Lebanon, for "long cloaks."

In addition to the above list, there are a number of undated inventions and labor-saving devices. Theodore Bates of Watervliet "invented" the flat broom. The broom industry at Watervliet and New Lebanon was expedited by an improved lathe with a screw feeder for turning broom handles, the invention of Jesse Wells of New Lebanon. "Machines" for filling seed bags and herb packages and presses for printing them were devised at both colonies. Elders Daniel Boler and Daniel Crossman of New Lebanon invented machinery for splint-making, "basket working," and box cutting. A pipe machine, a pea sheller, a "butter worker," and a machine for twisting the handles of "sopus whips" were made at Watervliet, and a water-powered machine for splitting stove wood either there or at New Lebanon. The first one-horse wagon used in this country is supposed to have originated at the Enfield, Connecticut, community. At an early date, dumb waiters, operated by pulleys and weights, were installed in Shaker buildings.

No less inventive, as our list indicates, were the western societies. At North Union, Ohio, a dough-kneading machine, a cream separator, a power-driven churn, and a "miniature railway" to transport milk to the milk cellar were all in early use. Union Village had an ox-powered "incline wheel" to run its fulling mill and a buzz saw. Some communities, both in the East and West, had cranes for lifting clothes from the boilers, presses for wringing out clothes, and ingenious methods of drying clothes. The Shakers, at some point, devised a method of dressing cotton and worsted cloth (drugget) to give it a glossy finish: sheet iron was warmed to the right temperature, then the cloth was folded around it and subjected to pressure.

Shaker tools, machines, and the furnishings of the shops were made with the same care as the furniture of the dwellings and meetinghouses. Commenting on the industrial installations at the Shaker Museum in Old Chatham, New York, a correspondent wrote:

> To people conditioned to the shiny inscrutability of modern machines, the museum exhibits are a restful contrast. The forged iron of their metal parts is shaped like fine wood, and the rock maple or oak of their frames is put together like furniture. In true Shaker fashion, there is no ornamentation, but no edge is left unfinished and even minor parts are turned and polished.[11]

159

# III  The Shakers and the Law

People who traded with the Shakers and those who lived in the neighborhood of their communities, as a rule, developed a respect for them as a sober, honest, and peaceful folk. They may have disapproved of the doctrine of celibacy, decried the eccentricities of their worship, and misunderstood the unorthodox principles of their faith. But the Shakers' industriousness, the excellent quality of their goods, their hospitality and far-flung benevolences, their solicitude in the care of children and their aged members—in short, their essential goodness and sterling character—came to be recognized by the unprejudiced and fair-minded observer.

From the very beginning of the movement until well after the middle of the last century, however, the society found it necessary to protect its constitutional and covenantal rights from legislative interference. Whether the issue was that of 1) military fines and requisitions, 2) the right to indenture children if one parent dissented, 3) the validity of the covenant when a seceder sought to recover compensation for his services, or 4) the amount of property and income which such a society should be allowed to hold, the Shakers were confronted with the problem of justifying, in courts of law, the tenets of their religion. All these issues affected, directly or indirectly, the economy of the sect, particularly in New York, where they were fully aired in the state legislature.

# Military
# Requisitions

In his "way-marks," Joseph Meacham gave the following instructions in regard to military requisitions:

> As we have received the grace of God in Christ, by the gospel, and are called to follow peace with all men, we cannot, consistent with our faith and conscience, bear the arms of war, for the purpose of shedding the blood of any, or do anything to justify or encourage it in others. But if they require, by fines or taxes of us, on that account, according to their laws, we may, *for peace sake,* answer their demands in that respect, and be innocent so far as we know at present.

Hoping that the time was near "when others will be so far enlightened that they will be willing to exempt us," Meacham felt that in the early stages of organization, when the society was still insecure, compromise on the issue was justified. For a number of years, therefore, the Shakers duly paid the muster fines required for exemption from service in the militia. Up to 1815, the New Lebanon society alone paid $2,000 in such fines.

The War of 1812 convinced the Shakers, however, that it was morally wrong not only to bear arms and pay fines, but even to hire substitutes or render any equivalent for military services. Accordingly, in 1815, twenty-four leaders of the parent society drew up, for legislative consideration, a declaration stating their reasons for refusing "to aid or abet the cause of war and bloodshed." A similar declaration was issued from the Enfield (Connecticut) society. This was followed, in 1816, by a memorial protesting the militia laws, and a pamphlet, published by the Watervliet community, entitled *Observations on the Natural and Constitutional Rights of Conscience, in Relation to Military Requisitions on the People Called Shakers.*

As soon as the Shaker position became known, authorities moved to uphold the law; on January 21, 1815, a sergeant came to New Lebanon to summon representatives of the society to appear at court-martial. On February 6, four delegates complied, but the "delinquents" were finally released. In October, however, horses and a wagon were taken in lieu of fines at Watervliet.

As a result of these declarations, which were followed by an interview with Governor DeWitt Clinton, a memorial (February 13) submitted to the Senate by Martin Van Buren, and a petition (February 20) drawn up in

163

favor of the Shakers by 120 citizens in Canaan, Watervliet, and other towns, the legislature, on March 29, passed an act exempting the society from "all manner of military service within this state, and from any commutation in lieu thereof in time of peace." But two years later, on April 21, 1818, influenced, it appeared, by the case of Eunice Chapman (who had been suing the Shakers to recover her children), the legislature repealed the act and substituted another imposing a four-dollar yearly fine, as the price of exemption, on every able-bodied Shaker between the ages of eighteen and forty-five. If the person refused to pay, or had "no goods and chattels, the body is to be taken and imprisoned and kept in close confinement till payment is made, with the additional cost of constable and jailors' fees, provided each confinement should in no case exceed the term of twenty days."

Although another act was passed on April 14, 1820, exempting the Shakers, we find that on November 7, 1822, fines were imposed at court-martial, the sentences being reversed, however, by Governor Clinton. In the revision of the military laws in 1823, in spite of another memorial (February 24) by the Shakers, the four-dollar fine was again imposed against conscientious objectors; and in an amendment (April 1824), they were made subject not only to fines but imprisonment. Twelve brethren at Watervliet had in fact been jailed on January 8, 1824, but were liberated the next day, and "the colonel of the regiment, on learning of the case, remitted their fines."

Faced with such harassment, the Shakers appealed for help to U.S. Senator J. Holmes, who had been instrumental in inserting a clause in the Maine constitution exempting the Shakers from requisitions, and to Martin Van Buren, then a U.S. Senator, who, although not in sympathy with the sect's religious views, admired "their charities, their sobriety, and industry."[1] In the meantime, beginning in 1823, the central ministry authorized the movement of twenty-seven brethren from New Lebanon and all the young men from Watervliet to the Hancock, Massachusetts, community where they were outside the jurisdiction of New York authorities, and where they issued the following statement:

> We have a just and lawful right to inhabit which state we choose.
> And it is our unquestionable privilege to fix our abode where we
> can best enjoy the free exercise of our faith and consciences.[2]

Despite further petitions in 1824 and 1825, nothing was done for the relief of the society. In a memorial sent to the legislature on January 10, 1826, the Shakers, represented by a Mr. Jordan, argued their case on several counts besides those of conscientious scruple:

> Their taxes were more than from the ordinary state of society,
> because less expensive to collect, the property was more compact,

the payment was prompt, and the articles exempted from taxation were much less numerous in proportion to the amount of property.

They maintained their own poor in addition to paying their full proportion of taxes for the support of paupers.

Accrued pensions relinquished by legal claimants (Revolutionary War veterans), exclusive of bounty lands, amounted to $10,000.

It is unjust to seize the consecrated property of a society "for the delinquency of an individual, who, perhaps, has never contributed one cent to that property, and never had any legal or just claim to it."

The memorial criticized the state constitution: the third section, seventh article, it pointed out, read that "the free exercise and enjoyment of religious profession and worship, without discrimination or preference, shall forever be allowed in this state to all mankind." But the militia law, predicated on the fifth section of the article, by levying a tax on the exercise of conscience, abridged such free exercise. Sections three and five, the Shakers contended, were contradictory. The fine for not paying the tax amounted to "a legal declaration that obedience to the law of Christ . . . is a transgression punishable by law."

A favorable committee report on this appeal was rejected by the House. Four years later, on March 20, 1830, another memorial was issued by the New Lebanon and Watervliet societies. This was a remonstrance against the passage of a certain law which would subject communal Shaker property to judgments and executions against individual members, prohibit fathers from turning over all their property to the United Society, and prevent evasion of the militia law by the Shakers. The proposed bill was so defamatory in character, and marked by such ignorance of the true nature of the society, that the leaders proposed, for the first time, to issue *A Brief Exposition of the Established Principles and Regulations of the United Society*. The exposition, presented to "all candid inquirers" and particularly to "the statesman, whether legislator, lawyer, judge, or jurist," went through nine editions, clarifying many points on which the public had been ignorant or misinformed. Hastily written, it was laid before the House in the session of 1830. But again the remonstrance failed; the muster fines remained on the statute books.

Many Shakers again moved out of the state into Massachusetts, which by law had exempted all who were "conscientiously averse" to bearing arms. New Hampshire had done the same. Maine and Connecticut had written such exemptions into their constitutions. Ohio had passed a militia law against the Shakers in 1818, but in 1821 passed another law relieving them from military service by working out an equivalent amount of duty on the public highways.[3]

# The Custody
# of Children

One reason for circulating the *Brief Exposition* was to explain the Shaker regulations regarding the acceptance of children when an unbelieving husband or wife was involved. The society had undergone extensive litigation and tribulation in two cases, one brought before the New York legislature in 1815 by Eunice Chapman, the other by Mary Dyer, who three years later petitioned the legislature of New Hampshire to interfere on account of the "mal-conduct" of the Enfield Shakers and "their unjust detention of her children in their custody." Eunice won her case. Mary lost hers.[1]

Both affairs were involved, with charges, counter-charges, and vivid accounts of marital dissension printed for the edification of court and public. There was blame on both sides, although in the Dyer case the mother at first agreed to join her husband in the order. Eunice, on the other hand, at no time was reconciled to the Shaker custody of her children, even though James, her husband, tried to persuade her to join the society and at one time she stayed for several weeks at the Watervliet community.

Failing in her own attempts to recover her two young daughters and son, with the help of friends she brought her case to the legislature, where, after prolonged debate, a law was passed (on March 7, 1818) that if a man joined the Shakers his children should go to the disbelieving wife. The law also allowed Eunice to divorce her husband, "the only divorce ever directly voted by the Legislature."[2]

The law was passed in spite of a strong demurral by the Council of Revision, composed of Governor DeWitt Clinton, Chancellor Kent, Chief Justice Smith Thompson, Judges Ambrose Spencer, W.W. Van Ness, Joseph C. Yates, and Jonas Platt, and Attorney General Martin Van Buren.[3] These eminent jurists reported that

> This special regulation is in the nature of a penalty; it is practically making a "discrimination" and giving a "preference" whereby the equality of civil rights (as between persons of different religious professions) is essentially impaired. If the Legislature can constitutionally deprive a man of his parental (or marital) rights, merely because he belongs to a particular sect; for the same cause it may disfranchise him of every other privilege, or banish him, or

even put him to death. If the principle be admitted it must rest in discretion alone how far it shall be carried in the measure of punishment.

The Shaker side of the case was thus expressed in Youngs's *Concise View:*

March, 1818. It appears that Eunice Chapman, by her subtle insinuations and *fascinating charms,* has so far allured the majority of the members of the Legislature that their servile passions and prejudices have become more than a match for manly wisdom and discretion. In consequence of this they have not only enacted a law to divorce her from her husband, James Chapman (which is indeed a welcome act to him), but they have made provision, in case a man joins himself to a Society of people called Shakers, to take his children from him and give them to his unbelieving wife.... After the passage of the act Eunice Chapman became so bold and

brazen, and her behavior was so utterly the reverse of all modesty,
that many who had voted in her favor became quite disgusted with
her conduct before the close of the session; but it was too late to
recall their votes, and this unconstitutional act, tho condemned by
the Council of Revision, still remains a blot upon the statute book.

We have noted that a few weeks after the act was passed another one
repealed the law of 1816 which had granted the Shakers exemption from
military requisitions.

The issue raised in the Chapman case was not provided for in the first
Shaker covenant (1795), which merely stated that "Youth and Children,
being under age, were not to be received as members, or as being under
the immediate care and government of the Church, But by the request
or free consent of both their parents, if living. . . . " The regulation, as given
in the *Brief Exposition*, is more explicit:

> No believing husband or wife is allowed, by our rules to separate
> from an unbelieving partner, except by mutual agreement; unless
> the conduct of the unbeliever be such as to warrant a separation
> by the laws of the land. Nor can any husband or wife who has
> otherwise abandoned his or her partner, be received into
> communion with the Society.[4]

The trouble, in the Chapman case, was that husband and wife could
not mutually agree. And if, as was contended, James tried to induce Eunice
to join him, could it be said that he had abandoned her?

It was against the rules of the society to aid a man or woman in deserting
wife or husband by joining the community,

> or that a deserting spouse bring children into the community
> against the will of the other parent. Occasionally, however, and
> presumably without the knowledge of the community, a child is
> brought in under such fraudulent circumstances. Once there,
> mingled with the other children and separated from its parents, the
> child is difficult to find, particularly if the community is loath to
> lend its aid. The statute . . . was aimed at this practice.[5]

The Chapman case was only one of several in New York in which children
were involved. On November 7, 1845, "a difficulty arose about two children
named Traver. The case was tried on the 19th in our favor. But the girls
were afterward taken from us, by duplicity and never returned."[6] In March
of the same year, in a case involving a certain Sarah Ogden, the Shakers
felt obliged to send a memorial to the state Senate replying to accusations
of "immoral practices" by the Shakers in a bill "to prevent the binding
of minor children to the society." And in another case, in 1847, this one

by a father, the Shakers were tried for an attempt to "restrain" the wife and three children of William Pillow.[7]

Again, in 1849, a committee from the New Lebanon and Watervliet societies had to remonstrate against what they feared would be a law that would deprive a man of his parental and marital rights merely because he belonged to a particular sect. A report of the judiciary committee of the Assembly was taking "cognizance of the fact of a husband or wife becoming a member of any religious sect holding and teaching certain doctrines and tenets, and imposing a penalty not applicable to . . . members of other religious societies. . . . "[8] The Shaker committee protested against the passing of any law which would make an individual "accountable for any religious tenets or doctrines, or make him answerable in any court for matters of faith and opinion." Although the United Society recognized the validity of the marriage contract, and since marriage was a civil institution, also the right of the legislature and courts to provide for "releasing . . . cases of hardship," it challenged the right "to examine and decide matters of conscience," and protested the discourtesy of stigmatizing, in a public document, the teaching of peaceable citizens as "religious fanaticism and frenzy."

# The Validity
# of the Covenant

The validity of the covenant was established in several legal tests, among them the Goodrich case in New York (1799), *Heath v. Draper* in New Hampshire (1810), *Wait v. Merril* et al., in Maine (1827), and *Gass and Banta v. Wilhite* et al., in Kentucky (1834).

In the first of these actions, Benjamin Goodrich, an apostate from the New Lebanon society, brought suit against Jonathan Walker for $3,000 which he contended represented wages withheld from him when he was a member. When the case was tried in the Supreme Court, the society produced the document, dated May 24, 1796, whereby, "in consideration of forty pounds to him in hand paid, by David Meacham and David Osborne, overseers of the church at New Lebanon, the plaintiff released and discharged the said overseers and community of the said church, jointly, and severally, from any further charges and demands whatsoever." In his charge to the jury, Chief Justice Lansing said that in his opinion the weight of the testimony was in favor of defendant and the jury so found.[1]

The defense in the Heath-Draper case before the Supreme Court of New Hampshire was similarly based. "Recovery" of some $2,000 by the plaintiff, John Heath, was "resisted" on the ground that there was "no *implied* promise" by the Shaker deacon, Nathaniel Draper, to pay wages, but, on the contrary, "an express agreement that plaintiff was *not labouring* for *hire* or wages: and as to the money put into the joint stock by the plaintiff, it was *given*, the gift was *complete and effectual*—possession delivered: it was not in the power of the donor to retract or reclaim it." Having signed the covenant, the action of the plaintiff was a breach of contract as well as of faith. Nor can it be contended, the court said, that the dedication of property and labor was "to a false religion and so not binding":

> No one can see the improvements made in husbandry and manufactures by this sect, and at the same time believe the existence of the sect to be against the policy of the law. Whatever we may think of their faith, their works are good, and charity bids us think well of the tree when the fruits are salutary. We cannot try the question, which religion, theirs or ours, is the better one. . . .[2]

The plaintiff "knowingly signed the covenant," it was established in the *Wait v. Merril* case. There was nothing illegal about the contract: it "does not contain a fact or a principle which an honest man ought to condemn; but it does contain some provisions which all men ought to approve. It distinctly inculcates the duty of honest industry, contentment with competency, and charity to the poor and suffering." In answer to the objection that the covenant was void because it was "in derogation" of the inalienable right of liberty of conscience, the court declared that the reply was obvious:

> The very formation and subscription of the covenant is an exercise
> of the inalienable right of liberty of conscience. . . . We must
> remember that in this land of liberty, civil and religious conscience
> is subject to no human law; its rights are not to be invaded or even
> questioned, so long as its dictates are obeyed consistently with the
> harmony, good order and peace of the community.[3]

In 1826, one John Whitbey, a member of Robert Owen's New Harmony society in Indiana, wrote a scurrilous anti-Shaker tract called *Beauties of Priestcraft, or a Short Account of Shakerism.* Two years later he submitted, on behalf of himself and others residing in or near the vicinity of Pleasant Hill, Kentucky, a petition to the General Assembly of the state asking for a redress of alleged grievances suffered under the "oppressive and despotic" government of the Shaker society. One of the key plaintiffs in the ensuing case was Samuel Banta, who had told Whitbey that in leaving the Shakers he lacked the remedy to recover the property which he took to them. The names of the other plaintiffs were Gass, Sasseen, and Burnett. The case was first tried in the Lincoln Circuit Court, and then appealed to the Court of Appeals.

Pertinent to an understanding of the case of *Gass and Banta v. Wilhite* et al. was an act, passed by the legislature in 1828, "to regulate civil proceedings against certain communities having property in common." The act declared "that it shall and may be lawful to commence and prosecute suits, obtain decrees and have execution against any of the communities of people called Shakers,—without naming or designating the individuals, or serving process on them, otherwise than by fixing a subpoena on the door of their meeting-house." What makes the case significant are two documents defining the peculiar nature of the Shaker institution: the speech of Robert Wickliffe in the Kentucky Senate (January 1831) on a bill to repeal the act of 1828,[4] and the opinion of the Court of Appeals as delivered by Judge Nicholas on May 5, 1834.[5]

Wickliffe condemned the act as unconstitutional: the constitution of Kentucky declared "that no law impairing contracts shall be made,"

that all free men, when they form a compact, are equal—that no

preference shall ever be given, by law, to any religious societies or
modes of worship—that the civil rights, privileges or capacities of
any citizen shall in no wise be diminished or enlarged on account
of his religion—that no human authority ought, in any case
whatever, to control or interfere with the rights of conscience.

His basic argument was that the Shakers were not a civil community,
one that was legally recognized. They were not an incorporated body. "Civil-
ly and politically, they are no community—religiously they are a society
of Christians." They were not a company or corporation, organized to
accumulate wealth or for any other temporal purpose: their purposes were
religious and pious only. They had, in short, no legal existence. Therefore,
because of their peculiar status, the state had no right to regulate their
temporal economy unless they violated some known law. More importantly,
in the present case, no contract could be made with them as a community;
they could neither sue nor be sued; contracts could be made with them
only as individuals.

"All laws, to be constitutional," the court held, "must be equal, and
to be equal, there must be mutual reciprocity." Because under the act of
1828 the whole society could be sued, but could not sue in turn, it was
unconstitutional.

In the case argued before the Court of Appeals in 1834, the ex-Shakers
Gass and Banta sought a "partition" or division of community property,
with their shares allotted to them either on the principle of equality as
two of its covenant members or according to the amount of property each
had brought into the society. Since they were "joint beneficial proprietors"
of the property, in their individual natural capacities "the covenants in
restraint of partition" were void. Gass and Banta were suing " to set aside
and vacate" the whole contract on which the society was based.

But Judge Nicholas pointed out that the Shaker covenant was a valid
contract and that it expressly precluded any claim to a division.

> Nothing could be plainer than the intent to keep the property
> together in perpetuity, for society purposes, free from any
> individual claims on the part of its members. . . . The import of the
> whole section [Article 3 of the covenant] being that the property
> bro't in should become the property of the whole society, as a
> society, with a several right of use conferred on each member as
> a member, and by consequence only whilst or so long as he
> remained a member.[6]

When a donation was made, the judge continued, it was

> not to each other in the nature of a community of goods among
> individuals, but to the society. They do not hold as individuals, but

as members of the society. Their proprietorship of the usufruct continues so long as they continue members. When they cease to be members, they cease to be propietors. . . .[7]

The result is, that, considering the objects and purposes of the trust under which the property of the Shaker society is held, as legitimate and valid, and that the complainants never had any interest therein by the terms of the trust, except as members, and so long as they remained members, they have no right to the partition which they claim, and consequently their cross-bill was properly dismissed.[8]

Court opinion was substantially the same in a suit brought against the society in Massachusetts in 1875 by Roxalana L. Grosvenor and Maria F. Grosvenor: the rights of a person who has been expelled from a religious society are to be determined by the constitution of the society. A person who has been expelled from the society cannot maintain an action for services rendered the society. The ministry and elders had the power to expel members who entertained opinions and promulgated doctrines "at variance with the established belief and subversive of the organization."[9]

Another case to dissolve the society occurred in Kentucky as late as 1909. Mary E. Porter, trustee for one Charity Hilton, the plaintiff, had filed a bill to dissolve the South Union society, distribute its property among the members, and "recover damages for breach of the Shaker covenant." But the bill for the defendants (the United Society), citing the Gass-Banta case, held that no one part of the society could be dissolved without the consent of the leading authority at New Lebanon, who had "the sole right to pass on what constitutes a breach." Just because the Shakers no longer had public worship was no proof that they had renounced or abandoned their covenant.[10]

# Distrust of
# Shaker "Wealth"

Pacificism, celibacy, common property—these unorthodox principles formed a barrier between the Shakers and the world. Bureaucrats resented their civil disobedience to military requisitions. Chastity was a dangerous doctrine—what would become of the world if all became Shakers? United inheritance—did that mean that man should have no compensation for his labors? And there was another area in which, due to suspicion of the Shakers or confusion over what to do about this peculiar institution, the legislature saw fit to regulate the sect's affairs: what should be done about the expansion of the United Society and its increasing "wealth"?

On July 15, 1841, the Shakers at Watervliet were visited by an Englishman who has been called "one of the most intelligent, energetic, and liberal of British visitors to America before the Civil War."[1] He was a former sea captain, a founder of the *Athenaeum*, a London literary weekly, a journalist, a member of Parliament, and an "untiring advocate of social reform." His name was James Silk Buckingham.

The Shaker experiment in communitarianism, as seen first-hand, convinced Buckingham that it was bound to succeed, and bound to be an increasing influence for the good:

> As far as the history of the Shakers can establish the fact, it has certainly shown that, where property is held in community, and not individually, the disposition to bestow it in works of charity and benevolence to others is greatly increased. And that property itself is better managed for accumulation and preservation, no one can doubt who has watched the progressive advancement which this society has made in the augmentation, as well as improvement of its possessions, and in the neatness, order and perfection by which everything they do or make is characterized: this is so much the case, that over all the United States, the seeds, plants, fruits, grain, cattle, and manufactures furnished by any settlement of Shakers bears a premium in the market above the ordinary price of similar articles from other establishments. There being no idleness among them, all are productive. There being no intemperance among them, none are destructive. There being no misers among them, nothing is hoarded, or made to perish for want of use; so that while production and improvement are at their maximum, and waste and

destruction at their minimum, the society must go on increasing the extent and value of its temporal possessions, and thus increase its means of doing good, first within, and then beyond its own circle.[2]

Buckingham was writing two years after the legislature of New York had passed a controversial act "in relation to certain trusts," trusts of real and personal estate "for the benefit of any United Society of the people called Shakers." His observations and those of other visitors during the 1830s and '40s call attention, however, to the fact that during this period the society was increasing the extent of its possessions, an issue of concern both to the Shakers and the world.

It concerned the world—that is, public officials and a segment of the public—because of the fear that the Shakers, by buying up large acreages, "were forming a dangerous monopoly of the lands of the State."[3]

It concerned the Shakers, because, as we have seen, they had had on several occasions to defend the validity of their covenant and the right of their trustees to hold property in trust. They feared that the Revised Statutes of the state of New York had invalidated their right to hold deeds of real estate.[4] The Trust Act, passed by the New York legislature on April 15, 1839, benefited the society in that it made "valid and effectual . . . all deeds of trust in relation to real and personal estate executed and delivered" prior to January 1, 1830; and "such legal estates and trusts may be continued so long as may be required for the purposes of the trust." On the other hand, the Trust Act protected "the people of the state" from the fear of monopoly or the rise of a "money power" by asserting that no Shaker society shall become "beneficially interested" in any property "the annual value or income of which, after deducting necessary expenses, shall exceed five thousand dollars."

Even this limited concession to the United Society was strongly opposed before its passage, the principle opposer being the Shakers' neighbor in New Lebanon, Samuel J. Tilden. The Shakers had memorialized the legislature in April 1838, for the right to hold property in trust. A committee had reported favorably, but the session closed before action was taken. In January 1839, the bill was reintroduced, with certain amendments.

It was about that time that Tilden began his campaign of opposition. On February 7, he wrote his father, Elam, that he had "partly written a letter on the Shaker business," mentioning a talk with William Cullen Bryant at the *Evening Post* office in which he (Tilden) had spoken of the Shaker bill, "an abominable violation of principle."[5] The New Lebanon Shakers, he said, wanted to have their property exempted from the operation of the general laws of the state applicable to trusts.

Tilden's *Considerations in regard to the application of the Shakers for certain special privileges* (first published in the next issue of the *Post*?) are worth examining in some detail as they expressed a conviction, current at the time, that the Shakers were anti-American in both their principles and practices.[6] Like many others, Tilden had been prejudiced by reading the anti-Shaker publications of William Haskett and other seceders who had had personal, and often unjustified, complaints against the government of the order.[7]

In five respects, the future governor wrote, the act would violate the general law of religious corporations:

1.  The general law restricts the property held by religious societies to what is necessary for strictly religious uses, and limits the amount. "This act would enable this Society to hold in perpetuity the aggregate of the individual property to all its members, and to an unlimited amount."

2. The general law defines the powers and duties of the trustees who control the property of religious societies, makes them elective, limits their term of office, etc., "thus conforming them to the character of the political institutions of our country." The act would give the society extensive powers without regard to such provisions. (The Shaker trustees were not elected and held office by appointment of the ministry for an undeclared duration.)

3. The act was "inconsistent with the general laws which regulate the descent of property. It involves the odious principle of entailment, which it was one of the first acts of our national independence to abolish as incompatible with institutions of freedom."

4. Because the Shakers' property was held for their "benefit and use" just as private property is (even though it was held in common), the act would be "analogous to entailment of private property, not the use of property for religious purposes or for public use."

5. The act was unconstitutional in that in operation it would be an *ex post facto* law. "All persons who were members of this Society when the trust terminated have a legal estate in the common property."

Tilden also objected to the word "clear" in the act's provision that no society should hold property "the whole clear annual income of which shall exceed five thousand dollars," contending (as it indeed did) that it would allow the Shakers to hold property producing an income of $5,000 *beyond* all expenditures. This, he wrote, was a special privilege not granted to other religious societies, where the law restricted them to the *whole* amount of property they could hold. In another objection, he construed the act as recognizing each *family* in a society as a distinct society, and thereby, if the Shakers multiplied the number of families, "the amount of property which the whole Society can legally hold may be increased indefinitely." Either because of this objection, or because Tilden was in error, the act specifically defined the word "society" as meaning and including all Shakers "resident within the same county." There were, then, three New York societies within the meaning of the act: New Lebanon, Watervliet, and Groveland.

One cannot but feel that Tilden's "observations" were based in part on prejudice and an ignorance of the true nature and intent of the Shaker institution. He concludes with a criticism of its "arbitrary" government, its "irresponsible" ministry, its "internal police" who had "supervision and     177 control of the minutest personal concerns," the "servitude" of its members, its denial of compensation for services when a member is forced to leave, its destruction of natural affections and "the relation of parent and child, husband and wife," etc. Such principles, he held, were "in perpetual conflict with the social duties which the civil law recognizes and enforces, and whose organization is an unmixed and unmitigated despotism."

That Tilden's reservations regarding the act found considerable popular approval is evidenced by the fact that ten years later a resolution was introduced in the legislature "inquiring into the propriety of rescinding" the trust held by the United Society. This resolution followed and probably was influenced by an Albany reprint, in February 1848, of Tilden's *Considerations*. In the reprint, the author stated that the principles established by the act of 1839 were

> at variance with the principles of our free institutions, [and] subversive of public and individual rights. . . . They have already a very large real and personal estate, estimated at over one million dollars, and [are] increasing it very fast; encroaching in their purchases upon other denominations, and threatening in time to embrace whole towns, and perhaps counties, in their possession.

The report of the select committee (headed by Assemblyman Daniel B. Taylor), to which the above resolution was referred, served to quiet, to some extent, the fear that the Shakers were a wealthy organization verging on a monopoly.[8] It acknowledged, however, that the report would probably not "silence the many tongues which have been raised in relation to this almost unknown people"—especially since it decided that the matter presented no cause for legislative interference. This decision was based on a personal investigation of the Shaker schools, workshops and "manufacturies," all of which met with their approval. The committee learned that all the witnesses who had testified *against* the Shakers were "persons who had been turned away from the Society for imprudent conduct, or had been those who had joined them under improper motives, and becoming disappointed, had left." Most important of all, they learned that the total number of acres owned by the three communities in the state was about ten thousand, a fraction over ten acres a person—"not one fourth the quantity held by the Papal Indians of this State, against which not a murmur has ever been uttered."

The Senate, however, was not convinced, and less than a year after this report was submitted, passed a resolution requiring the trustees of the societies at New Lebanon to report on:

1. The amount of real estate belonging to the society on April 15, 1839;

2.  Real estate purchased in the state since that date, with the cost, number of buildings, etc.;

3.  Real estate sold since that date, to whom sold, and the price received for each separate tract;

4.  The value of all personal property, of every description, now owned or possessed by or for the society;

5.  The amount of money on hand or deposit, stocks, mortgages, bonds, and evidences of indebtedness;

6.  The amount of money or other property received since February 1849 for the sale of property and the amount paid out since that period; and

7.  An accounting of all money or other property expended since February 1, 1849, in buildings and "permanent erections upon the real estate of the society."

With this difficult demand, the Shaker trustees conscientiously sought to comply. To summarize as regards the New Lebanon society:

On section 1. real estate, as of April 1839, according to assessors' returns: 2,292¼ acres; value, including buildings: $68,225.

On section 2. real estate purchased: 14 lots, totaling about 760 acres, amounting to $19,628. (Very few buildings on land or erected since purchase.) Money paid for lands was "necessary expenditure," as they were used for grain and animals needed for home consumption.

On section 3. real estate sold since April 1839: three tracts at $2,350.

On section 4. "strict compliance. . . is utterly beyond our ability, but we will cooperate with any committee appointed." Livestock "only sufficient for the necessary supply of teams, animal food, butter, cheese, wool, etc. for the society's consumption." Occasionally some sold. "Our dwelling houses . . . are built and furnished in the most plain and simple style; and while all unnecessary and superfluous articles of furniture are avoided, the actual cost of furnishing one of our dwellings for the comfortable accommodation of 60 or 70 inmates would

179

fall far short of the sum often expended in furnishing some single parlors in the cities of New-York and Albany." "Our shops are fitted up only with the necessary conveniences and tools to carry on several branches of mechanical trades."

On section 5. monies on hand, stocks, etc.: $13,754, about $2,000 more than in 1839.

On section 6. amount of sales since February 1849: $38,405.35; amount expended: $37,810.07. Balance: $595.28. There are valid reasons why five to six hundred people are not able to increase their yearly income beyond the statements given in the report: first, the principles of the society forbid speculation, and "tolerate only such branches of industry as are useful to the public, instead of those which tend to superfluity and extravagance, though generally the latter yields vastly the most profit to the manufacturers"; secondly, the society supports its own poor, pays its share in supporting the county poor, and daily extends "such other deeds of charity to our fellow men, the yearly amount of which would be more than $2,000."

On section 7. built since February 1, 1849: one wool and dye house, one saw mill, and one dry house of stone. Cost: about $696.

Summing up, the trustees stated that the total real estate, including all the additions made in eleven years under the Trust Act, was 3,053 acres,

> which, were they divided among 110 families of five persons each
> ... then, for each one of such families of five persons there would
> be less than 38 acres! Also if the increased value of the society's
> property, for the last 11 years should amount to $25,000, the annual
> gain to each individual would be but a trifle over ($4), four dollars,
> a sum that might have been absorbed by a single useless article
> of dress.
> So, if any fears have been entertained that the society is becoming
> a dangerous money power; or, that it is extending its possessions
> beyond a reasonable land limitation, it is hoped that they may now
> be dispelled.

A similar report was made by the trustees at Watervliet. In 1849, that society owned 2,547 acres valued at $46,900. Net income over the eleven years since the passage of the Trust Act averaged $1,217.53.

In 1852, in reply to the requirement for a stricter report, the Shakers presented a "remonstrance" with 150 signatures and "a writing" signed at Hudson in their behalf. A petition *against* the Shakers was also sent to the legislature, but turned down by that body. And though the Shakers did not ask for it, the legislature extended their charter to allow a $25,000 annual income! A final effort to regulate the personal and real estate of the Shakers in 1855 (No. 115, In Senate) failed to pass.

Although the vexing question of income was finally settled in New York, the Shakers, in the country as a whole, were again involved in tax problems when the federal government passed its income tax law in 1861. The society was willing to pay its just share in federal taxes, but objected to alleged discrimination and overtaxation. In 1869, therefore, they engaged a lawyer, Durbin Ward, to present their case to Commissioner of Taxation Delano. Ward's brief is an interesting discussion of the legal state of the United Society.[9]

Counsel introduced his brief with a statement of the current wealth of the eighteen Shaker societies: about 65,000 acres of land, valued, with houses and "factories," at about $2,267,000; personal property, about $364,528. He then pointed out that as far as the federal government was concerned, there was no statute enjoining or forbidding "the amount, or the nature of property a citizen may hold, nor the form of tenure":

neither Fourierism, communism, cooperative associations, nor any form of industrial organization or development, has been sanctioned or condemned by law. The right of the Shakers, therefore, to their own social system, is as full and perfect as that of any other class of citizens. . . .

Addressing himself to the Shaker covenant, he argued that the society was "essentially a charitable institution," and that the covenant members were the owners of the whole consecrated property or interest. "No member of any company or association in business, or civil concerns," the revised covenant read, "no co-partner in trade, no persons under legal involvement, or obligation of service, no slave, no slave-holder" could enter into covenant relations.

Legally, Ward continued, they were charities and ought to be exempted from taxation. Since there was "no specific provision of the statute on the subject," he doubted whether charitable societies, with funds or endowments, were subject to taxation, or whether they were "in the contemplation of the statute at all." Nor within the meaning of the statute was the society either a person or corporation.

Ward proposed a rule which would assimilate the Shakers with the rest of the population: "families on the average consist of about five members, old and young, producing income, or helpless"; there was also a "non-producing" element in the Shaker society, the old and infirm; so divide them for taxation purposes into families of five.

And also give them just exemptions. Under a recent ruling of the commissioner, the whole society was treated as one person, with a single exemption of one thousand dollars. Since the average membership of the eighteen societies was about two hundred, this exemption would amount to only five dollars per capita whereas the general average in the population was about two hundred dollars. The object of the thousand-dollar exemption was to give a person "before he is required to return a taxable income that amount as a naked support, food and clothing, for his family." Is it just, then, asked Ward, to give no greater exemption to a social community of two hundred members "which performs the functions of a family by feeding, clothing, lodging, educating, and protecting its members?" In addition, Ward stated, in the 117th section of the tax law, a "person" is allowed to deduct "the amount actually paid for labor to cultivate land or conduct any other business from which income is actually derived." If the Shaker societies are treated as "persons," then, "by the same reasoning they are hired, their services are labor, even though the members are paid in food, clothing, lodging, medical attendance, etc., instead of money. Also, the society supports those who cannot work at all." From these considerations, it appears that "the whole expense of running the establishment ought to be deducted before the society can be said to have any income."

Ward won his case, although the issue of course became an academic one when the law was repealed.

The problem of military service came up again with the Civil War and the draft law of 1863. As this was also a federal law, the Shakers presented their familiar appeal for exemption directly to Lincoln and Secretary of War Stanton. The sum of money in the national treasury legally belonging to the society through those who had served in the Revolution, but had not because of their faith claimed their pensions or bounty lands, now amounted, with interest, to $439,733. Since only about seventy believers were liable for military service, the government would receive in fines an amount equivalent to only 4½ percent of the unclaimed money. The petition for exemption was granted.

Nevertheless, the Shakers, although non-combatants, aided the Union in other ways. As Durbin Ward pointed out in closing his brief,

> The Soldier's Aid societies, the Sanitary Commission, and the other organizations to minister to the suffering soldier, always found willing coadjutors in these communities. The needy wives and children of the soldiers found homes with these people whenever they asked shelter and were cheerfully supported without "money and without price." They supply the place unattended by the corruptions and evils of the old monastic institutions of the middle ages, and though they can never become numerous, supply a want which exists in all countries and ages.

183

# Landholding

The charges that the Shakers were becoming land monopolists were disproved by the court cases just cited. Certainly they never deliberately set out, for reasons of aggrandizement, to obtain control of as much land as possible. In the matter of inventions, we have seen that in most cases they abjured acquiring patents just because patent rights savoured of monopoly.

At first, it is true, they extended their landholding around the home farms with whatever surplus capital was available. Basically they were agriculturalists, with an economy based, directly or indirectly, on the soil. They must also have felt more secure from a hostile world with extensive farm lands serving as a sort of buffer. Nor should it be forgotten that the Shakers held their land in trust, "not only for themselves, but for all who may hereafter join their order, and they are therefore bound to keep a large surplus in hand for the purpose of forming new communities."[1]

Another factor, one of lesser importance, entered into the policy of land acquisition: the Shakers were not unaware of the fact that their well-tilled lands, and their prosperity as skilled agriculturalists, served as an added, and not illegitimate, magnet to draw people into the order, often those who failed to make a go of farming as individuals. "The surplus invested in new lands," was one writer's somewhat cynical observation, "will increase the temptation of converts to share the abundance, and in short the thing grows because it is. . . ."[2]

It was only when they began, more and more, to acquire "out-farms" detached from and sometimes quite remote from the home community that rumors began to spread. Tilden, for instance, was undoubtedly influenced by the fact that there were Shaker lands all around his neighborhood (as well as a medicinal herb industry competing with the Tilden company). When the legislature of New York limited the income of the society in 1839, and required an accounting ten years later, the Shaker movement was at its height, and its zenith reached in membership. From about 1850 on, membership began to decline, a trend accelerated by the Civil War, the westward movement, and the far-flung influence of the industrial revolution.

The decline in manpower had drastic effects on the land policies of the United Society. It found itself over-extended in acreage, and to keep up its farming operations had to resort to hiring labor and renting lands in the *métayage* system, the Shakers supplying capital and receiving half the crop in return. When we consider the convictions of the Believers regarding separation from the world, and the stringent early regulations to implement that principle, it can be seen that this system was, to use Dixon's phrase, "foreign to the genius of their order." "Even their wish to do good among the Gentiles," he wrote in 1870, "must not lead them into what is wrong; and they are now considering whether it may not be wiser for them to part with all their surplus lands."

It was not only a matter of principle, but also of good economy, good business. Speaking to Charles Nordhoff in 1875, Elder Frederick Evans of New Lebanon observed that it was a mistake for the Shakers to have farms outside the home domain:

> If every out-farm were sold, the Society would be better off. They
> are of no real advantage to us, and, I believe, of no pecuniary

advantage either. They give us a prosperous look, because we do improve them well, and they usually return a fair percentage on the investment; but on the other hand this success depends upon the assiduous labour of some of our ablest men, whose services would have been worth much more at home. We ought to get on without the use of outside labour. Then we should be confined to such enterprises as are best for us. Moreover, we ought not to make money. We ought to make no more than a moderate surplus over our usual living, so as to lay by something for hard times.[3]

Speaking at a time when the Shaker *industrial* economy was suffering from outside competition, Evans had concluded that "every commune, to prosper, must be founded . . . on agriculture. Only the simple labors and manners of a farming people can hold a community together." Yet he clung to the opinion that the Shakers should still make, as far as possible, all they used:

We used to have more looms than now, but cloth is sold so cheaply that we gradually began to buy. It is a mistake; we buy more cheaply than we can make, but our home-made cloth is much better than we can buy; and we have now to make three pairs of trousers, for instance, where before we made one. Thus our little looms would even now be more profitable—to say nothing of the independence we secure in working them.[4]

As time went on, Evans and another New Lebanon brother, Daniel Fraser, became outspoken advocates of landholding and land reform as a cure-all for social and economic evils. "Land monopoly," Evans once observed, "is the primary cause of poverty, and poverty of war." And Fraser, in a letter from Mount Lebanon on October 1, 1885, advised Joseph Chamberlain, member of Parliament, to

Declare through all nations that land, being the source of human subsistence, of social and judicial equality, and a regulator of the exchange and values of commercial equivalents, every person should have access to the land at all times. Declare that the possession of land operates as a break on the fly wheel of destructive competition and as a nullifier of the causes of panics, strikes, want and crime. . . .[5]

Around that time, Evans put his ideas on land limitation into concrete proposals. In a letter to Henry George (c. 1886) he suggested the advisability of a law (to apply to Indians, Negroes, and whites, both male and female) to prohibit the acquisition of any land that could not be or was not being made use of: "When a land holder dies the legal heirs may inherit, with the proviso that within two years they shall sell down to the legal limit of 100 acres. . . . " Then the landless, by right of birth, could acquire land, and in fifteen years, freeholders would be doubled. "It would make the whole country what New England used to be—a hive of busy, industrious freeholders who made good neighbors and helpful friends to each other."[6]

# IV The World's Appraisal

Although the law operated both for and against the Shakers as an experiment in association, the observations of visitors on the *economy* of the sect, as distinct from its religious principles and practices, were with few exceptions favorable and often laudatory. Since the economy was an expression of principles which were often condemned, such approval presents a paradox. For the commentators are placed, it seems, in the position of censuring doctrine and at the same time finding great merit in its "fruits." Could a society endure and be united, one asks, if it were composed of two contradictory sets of principles, one right and progressive, the other reactionary and wrong? Did these critics fail to understand the strange ways in which, as the Shakers put their hands to work, they put their hearts to God? Or were they merely trying to express a balanced, objective judgment?

Examples are numerous. Thus, the president of Yale, Timothy Dwight, after a visit to New Lebanon in 1799, voiced his strong disapproval of their "gross," "extravagant" doctrines but confessed that "the industry, manual skill, fair dealing and orderly behavior of the Brotherhood, render them useful members of society."

After praising the Shaker principle of *combined labor* and *expenditure*, W. S. Warder, a Philadelphia Quaker, in a letter to Robert Owen in 1817, wrote:

> the only objection in the mind of the liberal and well-informed is grounded on the degrading superstition, and consequently low state of intellect, exhibited in the religious notions and relative conduct of the Shaking Quakers. Even this, however, it seems, does not prevent—the limited progress of the useful inventive talents among them—an uniform and peaceable demeanor as subjects of the state—the exercise of the principles of veracity, honesty and sincere dealing towards everyone, kindness and hospitality!
> The defects, which create disgust and feeling, afford the most triumphant and abundant proofs of the truths developed in the work entitled *A New View of Society* where it is laid down as an undeniable principle that "the character is formed *for*, and not *by* the individuals!"[1]

In other words, in spite of its faults, a "moral character" had been developed by the virtues of the order which raised its members above their former lot, and the society itself above society at large.

Similar statements were included by Owen in the issue of *The Economist* for June 2, 1821. One was by Morris Birkbeck, the English reformer who had set up an agricultural colony in Edwards County, Illinois, in 1818, for the benefit of the working class in his own country. Birkbeck had been

struck with admiration at the astonishing results of their

combinations; and thought their settlements worthy of general imitation, but for the absurd puerilities of some of their peculiar tenets, and the revolting and unnatural regulation which prohibits marriage.[2]

In the same vein was the comment of Harriet Martineau, the English political economist:

> Whatever they have peculiarly good among them, is owing to the soundness of their economic principles, whatever they have that excites compassion is owing to the badness of their moral arrangements.[3]

Miss Martineau conceded that the Shakers (and the Rappites) were the "most remarkable order of landowners" in the United States. She praised their "cooperative principle." But there is a note of puzzlement in her appraisal:

> There must be something sound in the principles on which these people differ from the rest of the world, or they would not work at all. . . . Like all religious persuasions from which one differs, that of the Shakers appears more reasonable in conversation, and in their daily actions, than on paper and at a distance. In actual life, the absurd and peculiar recedes before the true and universal.[4]

Speaking of American communities in general, George Holyoake, the historian of cooperation in England, also admitted that "though caricatured by celibacy and defaced by religious and sexual eccentricities, [they] show that wealth, morality, and comfort can be had in them."[5] One should not call any people "enthusiasts" who seek to reduce to practice the principle of common property advocated by Christ and the early Christians.

One more example of this point of view. No one could have admired more the spirit of Shaker workmanship than the French lady Madame Thérèse Blanc, who visited the Alfred society late in the century:

> Nothing can give a [fair] idea of the order, of the tidiness, of the extraordinary calm of a Shaker village. It was a favorite saying of Mother Ann, it seems, that one should "Work as if you have a thousand years to live, and as if you have to die tomorrow. . . ." That is to say, undertake with spirit the longest and most difficult of tasks, and make haste to accomplish them. . . . [In the village there is] not a sound; the workers scattered about are as silent as shadows; never [is] a voice raised in anger to spur on a lagging horse, or for any other reason.

Yet Madame Blanc was critical of the spirit she praised. Comparing "our 191 monks and nuns" with the "good Shakers," she noted this difference:

> that a concern for material gain is too often mingled, among the
> Shakers, with the loftiest thought, that business occupies too large
> a place in their minds, that in the picture of the customs of the
> primitive church, "And they lived together, they bought and sold,
> and held all in common," the two traits, "they bought and sold"
> seem too greatly emphasized.[6]

Two other contributors to *The Economist* endeavored "to extenuate their
[the Shakers] peculiarities, on the ground that the society conforms to them
voluntarily, and from conscientious feeling." In a letter dated Edinburgh,
August 1819, a Mr. Courtauld, who had visited the community in Busro,
Indiana, reported that

> There are a few remarkable settlements [those of the Shakers]
> where a rapid increase of wealth, by the judicious application of
> capital and labor, arrest general attention; and which ... command
> the admiration of all who have witnessed their wonderful success,
> and can duly appreciate habits of industry, temperance, order, and
> neatness, with peaceable and unobtrusive manners, apparently
> flowing from a state of ease and contentment, and a serious sense
> of religion.[7]

Courtauld found particularly noteworthy the difference between the prosperity of the Shaker community and "the hardships to which isolated families and individuals are frequently exposed in the remote and infant settlements of North America."[8]

A favorable report was also made by a Mr. Melish, who visited the same
colony:

> It is impossible to convey any adequate idea of the diligent industry
> and perseverance of this people. Wherever we went we found them
> all activity and contentment. But they have every inducement to
> perseverance. They are all on an equal footing. Every member is
> equally interested in the good of the society.... There are no vicious
> habits among them....
>
> There is not an instance of swearing and lying, nor debauchery of
> any kind; and as to cheating, so commonly practised in civilized
> society, they have no temptation to it whatever. As individuals they
> have no use for money; and they have no fear of want....[9]

Melish believed that the Shakers would not only continue united, but would
be a model for other societies:

> They have the mutual aid of each other.... They can attend to the

worship of God with single hearts and undivided minds; and all
the duties of life are easy, because they go hand in hand with
self-interest.[10]

After reviewing all the reports, pro and con, from his correspondents
in America, Owen concluded:

No reasonable man, then, can doubt, whether society has the
means, even with its present limited knowledge, to enable the
human intellect to rise as much above the present level of its
powers and relative prejudices, as the conduct and comforts of
these simple-hearted Shakers, are superior to those of the lower
orders of the best-regulated city or village, under the existing
system, in the world.[11]

"A useful institution," Barnabus Bates believed. Government was founded on public opinion. There was no external compulsion.

> Conscience and the example of others are the only incitements to
> labor. . . . It is true they cannot have many distinguished scholars
> among them by this [the aforementioned] mode of education, but
> they will have, what is of much greater value, well-informed,
> practical, prudent men, who will be qualified to discharge the
> various duties of life with propriety and fidelity, and thus contribute
> their quota to the sum of human happiness, which is the great end
> of our existence.[12]

It is true, observed Charles Lane, one of the transcendentalists at Fruitlands, that there was little provision for literature, the fine arts, or intellect in the Shaker scheme of things. "Yet the truth must be affirmed that. . .they seem to be far on the road, if they have not already attained the solution of a chaste, scientific and self-sustained life. . . ."[13]

In a letter about a year later, Lane labeled as "perfectly ridiculous" the idea that the unity of the society was due to "lack of personal or mental attractions. . . . Both men and women are superior to the average of society in these respects as well as in purity."[14] When the Con-sociate family at Fruitlands broke up, Lane and his son joined the Shakers.

In a thoughtful work entitled *Old World Questions and New World Answers,* Daniel Pidgeon deplored, some forty years later, the passing of such institutions as the Slavic *mir*, the Swiss *allmend*, the English common, and the Shaker village, where "everyone had access to the soil, when fellowship lightened the labours of the field, and the commonwealth shared equally in the common store." The Shakers, he wrote, were rebels, but they "rebelled against society with churches and ploughs instead of fire and sword."[15]

To judge fairly the progress and success attained by the Shakers in their "temporalities," one should compare their condition with that obtaining among *contemporary* mechanics and agriculturists in the world. From this point of view, most observers, like Courtauld, passed judgments highly favorable to the order. Thus, Edward Everett, in 1823, reported, "The lands about this settlement [New Lebanon] he will find to be more neatly cultivated, than the majority of American farms."[16]

In the notes left by A. J. MacDonald, the wandering student of American socialism, who visited Watervliet in 1843, is the following observation:

> We see from 400 to 600 Men and Women living together in a
> community, with better physical circumstances surrounding them,
> and more wealth to each Individual (if divided) than any other 400
> Men and Women who have to work from ten to twelve hours per

day, in the outer World. We see such arrangements practically
carried out every day, as provide each Member of the Community,
with an abundance of all the necessities of life, and these
necessaries superior in quality to what is obtained by the great mass
of people who work for their living in old Society.

John Finch, the English economist, in 1844 found many useful lessons
in the Shaker society and other American communities, among them the
attention given to cleanliness and order. Neither man nor beast, he wrote,
is "permitted to live in wretched, filthy huts, cabins, cottages, garrets, and
cellars, such as are at present occupied by the majority of the work-
ing-classes in England, Ireland, and many parts of America."[17]

195

Commenting on such virtues as variety of employment, relief from "earking cares," and dread of misfortune in old age, Charles Nordhoff went on to say,

> If I compare the life in a contented and prosperous, that is to say
> a successful commune, with the life of an ordinary farmer or
> mechanic even in our prosperous country, and more especially with
> the lives of working-men and their families in our great cities, I
> must confess that the communist life is so much freer from care
> and risk, so much easier, so much better in many ways, and in all
> material aspects, that I sincerely wish it might have a farther
> development in the United States.[18]

"It is certain that the outside world has much to learn from these pure simple people," Professor Richard Ely of Johns Hopkins wrote. "I suppose they must be compared with people in the ordinary walks of life; for example with the average farmer's family, and they shine by comparison."[19]

It was Ely who illustrated the effect of communal principle on character by relating that he was taught at Mount Lebanon how "to shut the door so as not to give the slightest disturbance to anyone."[20]

The environment in which the labors of the brethren and sisters were pursued had, one is certain, its beneficent effects on the temper of the Shaker mind and the quality of their work. Visitors were unfailingly moved by the peaceful tenor of industry, the absence of stress and strain, the atmosphere of harmony and quietude. We close the present chapter with a few typical impressions of the setting in which the work of the Believers was carried on, from day to day, and year to year.

In his speech before the Senate of Kentucky in 1831, Robert Wickliffe gives this sketch of Pleasant Hill:

> In agriculture they excel every other portion of your State; and in
> architecture and *neatness,* are exceeded by no people upon the
> earth. Sir, your towns and villages bear testimony everywhere of
> their skill in the mechanic and manufacturing arts. The whole
> society live in unexampled neatness, if not elegance—not a pauper
> among them—all alike independent, and as happy as that
> independence and innocence can make them. . . . Who has visited
> one of the Shaker villages, that has not experienced emotions of
> delight at the peaceful, harmonious, but industrious movements of
> the villagers? Who can look upon the splendid edifices, the green
> pastures, and golden fields, the producc of their industry and
> art—who can look upon their flocks of fat cattle and extensive
> herds, and not admit that the blessing of a kind Providence rewards
> their innocent labors? . . . Let a stranger visit your country, and
> enquire at Danville, Harrodsburgh or Lexington, for your best

specimens of agriculture, mechanics and architecture, and sir, he
is directed to visit the society of Shakers at Pleasant Hill.[21]

"Nothing has been seen," Miss Martineau wrote, "equal to the perfection
of the Shaker and Rappite arrangements in their fields, vineyards, gardens,
and homes. . . ."

They have the best crops, the best wines, the best provision for the table, the best medicines, furniture, house-linen, roads, fences, and habitations in the country, with an enormously increasing amount of wealth, and very moderate labour....

The road through the settlement had not a stone bigger than a walnut upon it. Not a weed was to be seen in any garden, nor a dunghill in all the place. The collars of the men, and the caps of the women were white as snow. The windows were so clear that they seemed to have no glass in them. The frame-dwellings, painted straw-colour, and roofed with deep-red shingles, were finished with the last degree of nicety, even to the springs of the windows and the hinges of the doors. The floors were as even and almost as white as marble. The long table, at which we had our meal, was covered with delicious bread, some wheaten, some of Indian corn, and some made with molasses; there was cheese, butter, spring-water, and excellent currant wine. We really thought we could have gone on eating such bread and butter all day.[22]

Others besides Miss Martineau commented on the good Shaker fences. Warder, for instance, was curious as to how the Believers managed with their neighbors regarding fences. He was told, "Without much difficulty—for we make ours good, and they generally follow the example; if they do not quite [do] their part, we do a little more than ours, and in time they come tolerably near to what they ought to be: sometimes we shame into compliance even at the outset:—in short, we do not find much trouble when we endeavor to avoid it."[23]

Each Shaker community, Finch reported in 1844,

is a handsome, well-built town, with wide streets, laid out regularly at right angles; the houses, factories, workshops, agricultural buildings, and public buildings, all large and well-built—the whole surrounded with beautiful and well-cultivated kitchen and flower gardens, vineyards, orchards, and farms, the very best that are to be seen in the United States; their horses, their milking-cows, their sheep, and their swine, of which they have large numbers, are some of the best bred and the best fed I ever saw; their long ranges of stacks of grain, well-filled barns, and well-filled stores, prove that they have neither want nor the fear of it. The neatness, cleanliness, and order you everywhere observe in their persons and their premises, and the cheerfulness and contented looks of the people, afford the reflective mind continual pleasure; here none are overworked, and none ever want a day's labour; none live in luxury, and no man, woman or child lacks anything. Here machinery of every kind is always among their greatest blessings; it lessens their toilsome labour, and multiplies their enjoyments....[24]

The day's labor had its regular routine, which was described by Mac-Donald in his manuscript, "Narrative of Four month's residence among the Shakers at Watervliet."

the hours for rising were 5 o'clock in the Summer, and half past 5 in the Winter [a half hour earlier in some communities]—the Family all rise at the Toll of the Bell, and in less than ten minutes, vacated the Bed Rooms;—the Sisters, then distributed themselves throughout the Rooms, and made up all the Beds, putting every thing in the most perfect order, before Breakfast;—the Brothers proceeded to their various employments, and made a commencement for the day; the Cows were milked, and the Horses were fed. At 7 o'clock the Bell rang for Breakfast, but it was ten minutes after, when we went to the Tables. . . .

After Breakfast, all proceeded immediately to their respective employments, and continued industriously occupied until ten minutes to twelve o'clock, when the Bell announced dinner. Farmers then left the field, and Mechanics their Shops, all washed their hands, and formed procession again, and marched to

199

Dinner.... Immediately after Dinner, they went to work again ...
and continued steady at it until the Bell announced Supper.... At
eight o'clock all work was ended for the day, and the Family went
to what they called a Union Meeting, this meeting generally
continued one hour, and then about nine o'clock all retired to bed.[25]

In contrast with the "wrack and riot" of New York, what struck the
senses first at New Lebanon was its order, temperance, frugality, tranquility,
worship, the kind of rhythm with which life moved. "No jerk, no strain,
no menace is observed; for in a Shaker settlement nothing is done, nothing
can be done by force." Such was Dixon's impression: "The people are like
their village; soft in speech, demure in bearing, gentle in face; a people
seeming to be at peace, not only with themselves, but with Nature and
with Heaven."[26]

The same note was struck by Charles Nordhoff, who visited Mount
Lebanon in the 1870s:

If you are permitted to examine the shops and the dwelling of the
family, you will note that the most scrupulous cleanliness is
everywhere practised; if there is a stove in the room, a small broom
and dust pan hang near it, and a wood-box stands by it; scrapers
and mats at the door invite you to make clean your shoes; and if
the roads are muddy or snowy, a broom hung up outside the outer
door mutely requests you to brush off all the mud and snow. The
strips of carpet are easily lifted, and the floor beneath is as clean
as though it were a table to be eaten from. The walls are bare of
pictures; not only because ornament is wrong, but because frames
are places where dust will lodge. The bedstead is a cot that is easily
moved away to allow of dusting and sweeping. Mats meet you at
the outer door and at every inner door. The floors of the halls and
the dining-room are polished until they shine.[27]

The domestic economy of the society was an integral part of its economy
as a whole. Since it was a Shaker precept that "order is heaven's first law,"
it was the accepted responsibility of the sisterhood to keep the household
clean and orderly and prepare and serve meals on time. In addition to
these basic duties (performed in rotation), each sister was assigned to a
brother to take care of his clothing, look after his washing, and exercise
a general sisterly oversight of his temporal needs. Although the gospel of
Christ's Second Appearing strictly forbade what the *Millennial Laws* called
"all private union" between the two sexes, in practice there was cooperation
in every department, a devotion to mutual well-being, and an abiding sense
of *spiritual* union.

The spirit of cooperation, ably organized by the leaders of the sect's
temporal affairs, arose out of the consciousness of a divine and consecrated

fellowship of interests. No motivation could exceed this one of religious devotion to task. The Shaker brethren and sisters were ever aware that theirs was a high calling, and that they labored for the greatest Employer of all. With such meaning attached to their work, wages and hours were insignificant, the honor of the vocation everything. Those whose sincerity was found wanting in such a test of true service soon tired of the rigorous regime and left to pursue their own aims in their own ways. The Believers, as practical idealists, carried on with zeal and, for a surprisingly long time, made a Utopian commonwealth of peace, equality, and prosperity a reality.

# V Diminishing Returns

As an economic enterprise, Shaker communitarianism seemed at the height of the movement in the 1840s and 1850s, to be eminently successful. "The fact stares us in the face," Horace Greeley remarked in 1853, "that while hundreds of banks and factories, and thousands of mercantile concerns, managed by shrewd, strong men, have gone into bankruptcy and perished, Shaker communities, established more than sixty years ago, upon a basis of little property and less worldly wisdom, are living and prosperous today."[1] J. S. Buckingham and other commentators had also concluded, in the same period, that the United Society would endure and increase, in prosperity as in good works. As a matter of fact (if one excepts the Mormon Church, founded much later), it did last longer than any other religious communitarian order in the United States. What were the reasons for this unparalled success? And why, if so successful, did the movement start to decline in mid-century, facing today, with just eleven living Shakers, imminent extinction?

The questions admit of no simple answer. John Humphrey Noyes was convinced that the bond of the Shakers' union was their religion. He and William Alfred Hinds, another student of American communities, agreed that the celibate principle, in particular, was the force that held them successfully together. There was no loophole for private or separate family interest, no occasion for disputes over property. Union was reinforced by frequent meetings, the singing and union meetings during the week, and the services on the Sabbath. "American experience," Noyes held, "certainly leads to the conclusion that religious men can hold together longer and accomplish more in close Association, than men without religion." The successful communities—Ephrata, the Rappites, the Zoarites, the Amana community, the Shakers—all had a deep religious basis. Their exclusion of marriage was proof, Noyes thought, that "there is some rational connection between their control of the sexual relation and their prosperity."[2]

Finch disagreed. Their religious opinions and practices, he asserted,

> instead of being their binding principles, and the cause of their success, have continually produced internal and external discussion and repulsion [and have] been the principal means of prejudicing the minds and blinding the eyes of the American people to the excellence and beauties of the Community System, and of preventing its more universal adoption in practice.[3]

The real binding principles, he thought, were "their obedience to their leaders, their great order, complete organization, and the many temporal comforts they enjoy."[4]

The same opinion was held by Harriet Martineau, who, deploring their "moral arrangements," wished

204        that the Shakers could admit the pursuit of knowledge in other

departments besides agriculture, horticulture, and domestic economy. The world might derive a valuable lesson from witnessing what might be done in science, literature, and art by a body so relieved from worldly cares, so possessed, through their principle of community of property, with wealth and leisure.[5]

There were those, however, who disputed such views. Greeley himself wrote, "Religion often makes practicable that which were else impossible, and divine love triumphs where human science is baffled." Baker argued that religion, the desire "to subordinate the lower self to all that is truest and best within us," was the one "constraining bond" in the Shaker society, and the very basis of that union, cooperation, and order, to which Finch "ascribes so much efficacy." And the Shakers themselves, pointing to the failures of the many experiments—Owenite, Fourieristic, and transcendental—which opposed religion or the celibate principle, contended that these were the primary causes for the duration of their faith. The private family relation, they freely admitted, "is necessary and must always exist—the seed garden of the human race—but they also recognize[d] that higher nature which makes communistic association as great a necessity—the harvest field of the race."[6]

In his objective survey of American communities, Nordhoff took a middle position. To be successful, he thought, the persons forming a community should be of one mind on some question of importance to them—not necessarily religion. Nor did they have to be fanatics. Also important, he felt, was "a feeling of the unbearableness of the circumstances in which they find themselves." Dissatisfied with their lot, many were drawn into these orders by the promise of a better life. Here was temporal comfort, health, order, independence, security—"the decency and dignity [of] humble life." Here all, regardless of sex or race, were equal. Here was sufficiency if not abundance. Although everyone worked, no one was overworked. The fact that societies such as the Shakers had abolished the middleman, bought wholesale, paid no wages, and commanded a reputation in the world's markets guaranteed, Nordhoff believed, progress and economic success. All were producers, capitalists and laborers alike. He was particularly struck by the Shaker skill "in contriving new trades."[7]

One important, perhaps paramount factor in the strength of the Shaker movement has been underrated, namely the impetus given it, at several periods in its history, by the forces of millennialism or evangelical revivalism. If it had not been for the New Light Baptist revivals in New York and New England, it is doubtful that the first "witnesses" would ever have found their long-sought "opening." The Baptists, as well as the Quakers and other separatists, had already paved the way for the Shaker faith by their principles of avoiding all unnecessary intercourse with the world and of modeling their institution on the apostolic Christian church. Although the Shakers went further by identifying sexual relations as the basic sin, it remained true that all the "radical" sects were deeply concerned with freedom from sin, purity and perfection, and personal salvation. The testimonies of the early converts to Shakerism provide convincing evidence of their disillusionment with the established churches and their hope of regenerating their lives through acceptance of Ann Lee's millennial gospel.[8]

The Shaker communities in Ohio, Kentucky, and Indiana were also the direct result of revivalism, the so-called Kentucky Revival. In this case, the missionaries could support the contention that theirs was the only true Church of Christ by citing the achievement of the eastern societies. It had

*The Shaker educational system stressed character training and the more useful subjects. Practical training in farming and trades under caretakers and a quasi-guild system was considered of primary importance.*

already been demonstrated, they said, that a way of life free from sin and worldliness could be established on a foundation of consecrated labor and property. Shakerism could offer the prospective adherent a dual lure: temporal security and eternal salvation.

Several times later the spirit of revivalism injected new life into the movement. One such "awakening" occurred in 1827, followed a decade later by the "Era of Manifestations," "Mother Ann's Work," or "Mother Ann's Second Appearing." Accompanied by visions, revelations, prophecies, and a diversity of "gifts," this was a forerunner, and probably a generator, of modern spiritualism, and had it "retained its religious affiliations, it might also have furnished a fertile soil for missionary activity."[9] More beneficial was the collapse of Millerism in the 1840s, when hundreds shifted their allegiance to the older millennial faith. As the Believers, later in the century, became increasingly conscious of the decline in membership, they often voiced the hope that another great revival would replenish their numbers.

The reasons for the decline of the United Society are as complex and accumulative as the reasons for its success. The one most often cited is the doctrine of celibacy, which prevented any renewal of numbers from within. But the Shakers themselves argued that instead of being a deterrent, that principle was a determining factor in the durability of the order, freeing it from the divisive forces of familism and property disputes; it did not affect, for over half a century, the steady growth of the society.

Before the middle of the nineteenth century, there was evidence, however, that the doctrine was a handicap. The religious or revivalist temper of the earlier period was giving way to the forces of secularism. With the passage of time and the passing of the "old Believers" who had known Ann Lee and the other founders, the afflatus attendant on the opening of the gospel could not be sustained. Inquiries never ceased, conversions continued, but fewer were willing, for salvation's sake, to bear the Shaker cross (i.e., the celibate life) and subject themselves to the disciplines of the order.

"Neglect of marriage" was, for many people, the great defect of Shakerism. In a letter to his Shaker friend, Robert White, Jr., the Reverend Theodore Parker expressed the commonly accepted view that

> God created men and women and left the perpetuation of the race
> to the union of the two—doubtless intending that the marriage of
> one man with one woman should continue as long as the race
> should endure. It seems to me also that some of the best qualities
> of human nature are developed by the connexion. . . . If they [the
> Shakers] could still preserve a family tie and then have all the other
> good things it would have all that the Associationists are contending
> for. . . .[10]

On the speculative level, people also wondered, "What would become of the world if all became Shakers?"—a question so often asked that the society published, in 1868, and reprinted several times a pamphlet explaining its position on the doctrine of "virgin purity."

The Shakers could defend, if not successfully propagate, that doctrine. But they had no control over those forces, increasingly operative after the Civil War, which lured members away and discouraged accessions: the abundant economic opportunities afforded by the Industrial Revolution, the drift to urban centers, the opening of the West. America looked to the future. Even though the United Society relaxed to some extent its disciplines, allowing some amusements and the pleasures of music, flower gardens, and reading, etc., it seemed to look in the main to the past.

Numbers were maintained for some time by the adoption of orphans, children from destitute homes, and children who were indentured and sometimes accompanied by one or both parents. But the society found that it could not continually rely on even this source of renewal. With the establishment of orphanages and good schools, the improvement in the conditions of the working class, and the wide-spread opportunities for employment, the class from which the society formerly drew recruits was becoming increasingly restricted. The problem was compounded by the inability of the society, with its decreasing membership, to care for and educate young people, some of whom proved to be undesirables and most of whom left when they were just becoming productive assets to the economy.

Employment of hired labor, necessitated by the lessening number of males needed to work the large farms, was one harbinger of the decay of Shakerism, spiritual as well as temporal. It was a breach in the line of separation, held so long, between the society and the world. Though it also involved substantial expenditures, a drain on financial resources, the Shakers were loath to sell their lands or let them lie fallow. They regretted the necessity of employing outside labor, of letting the world in, but there seemed to be no alternative. They still believed, in the post-Civil War period, that the society would last indefinitely and that the United Inheritance entrusted to their keeping should be held for the use of those to come. As Howells once noted, "None of us can bear to think of leaving the fruits of our long endeavor to chance and the stranger."[11]

According to Nordhoff, these lands—not counting the out-farms, wood lots, sheep walks, and other holdings in "distant states"—amounted in 1875 to about 50,000 acres, and the total number of hired laborers to about 370. Hinds thought that their "aggregate landed estate" might reach 100,000 acres. The most profitable crop was timber.

The economy suffered in other ways. Severe losses by fire, many of them incendiary, were the Shakers' fate from the beginning. There were cases of defalcations by trustees unwisely chosen, and other cases where the naiveté of trustees was exploited by unscrupulous outside interests. Although grievous, these were temporary set-backs. More injurious to the economy was the loss of markets. The Shakers—with their economy based on the family unit—could not compete, in their seed and medicinal herb business and other enterprises, with factory production and cheaper prices.[12] Quality was submerged by quantity, creativity by commercialism. They were not equipped, in short, "to combat the force of secularization and the growing importance of a pervasive economic and social interdependence," of existing in a society but not of it.[13] As the present century advanced, Shaker industry in the few surviving communities was reduced to shops selling fancy work, postcards, confections, and in one store, chairs. In the end, the sale and rental of real estate provided the main source of revenue.

In 1824, after a visit to two societies in Massachusetts and Connecticut, an English traveler, Isaac Candler, observed that the Shakers were bound to become wealthy. For "when property more than sufficient for its object is possessed by those who have no intellectual pursuit, the danger of its abuse is increased." To Candler, the Shaker system appeared "like some complex piece of mechanism, beautiful and regular, but liable to be put out of order if any of the concealed springs lose their elasticity."[14]

Many years before, John Wesley, the founder of Methodism, had posed a similar question:

> I do not see how it is possible, in the nature of things, for any
> revival of true religion to continue long. For religion must
> necessarily produce industry and frugality, and these cannot but
> produce riches. But as riches increase, so will . . . love of the world
> in all its branches.[15]

The "riches" of the United Society at various stages in its history are not recorded. Nordhoff estimated its "wealth" in 1875 at twelve million dollars, but Hinds believed that figure far too high, and that with the declining value of its landholdings, losses by fire, and other causes, it was not as well off as commonly supposed. That the Shakers became *prosperous*, in terms of property ownership, cannot, however, be gainsaid. The questions then arise: was there the abuse of property which Candler prophesied and which Wesley felt was inevitable? Did they acquire more property than was "sufficient for its object"? Did they tend to become worldly minded, "resting on a mere profession," as they once accused Quakers of becoming?

Any answer must be qualified. We have seen, in the reports submitted to the New York legislature in mid-century, that the surplus of income over expenditure was then small, that income was legitimately used for expansion and improvement, and notably for charitable purposes. The record of Shaker benevolences is a long and honorable one.

The society has been criticized, nevertheless, for its "concern for material gain." "Business occupies too large a place in their minds," Madame Blanc thought; "They lack the divine flight of disinterestedness, the poetic love of voluntary poverty." But the French woman, it should be noted, was comparing the Shakers with the Catholic monks and nuns, who—in Dunlavy's words—were "an excepted and dependent branch of the body supported mainly by the gratuities and other contributions of the Church." The Shakers, on the other hand, had to support themselves by their own industry. Whatever shrewdness, acquisitiveness, and suspicion of the business world they were reputed to have could be explained by their status as a separatist order, one that was misunderstood, often persecuted, and totally dependent on its own efforts for survival.

Being human, they had their faults. There were jealousies between and within families and communities, examples of false pride and weak leadership—especially noticeable as groups became smaller and less isolated from the world. Less and less did religion and ritual serve as a cohesive force. More and more did they accede to the ways of the world. Although they might argue that saints as well as sinners should be possessed of the good things of this world, it remains true that in the end the traditional "gift to be simple" was to an extent abandoned for other values.

# Notes

## I. Hearts to God

1. General W. W. H. Davis, *History of Bucks(?) County, Pennsylvania*. The date 1773 is incorrect. It was probably a year later.
2. Shaker records make no mention of Mother Ann's presence in the Philadelphia area, either before the settlement in Niskeyuna or during the missions she later undertook. However, in *Travels in North-America*, by the Marquis de Chastellux, the translator wrote in a footnote: "General Gates told me he heard her preach at Rhode Island, and I made an attempt to hear her at Philadelphia in October, 1782, but the crowd was so great, and, what is very uncommon in America, so turbulent, that it was impossible to get near the place of worship. Two of her apostles came to the house I boarded in, to obtain lodgings for her, and some of the brethren; by which means I had an opportunity of seeing a specimen of them but they would enter into no conversation; they were tall, handsome men, the youngest not above nineteen, with large round flapped hats, and long flowing strait locks, with a sort of melancholy wildness in their countenances, and an effeminate, dejected air. ... " Marquis de Chastellux, *Travels in North-America, in the years 1780, 1781 and 1782*, Vol. 1. London, 1787, pp. 288-289.
3. Vernon Louis Parrington, *Main Currents in American Thought*, New York, 1930, p. 161.
4. Rev. I. D. Stewart, *The History of the Freewill Baptists ... Dover* [N.H.] 1862, Vol. 1, pp. 110-111.
5. William Plumer, "The Original Shaker Communities in New England," *The New England Magazine* (May 1900), Boston, pp. 306-308.
6. Rufus Bishop and Seth Y. Wells, *Testimonies of the Life, Character, Revelations and Doctrines of Our Ever Blessed Mother Ann Lee, and the Elders with Her; through whom the word of eternal life was opened in this day of Christ's second appearing: collected from living witnesses*, second edition, Albany, 1888, p. 207.
7. *Ibid.*, p. 233.
8. *Ibid.*, p. 214.
9. Isaac N. Youngs, *A Concise View of the Church of God and of Christ On Earth, Having its Foundation In the Faith of Christ's First and Second Appearing.* (MS.), New Lebanon, 1856.
10. "Another article of their faith is one I did not expect to find among the advocates of celibacy, namely: That all human action is imperfect that is not the result of the combined efforts of what they consider the two halves of humanity—man and woman" (Marianne Finch, *Englishwoman's Experience in America*, 1853, p. 126).
11. See also Gibert Seldes, *The Stammering Century*, New York, 1928.
12. In 1850, Meacham's way-marks, written between 1791 and 1796, were collected by Elder Rufus Bishop but never published.
13. Richard McNemar, *The Kentucky Revival*, Pittsfield, Mass., 1808, p. 91.
14. *Ibid.*, p. 101.
15. America has always been a proving ground of Utopias, "projects of people who insisted that in the greater world, the world of governments and power politics, secularism, materialism, and competition, there was too great a gap between the rich and the poor, the talented and the talentless, the seemingly wise and the seemingly foolish, and that man, somehow, had failed His purpose.... Most of these [experiments] were Christian, arguing for the fact that the Christian church itself was a utopian attempt" (Marcus Bach, *Strange Sects and Curious Cults*, New York, 1961, pp. 179-180).

## II. Hands to Work

1. Andrews Manuscript No. 1. *Millennial Laws, or Gospel Statutes and Ordinances....*
2. William Bentley, *The Diary of William Bentley, D.D. ...*, Vol. 2. The Essex Institute, Salem, Mass., 1905-1914, pp. 149-155.
3. Richard T. Ely, *The Labor Movement in America*, New York, 1969, p. 11. Reprint of 1890 edition.
4. Authors' correspondence with William B. Bennett, Adams, Mass., May 13, 1931. Three sons of William Bennett, Sr. (1723-1788), played conspicuous parts in the development of the parent society. Joseph, Jr., was the first deacon before the appointment of David Meacham.

Henry was the co-inventor of a "matching boards" (tongue-and-groove) machine. Nicholas was one of three carpenters or joiners—Amos Bishop and Anthony Brewster were the others—who in 1821 drew up the plans for the famous barrel-roofed meetinghouse at New Lebanon (built 1822-24).

5. Bentley, *Diary*, pp. 149-155.
6. Letter written from West Roxbury, Mass., July 31, 1848.
7. *The Gardener's Journal of Various Things* . . . . Entry of July 24, 1843. New Lebanon.

## THE CULTURE OF THE LAND

1. James F. W. Johnston, *Notes on North America. Agricultural, Economical and Social*, Vol. 2. Edinburgh and London, 1851, p. 264. Johnston's visit was to Watervliet.
2. William Hepworth Dixon, *New America*, third edition, Philadelphia, 1867, pp. 301-302.
3. The Shakers at Pleasant Hill, Kentucky, were among the first in the West to develop the so-called Leicester or Bakewell sheep. This was in the middle 1830s.
4. Horace Greeley, in *Hints Towards Reform*. Quoted by F. W. Evans in *Shaker Communism*, London, 1871, p. 118.
5. John Finch. Quoted in Arthur Baker, *Shakers and Shakerism*, London, 1896, p. 23. Similarly, in speaking of a western Shaker community, Harriet Martineau wrote: "The land is cultivated to a perfection seen nowhere else in the United States, except at Mr. Rapp's settlement on the Ohio, where Community of Property is also the binding principle of the Society" (quoted in Baker, *Shakers and Shakerism*, p. 18).
6. Dixon, *New America*, pp. 321-322.
7. Hervey Elkins, *Sixteen Years in the Senior Order of Shakers*, Hanover, N.H., 1853, p. 130.
8. Andrews MS. No. 1.
9. Andrews MS. No. 11. Farmer's Journal, 1857-67. (Includes an annual "recapitulation" of sales, stock, events.)
10. Andrews MS. No. 1, p. 77.
11. Russell H. Anderson, "Agriculture Among the Shakers, Chiefly at Mount Lebanon," *Agricultural History*, Vol. 24 (July 1950), p. 120.
12. Dixon, *New America*, p. 303.
13. Morgan Bulkeley, "Shaker Horticulture," *Horticulture*, June 1967, Boston, Mass.
14. Dixon, *New America*, p. 322.
15. D. A. Buckingham, "Epitomic History of the Watervliet Shakers," *The Shaker*, July 1877, pp. 49-50. (A monthly periodical of the society appearing under that title, and later as *Shaker and Shakeress*, *The Shaker Manifesto*, and *The Manifesto*, published at Shakers, N.Y., and Shaker Village, N.H., through December 1899.)
16. Andrews MS. No. 8. Seeds Raised at the Shaker Gardens. New Lebanon Church family, 1795-1884.
17. Andrews MS. No. 9. Price List of Seeds. 1807.
18. Andrews MS. No. 21. Trustee's Account or Day Book, 1831-46. Hancock. See also Anna White and Leila Taylor, *Shakerism: Its Meaning and Message*, Columbus, Ohio, 1905, p. 315.
19. Andrews MS. No. 22. Letter to Brother David [Goodrich] from Brother Morrell. Dated Watervliet, December 26, 1822.
20. Andrews MS. No. 10. A Journal of Garden Accounts Commencing July 27, 1840. New Lebanon Church family.
21. *The Manifesto*, March 1890, p. 50.
22. From an article in the Chatham (N.Y.) *Courier* printed in *The Manifesto*, April 1879, p. 88.
23. Benjamin S. Youngs, *The Testimony of Christ's Second Appearing*. Many cases of miraculous faith cures by Ann Lee and others are cited.
24. White and Taylor, *Shakerism*, p. 315.
25. Andrews MS. No. 3. Trustee's Account or Day Book, 1805-23. New Lebanon Church family.
26. *The American Journal of Pharmacy*, Vol. 18, 1852, p. 89.
27. *The Manifesto*, Vol. 20, p. 195.
28. *American Journal of Pharmacy*, p. 89.
29. Benson J. Lossing, "The Shakers," *Harper's New Monthly Magazine*, July 1857, New York, pp. 173-174.

30. George Niles Hoffman, *Pharmaceutical Era*, 1920, pp. 53, 197.
31. *American Journal of Pharmacy*, p. 90.
32. *Ibid.*, p. 188.
33. Edward D. Andrews, "The New York Shakers and Their Industries," Circular 2, New York State Museum, 1930, p. 6.
34. Sister Marcia Bullard, *Good Housekeeping*, July 1906, p. 37.
35. Andrews MS. No. 16. Journal Kept by the Deaconesses at the [Church] Office. New Lebanon, 1830-1871.
36. Andrews MS. No. 12. Ledger No. 1, 1827. Herb department, New Lebanon Church family.
37. Andrews MS. No. 19. Journal Kept by Elizabeth Lovegrove. Begun in March 1837.

### THE MECHANICAL ARTS

1. Andrews MS. No. 14. Tannery Journal and Account Book, 1835-78. New Lebanon Church family.
2. Andrews MS. No. 5. Trustee's Account or Day Book, 1830-36. New Lebanon Church family.
3. *The Manifesto*, April 1890, pp. 74-75.
4. Andrews MS. No. 15. A Journal of Domestic Events Kept by Benjamin Lyon, 18, Began, Dec. 21st, 1838.
5. Andrews MS. No. 6. Trustee's Account or Day Book, 1835-39. New Lebanon Church family.
6. *The Manifesto*, June 1887, p. 138.
7. Alice Morse Earle, *Home Life in Colonial Days*, New York, 1898, p. 193.
8. *The Manifesto*, September 1890, p. 193.
9. N. A. Buckingham, in *The Shaker*, July 1877, p. 50.
10. *Ibid.*
11. Charles Nordhoff, *The Communistic Societies of the United States*, New York, 1875, p. 149.
12. *The Manifesto*, May 1890, p. 98.
13. *The Manifesto*, September 1890, p. 193.
14. *The Manifesto*, August 1890, p. 170.
15. Andrews MS. No. 3.
16. Andrews MSS. Nos. 3, 5, 7. No. 7: Trustee's Account or Day Book, 1853-57. New Lebanon Church family.
17. Nordhoff, *Communistic Societies*, p. 139.
18. Andrews MS. No. 3.
19. Andrews MS. No. 10, p. 124.
20. *Scientific American*, Vol. 39, No. 21 (November 23, 1878), p. 325.
21. Andrews MS. No. 4.

### THE CLOTHIER SHOPS

1. Andrews MS. No. 3.
2. *The Manifesto*, June 1890, pp. 121-123; July 1890, pp. 145-146.

### OCCUPATIONS OF THE SHAKER SISTERS

1. Andrews MS. No. 20. Seth Y. Wells, Importance of Keeping Correct Book Accounts, 1836. (Copy of original MS.)
2. Andrews MS. No. 17. A Weaver's Memorandum; or An Account of Weaving, etc. Kept by Hannah Treadway, A. D. 1833 & 34.
3. Andrews MS. No. 18. Weaver's Journal. 1835-1865.
4. *The Manifesto*, July 1890, pp. 146-147; August 1890, p. 169.
5. Andrews MS. No. 16.
6. Andrews MS. No. 13. Ledger, 1834-38. Herb department, New Lebanon Church family. (Includes also trustees' accounts at Canaan Lower Family, 1838-1868, and miscellaneous Church records.)
7. Bullard, *Good Housekeeping*, p. 36.
8. The fact that the price of such products as apple sauce, jellies, preserves, catsup, stewed tomatoes, and cheese are computed in the early shilling currency inclines one to the belief that these commodities may have been prepared for market at an early date.
9. Andrews MS. No. 16.
10. Andrews MS. No. 19. The word "buck" is a bleaching term. The flax was cleaned by being

beaten with a stick or bat while it was in the water. Then it was steeped and boiled in lye.

11. Andrews MS. No. 23. A Little Book Containing a Short Word from Holy Mother Wisdom, Concerning the Robes & Dresses. . . . Copied July 20, 1842. . . .

## SHAKER CULTURE AND CRAFTSMANSHIP

1. *The Shaker*, August 1876, p. 58.
2. Nordhoff, *Communistic Societies*, pp. 164-165. See also *The Shaker*, June 1876, p. 46.
3. David Lamson, *Two Years' Experience Among the Shakers*, West Boylston, Maine, 1848, p. 17.
4. Andrews MS. No. 25. Remarks on Learning and the Use of Books. Watervliet, March 10, 1836. Signed by Seth Y. Wells. In his instructions to teachers he adds: "Letter learning is useful in its place, provided a good use be made of it by those who possess it. But there is much useless learning in the world, which only tends to clog the mind and sense, and shut the gifts of God out of the soul." See also Andrews MS. No. 24. Letter to the Elders, Deacons, Brethren, & Sisters of the Society of Watervliet, Watervliet, Jan. 26th 1832. Signed by Seth Y. Wells. Before joining the society, Wells had taught in the Albany public schools and at Hudson Academy. In 1821 he was appointed "General Superintendent of Believers' Literature, Schools, etc. in the first Bishopric, which included Watervliet, Hancock and Mount Lebanon" (White and Taylor, *Shakerism*, pp. 132-133).
5. Anna White, "Instrumental Music," *The Manifesto*, August 1890, pp. 177-178. The earliest worship of the Shakers, however, was attended by chant and song as well as by rhythmic, but often unrestrained dancing. The songs were said to have been inspired. The first songbook, *Millennial Praises*, was printed by Josiah Talcott in Hancock in 1813.
6. The Shakers often referred to their religion as a practical faith, combining "science, religion and inspiration" (*The Manifesto*, March 1886, p. 63). When Charles F. Wingate, editor of the *Sanitary Engineer*, visited New Lebanon in 1880, he was informed by the elders "that their careful attention to hygiene has a theological basis," and that they believed "that science and religion, 'truly so called,' are one and the same."
7. Robert Wickliffe, *The Shakers*. Speech of Robert Wickliffe. In the Senate of Kentucky, January 1831. Frankfort, Kentucky, p. 25.
8. John Hayward, *The New England Gazetteer*, Boston, Mass., 1839.
9. Dixon, *New America*, pp. 304-305.
10. William Dean Howells, *Three Villages*, Boston, Mass., 1884, p. 110.
11. William Alfred Hinds, *American Communities*, Oneida, N.Y., 1878, p. 101.
12. Aurelia C. Mace, *The Aletheia: Spirit of Truth*, Farmington, Maine, 1907, p. 74.
13. "The Trustees were very particular in regard to [all] articles when sent to the market. Everything must be free from blemish while that which was defective must be retained at home or given to the poor" (Abraham Perkins, *One Hundredth Anniversary of the Organization of the Shaker Church*, Enfield, N.H., 1893).

## CRAFTSMANSHIP IN WOOD

1. Price List of Shaker Chairs, Manufactured in the United Society, New Lebanon, Columbia County, N.Y. For the Year 18_ .
2. *The Manifesto*, November 1889, p. 252. The authority is the Canterbury and Enfield (N.H.) ministry. In as much as the Shakers at New Lebanon were not organized until 1786-87, and Shakerism itself in 1776 was isolated in the little group at Niskeyuna, the latter date can hardly be accepted. The craft of course may have been plied in the vicinity, and by one or more persons who later joined the society.
3. Andrews MS. No. 2. Trustee's Account or Day Book, 1789-92. New Lebanon Church family.

## SHAKER INVENTIONS AND IMPROVEMENTS

1. MS. in library of the Shaker Museum, Old Chatham, N.Y.
2. Recorded by Elder Rufus Bishop, May 10, 1850.
3. F. Gerald Ham, *Shakerism in the Old West*, MS., 1962. For information on a number of patents, we are indebted to Dr. Ham, who searched the reports of the Commissioner of Patents for items relating to the Shakers.

4. In his 1860 catalogue, Alexander L. Shaw of New York City advertised both "genuine and imitation Shaker brooms" and "genuine Shaker whisks."
5. Isaac N. Youngs, *A Concise View*, entry of December 17, 1808.
6. *Niles' Weekly Register*, March-September 1821, Baltimore, Maryland, p. 406.
7. MS. in Boston Public Library.
8. White and Taylor, *Shakerism*, p. 312.
9. Journal of Rufus Bishop and Benjamin Youngs, through the states of Ohio and Kentucky, 1834.
10. *Scientific American*, March 10, 1860, New York.
11. Richard Shanor. In *The New York Times*, April 26, 1964.

## III. The Shakers and the Law

1. John C. Fitzpatrick, ed., "The Autobiography of Martin Van Buren." Annual Report of the American Historical Association for the Year 1918, Vol. 2, pp. 153-154. Washington, D.C., 1920. In discussing the Shaker petition, Rufus King, Van Buren's colleague, said that it should be laid on the table, "adding that it should be thrown under the table."
2. Pittsfield (Mass.) *Sun*, May 8, 1823.

### THE CUSTODY OF CHILDREN

1. For a detailed account of the Chapman case, see Nelson M. Blake, "Eunice Against the Shakers." In *New York History*, October 1960, pp. 359-378.
2. *Ibid.*, p. 359. As early as 1812, when "the spirit of persecution" was rampant against the western Shakers, the legislature of Kentucky passed an act that would allow instant divorce to a man and wife if either party joined the Shakers. Commenting later on this act, Robert Wickliffe said that it made membership in the society "a greater crime than simple adultery, drunkenness and total abandonment." Robert Wickliffe, *The Shakers*, pp. 28-29.
3. Domestic relations law, Art. 5, Section 71, Laws of 1818, New York, entitled "Habeas Corpus for Child Detained by Shakers." The law provided that "If it shall appear ... that the husband or wife of the applicant [for writ of habeas corpus] has become attached to the society of Shakers, and detains a child of the marriage among them, and that such child is secreted among them, the court may issue a warrant in aid of such writ of habeas corpus, directed to the Sheriff of the county where the child is suspected to be, commanding such Sheriff, in the day-time, to search the dwelling houses and other buildings of such society ... for such child." (See also The Revised Statutes of the State of New York, Vol. 2. Albany, 1836, pp. 82-83. Also, Laws of 1909, Chapter 19, as amended June 1, 1938.)
4. *A Brief Exposition of the Established Principles, and Regulations of the United Society of Believers called Shakers,* Watervliet, Ohio, 1832, second edition, p. 6.
5. "Special Laws Rule Society of Shakers," *The New York Times*, January 17, 1832.
6. Isaac Youngs, *A Concise View*.
7. For an account of this case, see Viola Woodruff Opdahl, "William Pillow. His Life Among the Shakers." In *The Yorker*, Vol. 15, No. 2 (November-December 1956), Cooperstown, N.Y. See also "Trial of the Shakers for an attempt to restrain the wife and three children of William H. Pillow; an exposure of their deceptions, and her final release, by a writ of habeas corpus." Extracted from *The True Wesleyan*, October 1847. n.p.
8. Remonstrance of the United Society Called Shakers, Against the Passage of a Certain Law. New Lebanon, February 26, 1849.

### THE VALIDITY OF THE COVENANT

1. William Johnson. Reports of cases adjusted in the supreme court of judicature of the state of New York, from January term 1799, to January term 1803 ... New York, 1846.
2. *Investigator, or a Defense of the Order, Government and Economy of the United Society called Shakers, against Sundry Charges and Legislative Proceedings.* Lexington, Ky., 1828. Reprinted, New York, 1846, pp. 49-51.
3. *Investigator*, pp. 40-44.
4. Wickliffe, *The Shakers*.
5. *The Decision of The Court of Appeals [In Kentucky], In a case of much interest to religious*

*communities in general, and to the Shakers in particular. To which is prefixed a brief illustration of the ground of action.* Dayton, Ohio, 1834.

6. *Decision of the Court of Appeals*, p. 55.
7. *Ibid.*, pp. 59-60.
8. *Ibid.*, pp. 61*f.*
9. *Roxalana L. Grosvenor vs. United Society of Believers. Maria F. Grosvenor vs. United Society of Believers.* Suffolk, Mass., March 10-June 23, 1875.
10. United States Circuit Court, Western District of Kentucky. *Mary E. Porter, Trustee for Charity Hilton* [Plaintiff] *vs. United Society of Shakers, and others* [Defendants]. South Union, c. 1909.

## DISTRUST OF SHAKER "WEALTH"

1. Allan Nevins, *American Social History as Recorded by British Travelers.*
2. J. S. Buckingham, *America, Historical, Statistic, and Descriptive*, Vol. 2, New York, 1841, p. 75.
3. Johnston, *Notes on North America*, p. 266. "It was asserted that they [the Shakers] were increasing, prospering, and buying land so fast, that they were forming a dangerous monopoly of the lands of the State."
4. "It was found," Youngs wrote in *Concise View*, "that apostates had taken advantage of this supposed deficiency in our Trust deeds, and congratulated each other on the present good opportunity to seize upon the joint property, and thus dissolve the society." (See also Revised Statutes, Vol. 2, Albany, 1836, pp. 82-83.
5. John Bigelow, *The Life of Samuel J. Tilden*, Vol. 1, New York, 1895, p. 79.
6. John Bigelow, ed., *The Writings and Speeches of Samuel J. Tilden*, Vol. 1, New York, 1885, pp. 89-100.
7. William J. Haskett, *Shakerism Unmasked*, Pittsfield, Mass., 1828.
8. State of New York, No. 198. In Assembly, April 2, 1849.
9. Shaker Income Tax. Application to Commissioner Delano. Brief of Durbin Ward, Counsel for Applicants. Albany, N.Y., 1869.

## LANDHOLDING

1. Baker, *Shakers and Shakerism*, p. 25.
2. Edward Everett, "The Shakers," *North American Review*, Vol. 16, January 1823, p. 95. Everett quoted Adam Smith: "Whenever there is money's worth, there will soon be money." "In like manner," Everett observed, "whenever there are man's food and clothing, there will be man."
3. Nordhoff, *Communistic Societies*, pp. 162-163.
4. *Ibid.*, p. 161.
5. Frederick W. Evans, *Shaker Land Limitation Laws*, Mt. Lebanon, N.Y., n.d. (1886?). In another treatise, the legal limit was increased to 160 acres, and the surplus to be sold within one year after the death of the owner.
6. *Ibid.*

## IV. The World's Appraisal

1. *A Brief Sketch of the Religious Society of People called Shakers.* [Communicated to Mr. Owen by Mr. W. S. Warder of Philadelphia, one of the Society of Friends.] London, 1818, Foreword.
2. *The Economist*, No. 19, June 2, 1821, London, p. 294.
3. Harriet Martineau, *Society in America*, Vol. 2, London, 1837, p. 55.
4. *Ibid.*, p. 59.
5. George Jacob Holyoake, *The History of Co-operation in England: Its Literature and Advocates*, Vol. 2, London, 1879, p. 293.
6. Th. Bentzon (Mme Thérèse Blanc), *Things and People in America*, Paris, 1898, pp. 67-68, 104-105.
7. *The Economist*, p. 291.
8. *Ibid.*
9. *Ibid.*, p. 293.

10. *Ibid.*
11. *Ibid.*, p. 296.
12. [Barnabus Bates] (Erroneously attributed to Professor Benjamin Silliman of Yale College), *Peculiarities of the Shakers, described in a series of letters from Lebanon Springs in the year 1832, containing an account of the origin, worship and doctrines of the Shaker's society. By a visitor*, New York, 1832.
13. C. L. [Charles Lane], "A Day with the Shakers," *The Dial*, Vol. 4, No. 2 (October 1843), pp. 171-172.
14. Letter, dated January 1844, to William Oldham, Pater at the Concordium, Ham, England. (Published in *The New Age.*)
15. Daniel Pidgeon, *Old World Questions and New World Answers*, pp. 129, 131.
16. Wickliffe, *The Shakers*, p. 25.
17. John Finch, *The New Moral World: and Gazette of the Rational Society*, Vol. 5, No. 40 (March 30, 1844).
18. Nordhoff, *Communistic Societies*, p. 163.
19. Richard Ely, *Labor Movement in America.* Ely was not the only one to refute the common charge that community life did not foster intellectual life and independent thinking. Referring to Frederick Evans and Daniel Fraser of New Lebanon, it has been observed that certainly in their case, "plain living and high thinking go together, and that in extent of reading, in mental vigor, in ready use of logic and in sincerity of utterance they are at least the equals of any two men of my acquaintance in the world" (*Among the Shakers.* Broadside, n.d.).
20. Baker, *Shakers and Shakerism*, p. 17.
21. Wickliffe, *The Shakers*, pp. 25-26.
22. Quoted by Baker, *Shakers and Shakerism*, pp. 18-19.
23. Quoted in *The Economist*, p. 290.
24. Finch, *New Moral World*, Vol. 5, No. 32 (February 3, 1844).
25. MacDonald MS. Yale University library.
26. Dixon, *New America*, p. 305.
27. Nordhoff, *Communistic Societies*, pp. 136-137.

## V. Diminishing Returns

1. Horace Greeley, *Hints Towards Reform*, second edition, Boston, Mass., 1853.
2. John Humphrey Noyes, *History of American Socialisms*, Philadelphia, 1870, pp. 139 *f.*
3. Finch, *New Moral World*, Vol. 5, No. 41 (April 6, 1844).
4. *Ibid.*, Vol. 5, No. 33 (February 10, 1844).
5. "The Shakers," *The Penny Magazine of the Society of Useful Knowledge*, November 18, 1837, p. 447.
6. M. Catherine Allen, *A Full Century of Communism*, Pittsfield, Mass., 1897, p. 5.
7. Nordhoff, *Communistic Societies*, pp. 385*f.*
8. *Testimonies concerning the character and ministry of Mother Ann Lee ... given by some of the aged brethren and sisters of the United Society, including a few sketches of their own religious experience*, Albany, 1827.
9. Stow Persons, *Socialism and American Life*, Vol. 1, Princeton, N.J., 1952, pp. 138-139. "But spiritualism," Persons noted, "turned in the direction of free love, anarchism, and materialism, which left the Shakers no points of contact."
10. Letter from West Roxbury, July 31, 1848.
11. William Dean Howells, "A Shaker Village," *The Atlantic Monthly*, June 1876, p. 707.
12. The Shakers came to realize that instead of each family composing a society "maintaining separate temporal interests ... much larger benefits might have accrued had they organized ... in large societies, having central industries and interests" (M. Catherine Allen, *Full Century of Communism*, p. 10).
13. Wilbert E. Moore, "Sociological Aspects of American Socialistic Theory and Practice." In Persons, *Socialism and American Life*, p. 547.
14. Isaac Candler, *A Summary View of America*, London and Edinburgh, 1824, pp. 231-234.
15. Quoted by Max Weber, *The Protestant Ethic and the Spirit of Capitalism*, London, 1952, p. 175.

# Bibliography

## Editor's Note

Many sections of *The Community Industries of the Shakers*, a handbook written by Dr. Andrews in 1933, have been incorporated into the text of *Work and Worship*. The handbook contains invaluable material on the Shaker industries and represents years of painstaking research by Dr. Andrews. Through the inclusion of portions of this handbook in the present work, it is hoped that *Work and Worship* will be the most complete work ever published on the Shakers and their relations with the world.

## Major Books by the Authors

*The Community Industries of the Shakers.* The University of the State of New York, Albany, New York, 1932.

*The Gift to be Simple: Songs, Dances and Rituals of the American Shakers.* J. J. Augustin, New York, 1940. Reprinted by Dover Publications, New York, 1962.

*The People Called Shakers: A Search for the Perfect Society.* Oxford University Press, New York, 1954. Enlarged edition, including bibliographical information on more than 300 text references, Dover Publications, New York, 1963. *The Millennial Laws,* never before printed, is reproduced in its entirety in this highly recommended in-depth history of the Shakers.

*Religion in Wood: A Book of Shaker Furniture.* Indiana University Press, Bloomington, Indiana, 1966.

*Shaker Furniture: The Craftsmanship of an American Communal Sect.* Yale University Press, New Haven, Connecticut, 1937. Reprinted by Dover Publications, New York, 1950.

*The Shaker Order of Christmas.* Oxford University Press, New York, 1954.

*Visions of the Heavenly Sphere: A Study in Shaker Religious Art.* Published for The Henry Francis du Pont Winterthur Museum by The University Press of Virginia, Charlottesville, Virginia, 1969.

## Manuscripts

Andrews MS. No. 1. Millennial Laws, or Gospel Statutes and Ordinances; Adapted to the Day of Christ's Second Appearing. Given and established in the Church for the protection thereof by Father Joseph Meacham and Mother Lucy Wright, the presiding Ministry, and by their successors the Ministry & Elders. Recorded at New Lebanon, Aug. 7, 1821. Revised and Re-established by the Ministry and Elders, Oct. 1845. (Undoubtedly this code of regulations is the most important unpublished record in the history of the sect.)

Andrews MS. No. 2. Trustee's Account or Day Book, 1789-92. New Lebanon Church family.

Andrews MS. No. 3. Trustee's Account or Day Book, 1805-23. New Lebanon Church family.

Andrews MS. No. 4. Trustee's Account or Day Book, 1817-35. New Lebanon Church family.

Andrews MS. No. 5. Trustee's Account or Day Book, 1830-36. New Lebanon Church family.

Andrews MS. No. 6. Trustee's Account or Day Book, 1835-39. New Lebanon Church family.

Andrews MS. No. 7. Trustee's Account or Day Book, 1853-57. New Lebanon Church family.

Andrews MS. No. 8. Seeds Raised at the Shaker Gardens. New Lebanon Church family, 1795-1884.

Andrews MS. No. 9. Price List of Seeds. 1807.

Andrews MS. No. 10. A Journal of Garden Accounts Commencing July 27, 1840. New Lebanon Church family.

Andrews MS. No. 11. Farmer's Journal, 1857-67. (Includes an annual "recapitulation" of sales, stock, events.)

Andrews MS. No. 12. Ledger No. 1, 1827. Herb department, New Lebanon Church family.

Andrews MS. No. 13. Ledger, 1834-38. Herb department, New Lebanon Church family. (Includes also trustees' accounts at Canaan Lower Family, 1838-1868, and miscellaneous Church records.)

Andrews MS. No. 14. Tannery Journal and Account Book, 1835-78. New Lebanon Church family.

Andrews MS. No. 15. A Journal of Domestic Events Kept by Benjamin Lyon, 18, Began, Dec. 21st, 1838. 1838-1878.

Andrews MS. No. 16. Journal Kept by the Deaconesses at the [Church] Office. New Lebanon, 1830-1871.

Andrews MS. No. 17. A Weaver's Memorandum; or An Account of Weaving, etc. Kept by Hannah Treadway, A.D. 1833 & 34. 1833-1834.

Andrews MS. No. 18. Weaver's Journal. Beginning in the year 1835. 1835-1865.

Andrews MS. No. 19. Journal Kept by Elizabeth Lovegrove. Begun in March 1837.

Andrews MS. No. 20. Importance of Keeping Correct Book Accounts. By Seth Y. Wells. (Copy of original MS.) 1836.

Andrews MS. No. 21. Trustee's Account or Day Book, 1831-46. Hancock.

Andrews MS. No. 22. Letter to Brother Daniel [Goodrich] from Brother Morrell. Dated Watervliet, December 26, 1822.

Andrews MS. No. 23. A Little Book Containing A Short Word from Holy Mother Wisdom, Concerning the Robes & Dresses That Are Prepared for All Such As Go Up to the Feast of the Lord, or Attend to Her Holy Passover. Copied July 20, 1842. For the Ministry of the City of Peace. 1842.

Andrews MS. No. 24. Letter to the Elders, Deacons, Brethren, & Sisters of the Society in Watervliet, Watervliet, Jan. 26th, 1832. Signed by Seth Y. Wells.

Andrews MS. No. 25. Remarks on Learning and the Use of Books. Watervliet, March 10, 1836. Signed by Seth Y. Wells.

Most of these manuscripts are now in The Edward Deming Andrews Memorial Shaker Library, a gift by the family to The Henry Francis du Pont Winterthur Museum.

## Selected Bibliography

Andrews, Edward D. *The New York Shakers and Their Industries.* Circular 2. New York State Museum, 1930, 8 pp.

Avery, Giles B. *Autobiography of Elder Giles B. Avery.* East Canterbury, N.H., 1891, 33 pp.

———. *Circular Concerning the Dress of Believers.* Mount Lebanon, 1866, 12 pp.

Baker, Arthur. *Shakers and Shakerism.* New Moral World Series. London, 1896, 30 pp.

[Bishop, Rufus, and Wells, Seth Y.] *Testimonies of the Life, Character, Revelations and Doctrines of Our Ever Blessed Mother Ann Lee, and the Elders with Her; through whom the word of eternal life was opened in this day of Christ's second appearing: collected from living witnesses.* Hancock, Mass., 1816, 405 pp.

Blinn, Henry C., ed. *Shaker Manifesto*, vols. 12-13 (January 1882 to December 1883), Shaker Village (also called Canterbury or East Canterbury), N.H.

———. *The Manifesto*, vols. 14-29 (January 1884 to December 1899), Shaker Village N.H.

Buckingham, J. S. *America, Historical, Statistic, and Descriptive*, vol. 2. New York, 1841.

Bullard, Sister Marcia. "Shaker Industries," *Good Housekeeping*, vol. 43, no. 1 (July 1906), pp. 33-37.

*Catalogue of Medicinal Plants, Barks, Roots, Seeds, Flowers and Select Powders. With their therapeutic qualities and botanical names; also pure vegetable extracts, prepared in vacuo; ointments, inspissated juices, essential oils, double distilled and fragrant waters, etc. etc. Raised, prepared and put up in the most careful manner, by the United Society of Shakers at New Lebanon, N.Y.* (No date is on this copy. MacLean refers to a catalogue with similar title dated 1860, published at Albany; Nordhoff records another dated 1873.)

Crossman, Charles F. *The Gardener's Manual; containing plain and practical directions for the cultivation and management of some of the most useful culinary vegetables; to which is prefixed a catalogue of the various kinds of garden seeds raised in the United Society at New Lebanon; with a few general remarks on the management of a kitchen garden.* Albany, N.Y., 1836, 24 pp.

Darrow, David, Meacham, John, and Youngs, Benjamin S. *The Testimony of Christ's Second Appearing; containing a general statement of all things pertaining to the faith and practice of the Church of God in this latter day,* 2nd ed. Albany, N.Y., 1810, 620 pp. (The actual writing of this book is credited to Benjamin S. Youngs, although the names of David Darrow and John Meacham are also signed to the preface. The second edition was revised by Youngs with the help of Seth Y. Wells.)

Dixon, William Hepworth. *New America.* Philadelphia, 1869.

Eads, Harvey L. *The Tailor's Division System, Founded Upon, and Combined with Actual Measurement; containing thirty diagrams and designs, reduced to mathematical principles.* Union Village, Ohio, 1849.

Earle, Alice Morse. *Home Life in Colonial Days.* New York, 1898.

Elkins, Hervey. *Sixteen Years in the Senior Order of Shakers: a narration of facts concerning that singular people.* Hanover, N.H., 1853.

Emery, Stewart M. "Shaker Sect Reduced by Its Own Doctrines," *The New York Times,* vol. 76, section 9 (November 28, 1926), p. 9.

Evans, F. W. *Shaker Communism; or, Tests of Divine Inspiration.* London, 1871.

[Evans, F. W.] *Shakers as Farmers.* Broadside. Reprint from Chatham (N.Y.) *Courier.*

Evans, F.W., and Doolittle, Antoinette, eds. *Shaker and Shakeress.* vols. 3-4 (January 1873 to December 1875), Mount Lebanon, N.Y.

*The Gardener's Manual; containing plain instructions for the selection, preparation, and management of a kitchen garden; with practical directions for the cultivation and management of some of the most useful culinary vegetables.* Published by the United Society, New Lebanon, N.Y., 1843, 24 pp.

[Green, Calvin, and Wells, Seth Y.] *A Brief Exposition of the Established Principles and Regulations of the United Society of Believers Called Shakers,* Revised edition. New York, 1846, 36 pp.

Green, Calvin, and Wells, Seth Y. *A Summary View of the Millennial Church, or United Society of Believers, Commonly Called Shakers,* 2nd ed. Albany, N.Y., 1848. (First edition published in 1823.)

Hayward, John. *The Book of Religions.* Concord, N.H., 1843.

———. *The New England Gazetteer; containing descriptions of all the states, counties and towns in New England; also descriptions of the principal mountains, rivers, lakes, capes, bays, harbors, islands, and fashionable resorts within that territory.* Boston, 1839.

Hinds, William Alfred. *American Communities.* Oneida, N.Y., 1878, 176 pp.

———. *American Communities.* Chicago, 1902, 433 pp.

Howells, William Dean. *Three Villages.* Boston, 1884. (Contains a sketch of the Shirley Shakers, pp. 69-113.)

Johnston, James F. W. *Notes on North America. Agricultural, Economical and Social,* vol. 2. Boston, 1851.

Lamson, David R. *Two Years' Experience among the Shakers: being a description of the manners and customs of that people; the nature and policy of their government, their marvelous intercourse with the spiritual world, the object and uses of confession, their inquisition, in short, a condensed view of Shakerism as it is.* West Boylston, Maine, 1848, 212 pp.

Lomas, George A., ed. *The Shaker*, vols. 1-2 (January 1871 to December 1872), Shakers (Watervliet), N.Y.

———. *The Shaker*, vol. 6 (January 1876 to December 1876), published jointly at Shakers, N.Y., and Shaker Village, N.H.

———. *The Shaker*, vol. 7 (January 1877 to December 1877), Shaker Village, N.H.

———. *The Shaker Manifesto*, vols. 8-11 (January 1878 to December 1881), Shakers, N.Y.

Mace, Aurelia C. *The Aletheia: Spirit of Truth.* 1907, Farmington, Maine.

MacLean, J. P. *A Bibliography of Shaker Literature, with an introductory study of the writings and publications pertaining to Ohio Believers.* Columbus, Ohio, 1905. (Items Nos. 159-185 refer to pamphlets and circulars advertising Shaker medicinal preparations, seeds, chairs, etc.)

———. *Shakers of Ohio.* Columbus, Ohio, 1907.

———. *A Sketch of the Life and Labors of Richard McNemar*, Franklin, Ohio, 1905.

[McNemar, Richard.] *Investigator, or a Defence of the Order, Government and Economy of the United Society Called Shakers, against Sundry Charges and Legislative Proceedings. Addressed to the Political World, by the Society of Believers, at Pleasant Hill, Ky.* New York, 1846, 84 pp. (Includes "Some account of the proceedings of the legislature of New Hampshire in relation to the people called Shakers, in 1828.")

"New Lebanon: Its Physic Gardens and Their Products," *American Journal of Pharmacy*, vol 18, no. 1 (January 1852), pp. 88-91.

Nordhoff, Charles. *The Communistic Societies of the United States.* New York, 1875.

Noyes, John Humphrey. *History of American Socialism.* Philadelphia, 1870.

Reist, Henry G. "Products of Shaker Industry," *New York History*, vol. 13, no. 3 (July 1932), pp. 264-270.

*Report of the Commissioner of Patents for the Year 1852.* Part 1, Arts and Manufacturers, 1853, 484 pp.

Robinson, Charles Edson. *A Concise History of the United Society of Believers, called Shakers.* Shaker Village, East Canterbury, N.H., 1893.

[Silliman, Benjamin.] *Peculiarities of the Shakers, described in a series of letters from Lebanon Springs in the year 1832, containing an account of the origin, worship and doctrines of the Shaker's Society. By a visitor.* New York, 1832.

"The Shakers," *Harper's New Monthly Magazine*, vol. 15, no. 86, (1857), pp. 164-77.

"The Story of Shakerism. By One Who Knows." East Canterbury, N.H., 1907, 16 pp.

[Wagan, Robert M.] *An Illustrated Catalogue and Price List of the Shakers' Chairs, Foot Benches, Floor Mats, etc.* Lebanon Springs, N.Y., 1875, 12 pp.

[Ward, Durbin.] *Shaker Income Tax. Application to Commissioner Delano. Brief of Durbin Ward, Counsel for Applicants.* Albany, N.Y., 1869, 21 pp.

White, Anna, and Taylor, Leila S. *Shakerism: Its Meaning and Message. Embracing an historical account, statement of belief and spiritual experience of the church from its rise to the present day.* Columbus, Ohio, 1905.

Wickliffe, Robert. *The Shakers.* Speech of Robert Wickliffe. In the Senate of Kentucky, January 1831. Frankfort, Ky., 1832, 32 pp.

# Index